Literacy and Intellectual Life
in the Cherokee Nation,
1820–1906

American Indian Literature
Critical Studies Series

Literacy *and* Intellectual Life *in the* Cherokee Nation, 1820–1906

JAMES W. PARINS

UNIVERSITY OF OKLAHOMA PRESS : NORMAN

Also by James W. Parins

(with Daniel F. Littlefield, Jr.) *A Biobibliography of Native American Writers, 1772–1924* (Metuchen, N.J., 1981)
William Barnes (Boston, 1984)
(with Daniel F. Littlefield, Jr.) *American Indian and Alaska Native Newspapers and Periodicals* (Westport, Conn., 1984–86); Encyclopedia of Indian Removal (Westport, Conn., 2011)
John Rollin Ridge: His Life and Works (Lincoln, Nebr., 1991)
Elias Cornelius Boudinot: A Life on the Cherokee Border (Lincoln, Nebr., 2006)

Publication of this book is made possible through the generosity of Edith Kinney Gaylord.

Library of Congress Cataloging-in-Publication Data

Parins, James W.
Literacy and intellectual life in the Cherokee nation, 1820-1906 / James W. Parins.
pages cm. — (American Indian literature and critical studies series)
Includes bibliographical references and index.
ISBN 978-0-8061-4399-6 (hardcover) ISBN 978-0-8061-9315-1 (paper)   1. Cherokee Indians— Intellectual life—19th century.   2. Cherokee Indians—Government relations— History—19th century.   3. Cherokee Indians—Newspapers— History—19th century.   4. Literacy—Social aspects—United States—History— 19th century.5. Authors, American—19th century—Biography. 6. Indian authors—United States—Biography. I. Title.

E99.C5P27 2013
975.004'97557—dc23

2013015584

Literacy and Intellectual Life in the Cherokee Nation, 1820–1906 is Volume 58 in the American Indian Literature and Critical Studies Series.

To my kids,

Claire, Craig, and James

CONTENTS

Illustrations   ix
Acknowledgments   xi
Introduction   xiii

1. Writing in Early America   3
2. Literacy in the Cherokee Nation   11
3. The *Cherokee Phoenix*   51
4. Education after Removal   68
5. The Cherokee Language and the Sequoyan Syllabary   101
6. The *Cherokee Advocate* and Other Indian Newspapers   127
7. Four Cherokee Writers   152
8. Political Writers and Feuders   190
9. A Steady Stream of Cherokee Writers   218
   Epilogue   246

Notes   255
Selected Bibliography   267
Index   271

ILLUSTRATIONS

Following page 126

Sequoyah

Cherokee Syllabary

Title page of William Chamberlin's *Cherokee Pictorial Book, With Catechism and Hymns*

Page from William Chamberlin's *Cherokee Pictorial Book*

Elias Boudinot

John Ross

Office of the *Cherokee Advocate*, Tahlequah, Cherokee Nation

"Southern" Cherokee Delegation: John Rollin Ridge, Saladin Watie, Richard Fields, E. C. Boudinot, and William Penn Adair

DeWitt Clinton Duncan (Too Quah-stee)

William Potter Ross

Edward (Ned) Bushyhead

Ora V. Eddleman

ACKNOWLEDGMENTS

Thanks go to the staffs of the Western History Collections at the University of Oklahoma libraries and the Oklahoma Historical Society. Much of the work was done at the Sequoyah National Research Center at the University of Arkansas at Little Rock, where Tony Rose provided inestimable assistance in the technical area. My stumbling prose was smoothed by the best editor I know of, my wife, Marylyn Jackson Parins. And, as always, my good friend Daniel Littlefield always found time to discuss the project with me and to lead me out of blind alleys.

Introduction

The story of Cherokee reading and writing in the nineteenth century is a fascinating one, from the beginnings of efforts to bring literacy skills to the people in both English and their native language to the proliferation of literary works by Cherokees. These efforts surpassed those of other North American Indians at the time, as well as those of most other communities of similar size on this continent and beyond. This is a story not only of a rapid increase in literacy—which was occurring in other societies at the same time—but also of reading and writing in two sets of systems, the English alphabet and the Cherokee syllabary. The literary outpourings that resulted from this rise in literacy in this relatively isolated locality of tribal people, moreover, provided a model for other Native peoples in the years to come.

The history of literacy and literature among the Cherokee people in the nineteenth century is intertwined with the great social and political events bearing not only on that nation but on all the Indian nations with roots east of the Mississippi. These include, but are not limited to, the effects of the U.S. government's "civilization" policy, resistance to Removal, continuing efforts to recover from Removal, attacks on sovereignty, the westward expansion of American settlement, allotment, and dissolution of tribal status. This narrative attempts to show how these actions shaped and motivated efforts to educate the people and how Cherokee writers responded to these events in their works.

From the beginning of the nineteenth century, many leaders in the Cherokee Nation recognized the benefits and importance of education, defined in much the same way as white society understood the process; as a result, they sought ways to bring schools to their people. Literacy took on a value at this time that it had not had previously. Early in the century, the assumption was that literacy and the English language were bonded; if a Cherokee wished to read and write, she or he would have to learn English first. Later, the dramatic development that changed the history of Cherokee intellectual life, Sequoyah's syllabary, eliminated this requirement.

Sequoyah's invention of the Cherokee syllabary, which empowered those who spoke the language to read and write, was far more than an extraordinary improvement of a communications system; the syllabary was a cerebral achievement that opened a new intellectual world to the Cherokees. Of course, communications were improved as people who had emigrated to other parts of the continent exchanged correspondence with friends and relatives back in the eastern nation. Another result of the syllabary's adoption was the cohesiveness among the Cherokee people that helped them avoid the near-total obliteration of their culture, in contrast to the fate of other eastern tribes after the whites had established hegemony in their former lands. These effects were more easily achieved because of the rapidity with which the Cherokees claimed the writing system as their own. In a matter of weeks, large numbers of the population became literate in their native language, a remarkable feat when it is measured against the time necessary to teach reading and writing to an American child in English. Thus the syllabary became a gateway to a world of intellectual possibilities and had profound effects on the political, social, economic, and educational affairs of the Cherokee Nation that continue to this day.

One consequence of Sequoyah's creativity, perhaps unintended, was to impress the Cherokees with the power and possibilities of written language and to make them realize that English was the language of commerce and, increasingly important as time went on, of politics. Although this fact was obvious to most of the nation's elite, it was less so to the common Cherokee untouched by "English" education. As the revelation dawned that facility in the white society's language was important to an individual's fortunes, as well as to those of the larger nation, people began to desire the acquisition of English for their children, if not for themselves. This desire, coupled with the efforts of English-language advocates such as Principal Chief John Ross, produced an educational program prominently featuring the teaching and learning of English that often surpassed educational initiatives in white communities. The resultant fluency in the more widely adopted tongue subsequently opened opportunities for the Cherokees to engage in intellectual discourse on an equal level with the white world and to share their thoughts and expressions with a wider audience. Cherokees gifted in writing, oratory, politics, philosophy, religion, and social theory were given the ability to converse persuasively with the larger society. The adoption of English as a "second" language greatly broadened intellectual horizons for those inclined to explore them.

Cherokees in the nineteenth century (and earlier) viewed themselves as at least intellectual equals of whites and other peoples. They had begun to prove their intellectual prowess in their relationships with colonial and later U.S. governmental entities, meeting them on equal terms (at least in Cherokee eyes) and bargaining for land and treasure. Moreover, the Cherokees took a place at the negotiating table when neighboring tribes had to deal with the whites. Their skills were not lost on their adversaries, as U.S. envoys made clear to the Creeks when the whites sought to take control of remaining Creek lands and to remove the inhabitants westward. Cherokee John Ridge's part in these negotiations perhaps secured a better bargain for the Creeks than they could have achieved if they had been left to reach a deal alone.

Ridge, among others, set the tone for Cherokee writers working later in the century. Their foes were much the same, and the stakes had changed little: control of Indian lands and negation of Cherokee laws and culture. These later writers, like Ridge, saw themselves as intellectual equals of their adversaries, just as skilled in the arts of argument and debate and just as able to see the consequences and ramifications of precedent-setting actions. For their part, strong Cherokee leaders had the foresight to help prepare the people for these tasks by organizing a first-class educational system and supporting the publication of Cherokee writings for debate and consideration. These are hallmarks of a civilized society, the Cherokees asserted, and their nurturing of them demonstrated to all the civilized nature of Cherokee culture. Thus the Cherokees saw their course as using brainpower and the pen rather than battlefield tactics, fast ponies, and rifles to protect their culture.

The invention, adoption, and continued use of Cherokee writing are parts of a series of Cherokee intellectual endeavors that served to unify what was perceived as a fragmenting society. The Cherokees thus sought to keep their people together, to preserve their culture and heritage, and to prove to the world that their society was viable and distinct. Other ways in which they attempted to do this were the formation of a written constitution, thus establishing a system of laws; provisions for education of all their citizens; and print publication of Cherokee thoughts and ideas. Their written language thus served as a cohesive bond to hold individuals together and to create expression of Cherokee intellectual life. The common use of the English language supported this concept.

The present study attempts to look at some of the ways the Cherokees achieved this. I examine each of these intellectual attainments: the development of writing, organization of an educational system, establishment of a national press, and the literary efforts of individual Cherokee intellectuals. First, however, the study will provide a brief examination of the history of writing in the Western Hemisphere.

Literacy and Intellectual Life in the Cherokee Nation, 1820–1906

CHAPTER 1

Writing in Early America

Humankind's decision to inscribe speech so that a more or less permanent record was created was not a one-time event whose ramifications later spread around the globe. However, various claims have been made for the birth of writing (using several definitions of the technology), including a recent assertion that the alphabet that led to Semitic writing was invented by the Canaanites in the nineteenth century BCE; most of these theories on the genesis of alphabets in the Middle East agree that writing was a refinement of Egyptian hieroglyphics. Early writing took many forms: letters or symbols carved on rocks, painted on walls, indited in ink on papyrus, or pressed into clay tablets using wedge-shaped tools.[1]

In Mesoamerica, scholars have long focused on Native arithmetic systems, especially as they relate to calendars and maps. In the past two decades, however, archaeologists have discovered tablets, walls, and other stone surfaces inscribed with figures that appear to be more than ornamental. Examination of patterns in the figures has led linguists to conclude that these figures represent syllables in various languages from the region that relate the histories of these civilizations. Many of the cultures of the region shared some common symbols that later became the basis for writing. The Olmecs used these symbols to create texts early on, according to the scholarship done in the 1990s and early 2000s based on artifacts. In particular, a small stone tablet called the Cascajal block contains a text dating to between 1000 and 800 BCE. Before 300 CE, the Zapotecs and

Mayas developed Mesoamerican writing systems that followed the general outline of the early Olmec writing. Later, down to the year 1500 CE, writing systems appeared among other peoples, all based on the earlier patterns. Mayan writing, which lasted until around 1700 CE, has been especially studied and is very rich. It consists of a full set of phonetic signs that represent all possible sounds of the language, long passages that represent linguistic units such as nouns and verbs, and units that represent actions and ideas, that is, clauses and phrases.[2] This system allowed Mesoamericans to create syllabaries for their various languages, a departure from the alphabetic approach favored among Middle Eastern peoples.

After the Spanish conquest, the new rulers regarded the Native texts as "pagan" and ordered their destruction, except for a few works that they considered valuable for the administration of the subjected peoples. These preserved examples of Native writing were often accompanied by glosses in Spanish. Native scribes were taught the Spanish language and the roman alphabet and began to write their languages in the new orthographic system of their conquerors. In this way, although the ancient method of writing was lost, creation and other myths, poetry, and religious texts were preserved. In time, the nation-states that grew out of the Spanish colonies became so assimilated that they emphasized their Spanish rather than their Indian traditions. Still, many of the people remained close to their roots and preserved their languages and traditions. In the 1990s, there was a revival of Mayan culture, including interest in and study of the ancient writing.

Among Mesoamericans after the Spanish invasions, the written word took on a cultural importance that portended Cherokee strategies later. The Spanish policy of putting an end to "pagan" practices did much to obliterate the Native cultures. Rituals were forbidden, including the singing of hymns and observances of recurring days of devotion. David Tavárez, however, reports that among the Zapotecs of northern Oaxala, tribal intellectuals appropriated some European literary practices, as well as characters from the Latin alphabet, to create an alphabetic representation of the Zapotec 260-day religious calendar and thus preserved important aspects of the Native culture. These calendars were distributed among Zapotec settlements and used as guides by their leaders. This operation presupposes literacy among these people, albeit only among the intellectual elite. Nonetheless, the calendars demonstrate that the Zapotecs understood the power and efficiency of the written word.[3] The Mayans of the Yucatán Peninsula had an elaborate system of writing in their language before the Spanish invasion. But like the Cherokees later, the Natives also saw the merit of adopting the conqueror's writing methods, and so in addition to their traditional symbolic system, the Mayans developed alphabetic literacy like that of the Spanish as early as 1570. Moreover, as John F. Chuckiak IV has pointed out,[4] the Mayan intellectual elite used these systems vigorously, compiling libraries in both symbolic and alphabetic characters. It is especially interesting that the Native people resisted their conquerors by using written words both to communicate in armed rebellions and to carry out surreptitious activities against the Spanish.

According to the noted linguist James Constantine Pilling, the study of Native American languages by whites seems to have begun in 1545 with the compilation of a Huron vocabulary by Jacques Cartier in Canada.[5] Around the same time in Mexico, the Spanish were furnishing paper to the Aztecs on which older Native texts were transcribed that served as property records. Scientists surmise that these older texts had been written on bark, leather, or cloth and had used symbols—for example, hearts, arms, arrows, and bones—to accompany drawings of land plots.[6]

In North America, some early attempts to write the Indian languages found there began in the seventeenth century. Many of the Christian missionaries who approached the Native tribes in North America, including the Cherokees, were eager to learn the native languages in order to preach the gospel in the vernacular. The Massachusetts language was written from the 1660s through the 1750s, when it apparently became extinct. John Eliot's *Bible* was written in an alphabetically rendered form of Algonquin dialect used as a trading language. These documents were produced by Christian Indians in the "praying towns" among the Massachusetts, Narragansetts, and Wampanoags in the present-day northeastern United States. Native ministers or elders taught reading and writing in the Native languages until the mid-eighteenth century, when they were replaced by white missionaries who taught in English. The Massachusetts speakers who produced these early documents learned their orthography from John Eliot and his associates. The documents consist largely of records of the praying towns. The Mahican language was written in orthographies that were invented by the missionaries and were based on English in the Stockbridge missions and on German in the Moravian missions. The younger Jonathan Edwards wrote in Stockbridge after moving there at age six in 1751.[7] Natives John Quinney and Hendrick Aupaumut translated the Congregational Assembly's Shorter Catechism into Mahican in the early nineteenth century, and other writings in Mahican were produced in both German and English orthographies.[8]

The English were not the only missionaries interested in bringing the word of God in print to the Indians in North America. Early on, the French learned Native languages to aid them in governing the Indians and to allow the priests to proselytize them. Expertise in the indigenous languages was also provided by intermarried couples, who were widespread in New France but unusual in the English-speaking colonies. Catholics early introduced presses for printing religious texts in Canada and the Great Lakes areas.[9]

A number of missionaries invented written forms of Native languages based on the roman alphabet in the late eighteenth and early nineteenth centuries,[10] relying on Native aides when they had difficulties with the languages. Asher Wright printed an astounding number of his own texts in Iroquois dialects in the early decades of the nineteenth century. Henry Spaulding produced texts among the tribes of the Columbia River valley a little later. Linguist John Pickering sought a way to bring the various orthographies together, and in 1820 he published his influential *Essay on a Uniform Orthography for the Indian Languages of North America*. His system was embraced by many of the mission societies because it allowed printing in the roman alphabet and negated the need to have expensive special type cast for each language. The missionary societies, working with Pickering and other linguists, devoted much time and energy to constructing a universal orthography that might be used for all of the Native peoples' languages, but although Pickering's orthography was modified for use in a number of languages, it by no means fit all Indian languages and was not as widely used as expected because of the variety of sounds in unrelated languages. Although publications in Native languages reached some of the people, they still required the teaching of alphabets and their corresponding sounds and demonstration of how they related to the spoken language. In time, educators began to have some success in teaching English, and once more uniform curricula and government schools were introduced, use of Native languages was discouraged.

With the Louisiana Purchase in 1803, the number of missionaries in North America increased for two reasons. First, a vast territory was now rid of domination by Catholic, non-English-speaking European nations and became open to missionary efforts that grew out of the United Kingdom. Second, the purchase coincided with the U.S. government's civilization policy, which sought to bring education and the word of the Christian God to all the Native peoples within the boundaries of the United States. The missionary societies that had organized to bring their religion to the "benighted" non-European peoples of the world were, by nature, evangelistic; that is, their doctrinal reliance on the word of God as revealed in the Bible led them to promote literacy so that their audiences could read the scriptures. They were aided in this effort around the beginning of the nineteenth century by technological advances in printing; presses had become power driven and designed for countless repeated operations, which made them much less labor intensive and faster and increased their productivity exponentially over that of hand presses. Other printing advances followed, including the use of stereotype, which eliminated much of the tedious typesetting work for long runs of publications, such as pages from the Bible. At the same time, advances in paper chemistry led to the introduction of cheaper, wood-based paper. The impetus for literacy and the availability of cheap reading materials allowed the missionaries to bring their efforts to the "foreign" missions, including the Native populations of North America.

The missionaries' campaign to bring literacy and printed materials to Indian country was supported to a great extent by their sponsoring agencies, such as the American Board of Commissioners of Foreign Missions, a Congregationalist/Presbyterian organization, and similar groups among the Baptists, Moravians, and Methodists. These governing boards, in turn, were supported in their printing efforts by two influential organizations, the American Bible Society, founded in 1816, and the American Tract Society, founded in 1825.

Although their aim was to bring affordable religious texts to all Americans, they had a significant effect particularly on Indian communities through their production and distribution of free or cheap materials. They were especially appreciated by missionaries who lacked the means to print their own Bibles, hymnals, and catechisms. All these factors were to influence Native literacy, writing, and the use of indigenous languages.

The study of linguistics was a popular but highly speculative undertaking in the late eighteenth and early nineteenth centuries. Part of the attraction of these studies was the common belief that languages of "primitive" humans were by definition less developed and therefore simpler and easier to learn than the "civilized" languages. Serious linguists, of course, soon discovered the highly intricate and heavily nuanced nature of most of the North American languages and gave them the scholarly attention and respect they deserved. However, the field was riddled with pretenders, often clerics who knew Latin, Greek, and Hebrew but had little other linguistic acumen. Europeans, many of whom never left their home continent, made various attempts to learn North American languages. Missionaries and other visitors to the tribes attempted to develop vocabularies and to publish translated word lists, using various Native informants. By modern standards, these publications were inaccurate to varying degrees, but this fact did not deter scholars, albeit mostly amateur ones, from creating highly speculative theories. One of the most prevalent of these speculations involved using Native languages, even though they were understood imperfectly, at best, to prove that the Indian nations were the biblical lost tribes of Israel. In some cases involving faux linguists and "antiquarians," linguistic hoaxes were manufactured that lived on for years. The most famous of these was the *Walum Olum* affair.

A self-styled antiquarian, Constantin Samuel Refinesque, allegedly translated some Lenni Lenape texts from birch-bark and cedar tablets around 1830. This translation was published as *Walum Olum* shortly after it was produced and has remained in print ever since, despite the fact that the translator had little experience with language and was a naturalist, trained in zoology, botany, and meteorology. Once revered as a sacred religious text from the Delaware Nation's ancient past, it purported to present the tribe's creation story, its account of an ancient flood, and other historical and religious texts. Although Refinesque's work aroused some suspicion in later years, no one undertook a detailed analysis until David M. Oestreicher's work in the 1990s. Oestricher found that Refinesque translated his own English text into Delaware using word lists that had been in print in 1830.[11] Although it was used for years to demonstrate Lenni Lenape writing, *Walum Olum* is today considered a fraud because Oestreicher's work has been corroborated by other authorities.

Some credence was given to Refinesque's claims because Native Americans of North America have been keeping birch-bark scrolls for centuries, according to Indian reporters and contemporary white observers. Henry Rowe Schoolcraft reported that the Mide societies, which were the caretakers of traditional beliefs and history among the Ojibwe people, used scrolls containing pictographs and cryptic symbols. Schoolcraft's informant, his wife, Jane Johnston, was an unusually accurate historian of her people, and the pair's assertions have been corroborated by later scholars. Obviously, these scrolls constitute texts employing writing known to those for whom the texts were created, and they were most likely passed down by the Midewewin, members of the Mide, from generation to generation as a means of preserving ancient knowledge. However, the writing systems used by the Ojibwe secret societies today are probably not shared with all members of the community. This practice differs from that of early European societies in which the priests and nobility withheld writing from the general population in that modern Ojibwes have other means of written communication.

An interesting topic in relation to writing in the Sequoyan syllabary within the context of earlier Native writing systems is the initial insistence of officials, missionaries, and white linguists (as well as a number of assimilated Indians with classical educations) on writing the Native language using various orthographies, that is, using alphabets, rather than attempting to invent syllabaries that would reproduce the sounds of speech. The whites and their converts were steeped in "Western" systems of writing, including Middle Eastern, Greek, and roman alphabets, and so were reluctant to abandon that methodology in favor of what they considered a less elegant or more "uncivilized" mode of expression, the syllabary.

This partially explains the initial opposition to Sequoyah's work and the efforts of John Pickering and others to develop orthographies for Native languages. However, the tradition of using syllabaries, as we have seen, lies deep in Native American history and learning. One of the major reasons for this tradition is the rapidity and ease with which any syllabary can be put to use. Once native speakers learn the relatively few (as opposed to, say, Chinese) symbols, they can read and write perfectly. Thus this system is extremely efficient in comparison with any system employing an alphabet. In the latter approach, the native speaker must learn the alphabet and its corresponding sounds, then learn to form words from combining these orthographic figures, and then, after years of study, become more and more proficient. Cherokees, on the other hand, learned to read and write in a matter of weeks or even days. Missionaries who were not native speakers of Cherokee did not share this advantage, however, and took the course that was easier for them than for the beginning reader. Moreover, these advantages were lost, for the most part, on missionaries and linguists, steeped in centuries of their own traditions. The adoption of an orthographic system over a syllabic one became an ethnic prejudice rather than an intellectual preference.

Sequoyah, however, was not hampered by preconceived ideas. His task, as he saw it, was to provide the sounds of his language with symbols, thus enabling it to be written down and read by any speaker who had memorized the symbols corresponding to the sounds. With this system, the process of learning to read and write took a very short time and in this regard was superior to the European and Middle Eastern models.

Although Sequoyah's syllabary was not the only or the earliest writing system invented by American Indians, it was easily learned and shared with the total population, not only with the holy men, scribes, and sociopolitical leaders. As a result, its use spread amazingly quickly among Cherokee speakers, who not only delighted in their ability to communicate with far-flung fellow citizens but also regarded the syllabary as a source of national pride, the spirit in which it is seen today.

CHAPTER 2

LITERACY IN THE CHEROKEE NATION

Present-day readers regard the value of the ability to read and write as a given, but people who had learned about their world in educational systems that relied on oral tradition did not necessarily consider literacy as important as European and other literate societies did. For all the surmises Euro-Americans make about Native peoples' natural envy of the white man's "talking leaves," it was only when certain conditions came into being that literacy for a wide portion of the Cherokee Nation became a desideratum. Leaders like John Ross, John Ridge, and Elias Boudinot had been educated in white schools, and they saw the advantages of literacy. Further, adversity came to the Cherokees in many forms, but all of them threatened the continuing viability of their nation. The same threats faced by the northeastern tribes years earlier that had led to their virtual extinction now confronted the southeastern tribes, including the Cherokees. Chief among these was the increasing proximity of white populations. As the Cherokee lands shrank through cessions by treaty, whites filled in the lands left vacant and brought with them political and social structures increasingly more organized along Euro-American lines. Soon, the former Cherokee lands contained not only scattered settlements of subsistence farmers but also larger towns and even cities with their concomitant trappings of "civilization." As time went on, the Cherokees and other tribal peoples near them were forced to deal, in various ways, with these unfamiliar people and their lifeways, and inability to communicate in

11

some written form became increasingly disadvantageous. Because the settlers showed no inclination to learn Cherokee or other Indian languages, any communication other than that done with the aid of translators depended on the Natives learning English.

This fact was driven home by the series of treaties Cherokees made with the whites that brought about the proximity of the settlers. The European style of treaty making, closely tied to European legal systems, had been perfected by the whites down through the centuries. Communication through language is the essential element in contractual agreements like these; the Indians soon came to recognize the importance of language in treaties, especially legalisms they did not fully understand. These concepts were invariably expressed first in the white man's language and were later translated into the Native languages, often only orally, with varying degrees of accuracy. Large segments of the Cherokee land base had been eroded, or "ceded," through these language instruments. The terms of these contracts, moreover, seemed to give one party to the treaties certain intrinsic privileges not accorded to the other. For example, one had only to look at the history of the agreements to understand that the white men could abrogate the terms of the latest treaty with no apparent qualms and demand the drawing up of a new one, complete with terms advantageous to the violators of the previous contract. No corresponding authority, however, was granted to the Indian nations. These instruments thus took on a power of their own, at once couched in the language of the increasingly demanding society of white people and serving mainly the interests of that group. It was not hard to see the disadvantages thus heaped on the heads of the second party. Translations were notoriously inaccurate, and many translators were under the influence of the whites, which almost ensured some degree of miscommunication between the contracting parties. As time went on, the advantage of becoming fluent in the language of the people with whom they were forced to deal became increasingly clear to Native peoples. Fluency for their purposes included the ability to read and write. As Cherokee David Brown put the issue to Cherokee students at Creek Path School in 1827, "Remember that the whites are near us. With them we have constant intercourse; and you must be sensible, that unless you can speak their language, read and write as they do, they will be able to cheat you and trample on your rights."[1]

These dealings became more and more important as the nineteenth century approached. The colonists' victory over the British meant that the Indians no longer could play off against one another the European nations that had been fighting among themselves for supremacy on the North American continent. Now the Cherokees and other Indian groups had to deal with a young, expansionist nation that regarded the tribes as a nuisance that must be dealt with to gratify the wishes of settlers, land speculators, and ambitious politicians. Cherokee leaders saw that to remain ignorant of the encroaching nation's language, values, and methods was suicide. If the Cherokee Nation was to escape the fate of the several extinct and "remnant" Native groups, it was necessary to learn what the white man knew in order to deal with him on a more advantageous footing than had been the case previously.

A key ingredient in all this that gave a sense of urgency to the situation as the Cherokee Nation lived through the first two decades of the nineteenth century was the threat of Removal. In the southeastern United States, the rapid growth of the cotton trade led planters to demand more land. Around the same time, since the Louisiana Purchase in 1803, European Americans had become more aware of the vast wilderness to the west, an area deemed too distant and unexplored for white settlement at present, but a perfect resettlement ground for the "benighted" Native Americans who were seen as obstacles to expansion. Even before the purchase, unprincipled land speculators and others campaigned noisily for Removal, joined ironically by those whites who were sympathetic to the Indians; many reformers saw Removal as a way of isolating the Natives from the whiskey merchants and swindlers who preyed on unsophisticated tribal people and encouraged decadent behavior among them. Among the Cherokees, the Removal threat was very real in the early part of the century. Many were lured to Arkansas, where they were promised a new life free of harassment by the whites. The Cherokee leadership responded by forbidding this piecemeal emigration, recognizing that the scattering of the nation's citizens could only weaken them. The Cherokees soon concluded that one of the best defenses they could muster for their nation as a whole was education; their strategy was to educate their people in the "English" way, take on many of the lifeways of their white neighbors, and in this way become "civilized." A civilized people, they reasoned, should be no threat to the larger society; on the contrary, it could become a functional part of the American nation, much as other groups, such as the Dutch in New York, had.

The "civilizing" of the tribal peoples had adherents in the political and religious structures of the United States, giving credence to the Cherokee plan. George Washington's "civilization policy," as it became known, drew many of the same conclusions that the Cherokee leadership adopted, although for different reasons. Washington's policy defined "civilization" as adopting white ways of life. For the Cherokees, it meant adapting to the rapidly changing political and economic landscape. Although the government's policy was not fully adopted until 1819, and then only selectively and halfheartedly, it provided a framework for the treatment of Indian peoples throughout the nineteenth century. The civilization policy attributed to George Washington was put forth by Henry Knox, the first president's secretary of war, in 1789 and advocated leading the Indians out of "barbarism" by using missionaries as the instruments of change. During and after the Second Great Awakening, church-state issues were not seriously considered, and once this policy was established, it lasted, in one form or another, throughout the nineteenth century.[2] Knox's original idea was to acculturate 125,000 Natives in eighty-five tribal groups east of the Mississippi within fifty years.[3] The policy's goals included teaching Indians English and training them to farm on allotted land, as well as converting them to Christianity. Once these goals were met, the Natives would be admitted to the United States as full and equal citizens. Washington outlined his ideas to Congress in 1791 and 1792. Congress responded the following year by including in the Intercourse Act twenty thousand dollars to pay agents who might bring some of the trappings of civilization, such as farm animals and implements, to the Indians. This support was also included in subsequent intercourse acts. Thomas Jefferson continued the policy throughout his administration, and provisions were made in several treaties with the tribes to supply them with support for agriculture and training in the "domestic arts," such as spinning cotton and weaving cloth.[4]

The frontier whites who were becoming the Cherokees' neighbors in ever-increasing numbers never embraced the civilization policy.

One reason this segment of whites opposed it was economic. The local whites saw the policy as an obstacle to Removal and the subsequent acquisition of the lands they coveted because "civilization" as seen by Knox and Washington presupposed a stable, sedentary life for the Indians, usually on what ancestral lands remained. Another reason the whites opposed the idea was fundamentally racist; as missionary Ard Hoyt wrote in the "Brainerd Journal," a day-to-day report to his superiors in the Northeast, the frontier whites believed that "the Indian is by nature radically different from other men and that this difference presents an insurmountable barrier to civilization."[5] Such deep-seated views led to increased friction between local whites and the Cherokees, but it also had some unintended effects. The first was that the missionaries and the Cherokees were brought closer together against a common antagonist. The second was that the proximity of hostile whites fueled the fires of Cherokee nationalism.

The civilization policy drove missionary efforts among the southeastern tribes, but it was opposed by many within the Cherokee Nation, by an influential number of elected officials and bureaucrats within the federal government, and by the great majority of frontier whites. Although the federal government continued to give nominal support to the idea, over time officials increased pressure on the tribes to remove west of the Mississippi. For example, a year after a treaty was put to the Cherokees to remove to Arkansas, James Monroe called for an Indian Civilization Fund in his 1818 Annual Message to codify the civilization idea into law. In the same year, the House Committee on Indian Affairs reported favorably on the measure. Pushed by Cyrus Kingsbury and other mission supporters, the fund was to support missionary efforts in the cause. However, by the time an appropriation intended to help civilize Indians on ancestral lands was passed by Congress in 1819, it was for only ten thousand dollars per annum, a sum to support education among all the tribes and a 50 percent reduction of what the intercourse acts had provided earlier. The bulk of this fund went to the American Board of Commissioners for Foreign Missions, and missionaries to the Cherokees received the largest share.[6]

Evangelical Christianity's missionary movement was coming into its own early in the century, and many of its tenets were identical to those of the supporters of a civilization policy or at least agreeable to them. Spreading from England to the subcontinent of Asia, the Mediterranean, and the Middle East early in the century, the movement was joined by American groups that looked to the Pacific rim and other areas. These missionary societies had a common goal: to teach the benighted people to read, thus paving the way for familiarity with the holy scriptures and eventual adoption of their precepts. Within England, the evangelicals were a major factor in reforming the educational system and bringing literacy to the working classes. Their efforts, along with technological advances in papermaking and printing, helped bring about the information explosion that occurred during the Victorian era. Through their missionary societies, the evangelicals sought to bring about the same results in Greece, Malta, Palestine, India, Ceylon (now Sri Lanka), and Burma by teaching people to read and providing them with reading materials. American missionaries traveled to Hawaii and Samoa, among other venues, following the lead of their English brethren.

A major force in these efforts among the Cherokees was the American Board of Commissioners for Foreign Missions (ABCFM). The ABCFM was founded by Congregationalists at Andover Theological Seminary in Massachusetts on June 29, 1810. It declared itself to be interdenominational (and indeed did later include some Presbyterians and Dutch Reformed), nonpartisan, and dedicated to moral improvement, especially of those who did not "enjoy the blessings of civilization and Christianity." In practice, however, the organization was Calvinistic and Federalist. It placed particular emphasis on the American aborigines as its members set out to evangelize and civilize the southern Indian nations, beginning with the Cherokees.[7] The Prudential Committee was its board of directors, and Secretary Jeremiah Evarts was its executive. Evarts served in this capacity during the period that saw the founding of the Cherokee missions and their language, translation, and printing efforts. The ABCFM was powerful in the new nation through its influence in Congress (several of its members were congressmen), but it had clout with the public as well, especially in the Northeast, where it disseminated information about its activities in a monthly journal and an annual report and was active in abolitionist circles.

Acting on a request from the Delawares, the ABCFM debated whether to begin a ministry to the Indians at its 1814 annual meeting.[8]

It considered the question carefully and decided to send Cyrus Kingsbury to visit the Cherokees, Muscogee Creeks, Choctaws, and Chickasaws to ascertain the need (a foregone conclusion) and the likely reception by the tribes. Kingsbury's report to the board was an enthusiastic go-ahead; he had determined that it was a perfect time to begin. The board petitioned the government for permission to approach the tribes, which was granted in 1816. In the following year, the ABCFM established its first mission and school at Chickamauga, Tennessee, christened Brainerd by the missionaries. By this time, the Cherokee leadership, especially the mixed-bloods, had determined that it was in the Cherokee Nation's interest to encourage the acquisition of the English language in both oral and written forms among its people.

It is important to note that when ABCFM emissaries visited the Cherokee National Council to propose opening their missions, the Cherokees questioned them closely about the promised schools. They showed little interest in the missionary churches, which were, in the missionaries' eyes, the center of the outposts. Moravian and Presbyterian missionaries had been allowed into Cherokee country in the first years of the century with the stipulation that they would provide education for the Native children; however, when the schools they had promised failed to live up to the expectations of the Cherokee leadership, mainly because the missionaries and teachers refused to learn Cherokee, the schools failed around 1810. The Moravian mission remained open but was largely ineffective for the next eight years, while the Presbyterians withdrew entirely.[9] When the ABCFM and Baptist missionaries arrived with plans for new schools, the Cherokees welcomed them as they had the Moravians and Presbyterians. They saw the mission schools as a means of reaching an important national objective, namely, self-sustainability as a nation. Many Cherokee leaders wanted to obtain the "arts of cultivation" that the civilization initiatives of the government and the missionaries promised. As William G. McLoughlin points out, the Indians believed that once they were self-sustaining, standing on their own legs, so to speak, they would cease to be likely candidates for Removal.[10] This idea was reinforced by the missionaries, who, for their own purposes, advocated an "English" education for the young Native people. So the education program commenced, with all its implications for literacy. In its early involvement with the Cherokees, the board vowed "to make the whole tribe English in their language, civilized in their habits, and Christian in their religion."[11] These ambitious aims, as we shall see, would need to be tempered as the ABCFM missionaries came to know the Cherokees.

The founding of the American Board School at Brainerd in 1817 was accompanied by the revival at Springplace, Georgia, of a school taught by Moravian missionaries. Thus the Moravians and the Congregationalists were established in Georgia, eastern Tennessee, and northeast Alabama, near turnpikes and the bigger Native settlements; in these areas, the population included a large number of mixed-bloods.

In October 1819, the Cherokee National Council gave the Baptists land for a mission in Valley Towns, a region in the Great Smoky Mountains of North Carolina and Alabama. The Baptists were placed in an area that was isolated from major roads and white settlements and was populated largely by full-bloods. The placement of these mission schools, as well as the individual missionaries who came to work there, had important consequences for Cherokee literacy and publishing in the years to come.

In the 1820s, the mission movement in the Cherokee Nation was advancing. Both the ABCFM and the Baptists opened new missions. As time went on, the missionaries never changed their basic attitude that Anglo-Saxons were leading the advancement of human progress and its corollary that other peoples lagged behind, but as they worked with the Cherokees, they came to respect them. They recognized that Cherokee children had the same ability to learn as white children. More important, perhaps, they recognized in Cherokee society a stability and a concern for the general welfare not shared by surrounding white settlements or local and state governments.[12] Thus encouraged, the ABCFM established new missions and schools at Carmel and Creek Path as the Baptists moved into the Valley Towns, or Overhill, as it was sometimes called, in 1819; the Moravians opened Tinsawatee and Oothcalogy in 1821; and the Congregationalists began operations at Etowah, Haweis, and Willstown in 1823 and several other places between 1824 and 1835, including the Cherokee capital at New Echota in 1827. Methodists taught in six schools on a six-month circuit basis beginning in 1831.

The mission schools presented a whole range of issues that were not fully considered until after the missions were established. These concerns quickly became evident, however, and intense debates ensued. First, the Cherokees had few large population centers. Traditionally, they had lived in small settlements strung out over some distance. As a result, establishing local schools was difficult, especially because the missions suffered from a lack of cash and personnel. According to the missionary society template that was used in other places, the mission establishment was to be as nearly self-sufficient as possible, raising its own food, erecting and maintaining its own buildings, and raising its own livestock. Ideally, personnel would include one or more preachers with wives, a male teacher for the boys and a female for the girls, a blacksmith, a carpenter, and a farmer. Natives were to be recruited and trained for most of these professions, and although some missions had Indians who stepped into these jobs, the missionaries' correspondence with their superiors in the East was filled with requests for more personnel. Thus the proliferation of missions was limited; subsequently, the larger settlements were served, but the more sparsely populated areas were not.

Some missionaries tried to remedy this situation by taking a page from the Methodist book and sending preachers out on horseback to minister to the people's spiritual needs, but this was an unsatisfactory way to deal with their educational efforts, so they established boarding schools as a way of concentrating their audience in fewer venues. Boarding schools also helped remedy the lack of teachers because the missionaries adopted the Lancastrian, or monitorial, system, in which one teacher presided over the school, moving from one class to the next, and the children were organized by comparable proficiency in a subject. When the teacher left one group to see to the next, he or she put a monitor in charge who continued the lessons. The monitors were nearly always older children who had mastered the material earlier. In the Cherokee Nation, however, many of the monitors were not masters of the English language and thus were not as effective as they might have been. Another problem that surfaced was that the monitors were often younger mixed-blood children who used English at home. In Cherokee traditional education, elders and full-bloods were in charge, but the Lancastrian system turned this tradition on its head. Although this alone might not account for the high dropout rate among full-bloods, it caused some consternation.[13]

The Cherokee conception of who was considered a full-blood and who a mixed-blood differed from the commonly held blood-quantum idea many white people hold. For example, whites (especially southern Americans) regarded people as African-descended American if they possessed "one drop of blood" from the minority race. Persons of "mixed races" were termed "mulatto," "half-breeds," "quadroons," or "octoroons," depending on the amount of minority blood they supposedly carried, but the social and political stigmas suffered by the "full-blood" African-descended Americans fell on their heads as well. For the Cherokees, however, the criteria were linguistic and cultural rather than racial or biological. A full-blood was any person whose primary and preferred language was Cherokee, even though the subject might have had a white ancestor. A good example is Sequoyah, or George Guess, who was descended from a white man but spoke no English and was considered a full-blood Cherokee by his fellows. The Keetoowah Society, a conservative full-blood organization, maintained this standard as late as the 1850s, when its membership rules stated that a successful applicant needed to be "uneducated," that is, not English speaking. Its members adhered to precontact ideals such as embracing tribal or ethnic identity and saw fluency in the ancient language as the center of their belief system.[14] Mixed-bloods were defined as those who might have had some knowledge of Cherokee, but who spoke English in the home. As might be expected, full-blood communities had a much lower percentage of English speakers than did mixed-blood communities. One estimate is that in mixed-blood settlements, the population had seven times as many English speakers as full-blood areas.[15] One reason for this was that most full-blood areas were farther from white settlements, major waterways, and turnpikes, so Cherokees did not need English. Another was that in general, full-bloods lived farther from schools and missionaries, so they had fewer opportunities to learn the new language. But perhaps the biggest reason full-bloods did not learn English was cultural: many of them made a conscious decision to resist acculturation and to preserve the old ways.

Boarding schools presented other difficulties as well. In keeping with the self-sufficiency obligation of the missions, students were expected to share in the chores, including helping in the fields, shops, mill, and kitchen. This did not sit well with the parents, especially with the full-bloods. Many were dismayed to see their children employed as laborers on the same level, in some cases, with the black slaves that many of the mixed-bloods had working on their farms and plantations. Full-blood parents also did not understand the costs they had to incur before their children were allowed to matriculate: each family was expected to bear the costs for school supplies and "appropriate" clothing. For most of the Cherokees, day schools were much to be preferred to the boarding variety. The children could spend their evenings and Sabbaths at home, where they were often needed to help with household chores, family members were not separated for long periods of time, and the parents were able to exercise greater control over the upbringing of their children. Another complaint many Cherokees voiced against the mission boarding schools was the duration of instruction. When the schools were first opened, the expectation among the parents was that the children would attend for a year or two, become sufficiently fluent in English and the other "arts of civilization," and then return home to take their places as productive citizens better able to deal with the ever-encroaching white settlers and agents of the government who seemed to be increasingly appearing among them. When it became clear that this timetable was unrealistic, and that children spent the first years learning the roman alphabet and the sounds of the letters, many parents became restless. In the Baptist mission school at Valley Towns, for example, it took the full-blood children four to five years to learn English with any fluency.[16] The goal of having most of the Cherokee Nation's children become literate in English was simply not going to be reached, in spite of the best efforts of their teachers.

Another topic of debate among the missionaries and teachers was the language in which instruction was to be given, English or Cherokee. Arguments for one or the other approach fill the pages of the correspondence between those in the Cherokee Nation and those in the East who controlled the purse strings, including government officials wedded to the civilization policy. Thomas L. McKenney, director of the Office of Indian Affairs, stated, "I believe the less of it [the Cherokee language] that is taught, or spoken, the better for the Indians. Their whole character, inside and out, language and morals, must be changed."[17] Some argued for the use of English on the grounds that it would require teachers to have less fluency in the Native language, thus aiding in the recruitment of teachers and the pace at which they could be trained. Another point was that students would learn the English language at the same time as they learned various other subjects, such as history, religion, mathematics, and science. An important advantage to evangelicals was that by using English as the instructional language, students would learn to master the language of the King James Bible and would thus be able to read the Bible in the "original." An important economic consideration was the ready availability of textbooks and teaching materials in English but not in Cherokee. Those who favored teaching in the Native language countered these arguments by pointing out that the use of English necessitated a much longer instructional period for full-blood children; it simply took longer to teach the subject matter in English when the students were burdened by learning the English language. This would have been an economic disadvantage if it were not for another difficulty posed by this method: full-blood children became bored and restless by the slow pace and simply dropped out in discouragement. This led to schools with mainly mixed-blood populations. The problem of Indian schools catering primarily to mixed-blood children continued throughout the nineteenth century all across the country.

Many of the missionaries saw the advantages of using Cherokee as the instructional language in the schools. For children who had many adjustments to make, one major source of pressure was removed. Full-blood children found learning nonlanguage subjects easier when they were taught in their native tongue. Missionaries also made the point that getting religious instruction in Cherokee meant that the children absorbed the precepts of Christianity more quickly than they would by having to learn English first. Once the scriptures were translated, children could read them readily. Isaac Proctor and others saw this as a great advantage that would bring godliness to the heathens more quickly and whet their appetites for civilization. Proctor also argued that literacy in Cherokee would encourage people to send their children to English schools once they witnessed the advantages of literacy and realized the world that being able to read and write English would open up. Some difficulties were inherent in this approach, however. The system required a high degree of fluency among teachers that could be obtained only through hard work and immersion among Cherokee speakers. Even then, teachers found that they needed the assistance of translators in the schools. As early as 1818, Humphrey Posey cited the difficulty of finding bilingual teachers for the missions.[18] Another issue was that textbooks and other materials were not readily available, and later, when translations were made, they were not printed but were distributed in manuscript form. Some teachers and missionaries thought that abstract concepts, for example, original sin or redemption, were not familiar to Cherokee culture and were impossible to transmit in the native language. They pointed out, most likely missing the irony, that the Cherokees had no words for sin, grace, repentance, baptism, depravity, forgiveness, heaven, hell, soul, salvation, or damnation.[19] Serious questions also arose about which instructional language would further the ultimate aims of the missions, namely, religious conversion, religious instruction, recruitment of Native preachers, and the retention of converts. The missionaries had to keep in mind as well that they were operating under the aegis of the federal government, which, since the Washington administration, had voiced a policy of civilizing and assimilating the Indians. Teaching in English supported both of these issues.

In time, however, both the ABCFM and the Baptist missionaries came around to the idea that teaching in Cherokee was more effective and suited their ultimate aims better than using English. By 1825, ABCFM officials in Boston had decided to do their work among the Indians in Native languages. The board began to heed the words of its own people in the field, like Cyrus Byington, who maintained that the easiest and quickest way to teach Native children English was to teach them to read their own language first.[20] The board took the positive step at that time of appointing Byington and Alfred Wright to learn and translate Choctaw and sent Samuel A. Worcester to do the same among the Cherokees.[21] Once this decision was made and they were able to sell the idea of bringing the scriptures to the Indians to their superiors, they turned to the task of translating the scriptures and teaching materials. The Baptists had already started on this huge work with the appointment of Evan Jones in 1822.

Evan Jones, born in Wales and educated in London, had emigrated to the United States at age thirty-three and had settled in Philadelphia. He became a teacher and was well versed in several languages, including his native Welsh and the clergyman's staples, Latin, Greek, and Hebrew. Jones and his wife, Elizabeth, were members of a Baptist church whose pastor, Thomas Roberts, was recruited by the Baptist Board of Foreign Missions to become a missionary to the Cherokees at their newly established outpost at Valley Towns. Roberts, in turn, enlisted several of his parishioners, including the Joneses, to accompany him, and the group traveled to the Cherokee Nation in September 1821. Jones remained with the Cherokees for the rest of his life. From the beginning of his missionary work, Jones recognized that he and his colleagues would never reach the full-bloods until they had learned their language; accordingly, he set about learning it from his Cherokee neighbors. He found the language very difficult and was further hampered in his effort by the lack of teachers and any kind of learning materials. With the conversion of bilingual Cherokee John Timson in 1823, however, he gained a tutor and began to make significant progress. Timson, the first Baptist convert, was a mixed-blood who lived near the Valley Towns mission, and because he was bilingual, he served as an interpreter to the full-bloods. Later, he helped Jones with his Bible translation attempts. Even with Timson's help, Jones did not reach a level of fluency at which he felt comfortable for ten years. Jones was convinced that literacy in their own language was the first necessary step on the path to religion and civilization for the Cherokees. He was also convinced that once they had reached this stage, they would have more incentive to learn English. This stance, of course, was directly opposite to that of those in the mission societies who maintained that tuition and literacy in the Native language would be to the detriment of an "English" education. Jones was so confident of his idea that he later organized schools in which Cherokees taught their own people the Sequoyan syllabary and how to use it. This project fell by the wayside, however, when it became evident that the method of one person teaching another wherever they happened to be was more efficient than the formal school arrangement. As time went on, Jones's promotion of Cherokee literacy seemed to bear fruit. "The Cherokees seem to take great interest in reading and give serious attention to relations [of Bible stories] which a few years ago, would have been treated as mere romance," he wrote in his journal in November 1829. "The Scripture in their own language seems to promote the exercise of their intellect and instead of retarding their progress in the learning of English, as was feared by some, seems to facilitate it."[22]

Jones was posted to the Valley Towns in the North Carolina and Alabama mountains in September 1821. Once he appraised the situation among the full-bloods there, he came to the conclusion that the only effective way to reach them was preaching and teaching in the Cherokee language. He and his colleague Thomas Roberts were "fully persuaded that all attempts to introduce the gospel amongst these benighted people in a foreign language must prove futile."[23] He threw himself into learning the language with an eye to translating the scriptures and teaching materials into Cherokee as soon as he became fluent; he expected that this would be relatively soon because he believed, as did most missionaries with little experience, that a "primitive" people would have a simple language. Even when Jones realized his mistake, he was undaunted and doubled his efforts to learn the language of his flock until it became "an obsession."[24] Still, it took him many years to master the language. Jones was committed to the idea of using Cherokee as the instructional language in spite of opposition from his superiors, who embraced the assumptions of those supporting the government's civilization program. He outlined his ideas in a letter to a "friend" of August 17, 1822, published in the *Latter Day Luminary*.[25] In the letter, he proposes to publish "a small book" to help teach full-bloods, predicting that books translated into Cherokee will accelerate learning "tenfold." He recognizes the objection that the supposed dearth of vocabulary of Cherokee makes it impossible to convey abstract ideas, but he points out that the language has "great facility of combination," which allows speakers to express new ideas. Jones dubs this ability "Native fertility." Another objection he refutes is that translation into Native languages slows down the civilization process. He objects that this is not true in Burma, India, and Africa, where Baptist missionaries had been engaged in translation and publication for some time. Jones says that those who oppose teaching in Cherokee often make the point that teaching in Cherokee slows the acquisition of English, a goal of the civilization plan. Not so, Jones answers, demonstrating that American children who speak and read English are quick to learn new languages; here, Jones anticipates modern linguists who maintain that advanced language skills in one language ease the transition into a second. At this point in his letter, Jones makes a rather inflammatory comment to his friend, opining that objectors to teaching in Cherokee do not want to go to the trouble of learning Cherokee without the assistance of grammars, dictionaries, and instructional materials. His missive then lists the advantages of teaching, translating, and printing in Cherokee: a thousand students may be taught for the cost of a hundred in English because no time will be lost in teaching the students English before other teaching can begin; texts in Cherokee will reach more people, especially the scriptures; students will be more eager to learn in their native language; the chiefs and leading citizens will be more enthusiastic about the schools; and social and Christian virtue will be advanced. Jones ends the letter with the comment that he and his colleague, Rev. Thomas Roberts, have a number of materials ready to be translated, namely, a spelling book and accounts from the Bible, including the Creation, the Flood, Babel, the story of Abraham, the birth of Christ, and the third chapter of the Gospel of John.

Because Jones had been in the Cherokee Nation less than a year when he wrote his letter, it is doubtful that he had satisfactorily translated these materials into the Cherokee language. Fluency was a major obstacle to the missionaries' goals, but another problem for would-be translators of texts surfaced as well around this time, namely, transcribing Cherokee into a readable script. Jones's idea at first was to represent the sounds of Cherokee using the roman alphabet, a common way of proceeding among missionaries in Hawaii and other places. The Moravians had tried this as early as 1802, with the aid of bilingual Cherokee Charles R. Hicks, but had abandoned their efforts because certain sounds of Cherokee could not be expressed in the roman alphabet.[26] Jones and Roberts collected, they thought, all the sounds of Cherokee and then "fixed characters to represent them." Jones then collected verbs and their forms, while Roberts prepared a dictionary. They discovered that Cherokee verbs were modified by suffixes and prefixes, just like Hebrew verbs. This fact was possibly of interest because of the previously noted widespread belief among many churchmen in the eighteenth and early nineteenth centuries that the Indians were one of the "lost tribes" of Israel. Jones claimed to find twelve thousand inflections of the Cherokee verb "to bring," which doubtless revealed to him the error of thinking that "primitive" people must speak "simple" languages. In spite of their work, the Baptist missionaries ran into the same problem as the Moravians had in finding a satisfactory script. They looked around for help and found it in Rev. Daniel S. Butrick, an ABCFM missionary.

Butrick had worked on the transliteration problem until he thought that he had invented a workable scheme based on the roman alphabet. Butrick, Roberts, and Jones joined forces and and created an alphabet from Roman characters which approximates all the sounds in the language. Butrick reported that he and the other translators had agreed on the tricky question of representing the distinct vowel sounds of Cherokee.[27] Using this system, he and Jones set about making their translations in the fall of 1822. With the help of James Wafford, Roberts and Jones translated the first chapters of Genesis, the second chapter of Matthew, the third chapter of John, and other passages on the Creation, the Fall, and the life of Jesus. When Wafford read the finished manuscript to a Cherokee audience, they understood it. Wafford had a white father and a Cherokee mother and had lived in a white settlement in Georgia before moving to the Valley Towns. Even after living with whites, he was unsure of his English and so had enrolled in the Baptist school in order to improve his skills.[28]

Daniel S. Butrick was born in Windsor, Massachusetts, in 1789. Ordained in 1818, he almost immediately left the East for the Cherokee Nation, among whose people he, like Jones, remained for the rest of his life. Although he believed that the Indians were derived from the lost tribes of Israel mentioned in the Bible, Butrick did as much as almost any other white man to learn the language and culture of the Cherokees. He determined early on that in order to serve the spiritual needs of his congregation, a minister must learn its language. To achieve his goal of learning Cherokee, he left the relative comfort of his assigned post at the Brainerd mission and moved in with a full-blood family. Operating at first under the naive assumption mentioned earlier that aboriginal languages must be simple ones, he soon was amazed at the richness he found as his fluency increased. "He found nine modes, fifteen tenses and three numbers, singular, dual, and plural. No prepositions or auxiliary verbs were employed, these adjuncts being in the verbs themselves. Pronouns were seldom used; instead the nouns were repeated," reports Grant Foreman.[29] Later, Buttrick reported to Jeremiah Evarts that he considered the Cherokee language "far superior" to English and saw no problem in translating subtle or abstract ideas into it. Butrick also differed from many of his colleagues in that he had a special feeling for the full-bloods, who, he thought, were being ignored by many of the mixed-blood leaders and by some missionaries. He was especially incensed by the growing riches of the mixed-bloods while most of the full-bloods lived in poverty.[30]

Although Butrick was in the Cherokee Nation under the auspices of the ABCFM, his superiors in Massachusetts did not agree with his linguistic methods. The board had appointed John Pickering, a linguist at Harvard University, to create an orthographic scheme, beginning with Cherokee, that would allow translations of all Native languages. Besides Latin, Greek, and Hebrew, Pickering had an extensive knowledge of Chinese, African, and Pacific dialects, as well as Native American languages. He had published a major work, *On the Adoption of a Uniform Orthography for the Indian Languages of North America*, in the series Memoirs of the American Academy in 1816,[31] so from the ABCFM's point of view, he was the perfect scholar to tackle the problem. David Brown, a Cherokee translator and student at Andover, was hired as his assistant. However, when Butrick learned how Pickering's work was progressing in 1821, he sent word via Jeremiah Evarts that the linguist should use a unique character for each distinct vowel sound because Cherokee had many of these.[32] Pickering's development of Native orthographies was a response to the political ideology of the time that dictated that Native languages were obstacles to communications between Indians and whites.[33]

In Butrick's letter to Evarts, he notified the secretary that he was pressing ahead with his translations in the modified roman alphabet he had devised, starting with the first chapters of Genesis, the predictions of the coming of Jesus in the Old Testament, an account of Jesus's miracles, and some psalms. He planned to devote "a few months" to memorizing what he had translated to use in his sermons.

At this point, he had finished the translation of a sixty-two-page book, *A Summary of the Doctrines of Jesus Christ*, with great assistance from fellow missionary Ard Hoyt and his wife, Sylvia. In addition, Butrick had plans to produce a Cherokee dictionary and grammar. He seems to have been acting more as a facilitator than as a translator at this time because he told Evarts that he was doing little more than writing down the translations of others. However, he seemed content to play this role as long as his work had practical value. There is little doubt that Butrick's idea was to use the Cherokee language to bring his religion to the Indians, and his linguistic work was devoted to that end.

Butrick and Jones needed help from native speakers of Cherokee with their translation efforts, of course, because they would not be fully fluent in the language until many years later. They enlisted in their efforts, in addition to Timson, John Arch (Asti) and David Brown. Arch had attended school for a while as a child and had begun to learn to read English but had never gone far enough to achieve reading fluency. However, he could speak English, and as a young man, he heard that a school had opened for the purpose of teaching Cherokees to read. According to one account, he traveled 150 miles on foot to reach Brainerd, where he became a student and also served as a translator. Later he was appointed a preacher at the Creek Path mission, but his health declined until his death in 1824 or 1825. David Brown had been a promising figure in the Cherokee Nation from early on and had been one of a group of young men who had been sent to Cornwall, Connecticut, to be educated.

In 1817, the ABCFM had established a school at Cornwall that would invite only the best scholars from its mission schools to continue their education, with the expectation that the Native students thus trained would return to their respective peoples to aid in the civilizing process that the missionaries had undertaken. The first class of students was made up of Hawaiians and students from the Indian subcontinent. In the next year, Elias Cornelius, a Congregationalist preacher who was interested in educating Indian students from the southeastern tribes, escorted three Cherokee students to the school, among them Leonard Hicks, son of Charles Hicks, and Elias Boudinot. The following year, John Ridge, David Brown, and other Cherokee young men entered as well, for a total of ten. At first, the townspeople welcomed the students, whom they saw as earnest young men seeking civilization and salvation. Ironically, though, after both John Ridge (in 1824) and Elias Boudinot (in 1826) married daughters of townspeople, the resulting uproar from citizens and the press forced the school to close in 1827. Earlier, however, David Brown had been sent to Andover Theological Seminary by Jeremiah Evarts, who saw in the boy someone who would make a fine missionary to his people. While Brown was at Andover, he helped Pickering develop his alphabet; he left Andover to return to the Cherokee Nation without completing his studies. Evarts encouraged him to return to the seminary, but Brown died before he could do so.

Arch and Brown were instrumental in the translation efforts into the roman-based alphabet of Butrick and others, and by 1824, they had translated passages from the New Testament that were then copied by Christian Cherokees. Arch finished the Gospel of John in the fall of that year, and Stephen Foreman reports that the translation was copied "hundreds of times" by Cherokees and distributed widely.[34] However, Brown and Arch were relatively new to Christianity, so they made mistakes.[35]

In early 1825, Butrick, the main promoter of the translation effort, wrote to Evarts proposing that the Prudential Committee hire David Brown at a salary of twenty dollars per month to work full-time on the translation, with Major George Lowery assisting.[36] Lowery was a mixed-blood leader of the Cherokees who later served as second principal chief under John Ross. He was an ardent supporter of education in the Cherokee Nation and was especially interested in establishing a school fund so that the Cherokees would control their own educational system. Butrick marked the team's progress in a letter to Evarts in May 1825 in which he expressed the wish that if the board had plans to send missionaries to the Arkansas Cherokees in the fall, they would take along the New Testament manuscript in the roman-based alphabet, because it would be finished by then.[37] He added that eight chapters of Matthew had been translated and that he was devoting all his time to the work.

Butrick was not Brown's only champion with the ABCFM. Charles Hicks, a prominent mixed-blood convert, promoted the idea of Brown's employment as translator, but he was adamant that the young Cherokee's first job should be the translation of the New

Testament from its original Greek. Brown had learned Greek as part of his seminary work, Hicks reasoned, so the task should not be beyond his means. Hicks also identified the federal government or the Cherokee National Council as potential sources for Brown's compensation.[38] Hicks's idea was rejected, but Brown continued to translate from English. However, Ard Hoyt, whose wife, Sylvia, had begun to help Brown in his work, reported that Brown generally followed the English version in his translation, although when that seemed to convey a different meaning from the Greek, he followed the latter. This work continued until Butrick was able to report in September 1825 that much of the New Testament had been translated into the roman-based alphabet; he anticipated completion sometime in October. The project had been slowed, he noted, because by this time Brown was working without assistance, except that of Sylvia Hoyt. In the late spring of 1825, Butrick had assembled a translation group consisting of Brown as chief translator and Lowery as reviewer, assisted by Elias Boudinot.[39] The work of these three was then checked by another native speaker, Whirlwind, and Charles Hicks gave the translation a final going over.[40] Charles Hicks was a prominent Cherokee who brought his interest in promoting the use of the Cherokee language to the tribal councils, serving as second principal chief and later principal chief. He had paved the way for National Council acceptance of the Baptist missions and was a vocal member of the frequent delegations that met with federal officials.

Another Cherokee who assisted in translating the scriptures into Cherokee was Jesse Bushyhead, whose parents were Cherokee; one of his grandfathers was a British army captain. Bushyhead grew up bilingual and attended the ABCFM school at Candy Creek in Tennessee. He was licensed to preach by the Baptists, and Evan Jones ordained him to the ministry in 1833, when he was employed by the Baptist Board. Bushyhead was a better linguist than Timson, so he was called on to assist Jones in the translation efforts. In 1835, he was elected to the National Council and later became chief justice of the Cherokee Supreme Court.[41]

But for all the missionary debates and attempts to craft a suitable script to convey the Cherokee language, in the end the Cherokees themselves chose the vehicle. Around 1821, an event took place that perhaps is unique in the history of nations, the introduction of Sequoyah's Cherokee syllabary. This invention was to challenge the assumptions of the missionaries and the proponents of a civilization policy and would bring about lasting and profound changes. It would transform the Cherokee nation, in a matter of months, from a largely illiterate people to one whose citizens could read and write. The syllabary was embraced by nearly all the Cherokee speakers immediately, and by the "civilizers" in a very short time. Invented by a man who could not read, spoke fluent Cherokee, and knew little or no English, the syllabary consisted of eighty-six characters, each of which represented a Cherokee syllable. Speakers of that language needed only to memorize the characters, and within days they could read anything written using the syllabary. Modern linguists agree that there are three requirements for a successful writing system: the symbols in the script should account for all sounds, each symbol should represent only one phoneme, and the total number of symbols must be limited so that the memory of the users is not taxed.[42] Sequoyah's syllabary met all the requirements.

When the system became known to the missionaries, some debate ensued, fueled largely by sheer disbelief that an unlettered aborigine could have invented a successful reading and writing process. The question was rendered moot, however, when the Cherokees adopted the syllabary with great enthusiasm and refused to entertain the thought of using Pickering's, or anybody else's, alphabet. For ordinary Cherokees, the system was a practical tool that allowed them to correspond directly with friends and family in Arkansas, an ability that was extremely important to them. Moreover, the Cherokees recognized that the syllabary allowed them to keep records of farms and business activities in which they might be engaged. Many of the leaders, especially among the full-bloods, saw that they now had the means to preserve tribal institutions and culture that were increasingly being eroded as more and more assimiliation and adoption of white practices took place. The mixed-blood leaders saw that they could use the system in the constitution project that they were promoting; if the constitution were published in both languages, most Cherokees would be able to read and understand it.[43] Sequoyah's system had advantages that the Cherokees recognized immediately; its practical advantage was that it was quicker and easier to learn than any alphabet, but the intrinsic quality that it was wholly Cherokee made it overwhelmingly popular among the people. By 1826, Elias Boudinot was able to report in his "Address to the Whites" that "those characters have now become extensively used in the nation; their religious songs are written in them; there is an astonishing eagerness in people of all classes and ages to acquire a knowledge of them."[44]

George Guess, or Sequoyah, the author of this remarkable writing system, grew up among full-bloods speaking only Cherokee. Several accounts of his life exist, some of which contradict others, but some biographical facts are undisputed. Emmet Starr, the Cherokee historian, reported that written language held a particular fascination for Sequoyah, even though at the time he began working seriously on his system, no Indian nation had a written language. Seeing the written page used by white people, he first thought that each letter represented a word, but he soon saw that this could not be true. Around 1809, he got the idea that letters stood for sounds; this idea was the seed from which the Cherokee syllabary grew.

Sequoyah, Starr reported in his September 12, 1905 biographical article published in the *Cherokee Advocate,* was born about 1760. The historian describes him as a man who was below medium height and slightly lame from a childhood affliction. Sequoyah adhered to the ancient beliefs of the Cherokees and wore the traditional shirt, leggings, moccasins, and turban. According to Starr and other biographers, he never acquired any knowledge of the English language. He had earlier been employed as both a blacksmith and a silversmith, but when he turned his full attention to developing his syllabary, his wife became unhappy because she considered his linguistic work a useless effort. Nonetheless, he pressed on, beginning with the idea that letters stood for sounds. He tested this theory by scratching out a character resembling the roman letter *G* and calling it "wa," a syllable in the Cherokee language, and then scratching next to it the letter *E,* which he called "ku." Together, the letters represented "wa-ku," the Cherokee word for "cow," thus affirming that he was on the right track. His task then was to assign symbols to all the syllables used in the language. For the symbols, he used characters from an old English spelling book, capitals, lowercase letters, and italics, sometimes placing them upside down; he supplemented these with symbols that were probably from his own imagination. By the time he had finished in 1821, he had created a syllabary of eighty-six characters, each standing for a Cherokee syllable, plus one to indicate a hissing sound.

Sequoyah's system was not immediately embraced once he revealed it. Starr reports that at one point, his wife gathered up all the pieces of bark on which he had penned a character, a couple of armfuls, and threw them into the fire. Luckily, Sequoyah by this time had consigned the syllabary to memory, so he could reproduce it without much difficulty. Others also thought that he was wasting his time, and some even said that he had come under the spell of witchcraft or was insane. In spite of these criticisms, he pressed on, knowing full well that he would make a fool of himself if he failed.

But he did not fail, completing this important linguistic work while he was living in a remote cabin in Arkansas Territory in 1820 or 1821. Once he had shown the Cherokees living there what he had done, he traveled back to the Cherokee Nation in present-day Georgia to share his work with the main body of the tribe. Here he was met with skepticism at first, but once he had taught the system to some Cherokee youths, who were able to learn it quickly and easily, tribal leaders became enthusiastic. Sequoyah was hired as a teacher to help spread the syllabary's use, and in a short time, any Cherokee speaker who desired to read the language could do so. Sequoyah did not stay in the eastern nation, however; he moved back west, settling in eastern Indian Territory, where the so-called Old Settler Cherokees had taken land after leaving Arkansas. Later, after the main body of Cherokees removed from the East, Sequoyah was active among his people, taking part in deliberations concerning several treaties and in the formulation of the Cherokee Constitution in 1839. In 1842, he accompanied his son Teesee to Texas, at the time an independent republic. Starr reports that he died there in August 1843, but his burial site is unknown. In one way, at least, Sequoyah died a disappointed man. He had hoped that his work would help preserve Cherokee "heritage, traditions, and religion" because he was an ardent nationalist. He was said to have been "bitterly disappointed" when the missionaries adopted the syllabary for translating the Bible and other Christian works.[45]

The creation of the syllabary has been universally hailed as a monumental work. It is noteworthy, as Starr points out, in that it is the only writing system created by one man. It is also remarkable in its completeness because everyone who understands Cherokee, once she or he has learned which syllables the characters represent, can read and write the language. Also, it gave the traditionalists a secret form of communication, a "code" beyond the perception of the authorities, white or red, enabling full-bloods in the eastern and western bodies of the Cherokee Nation to exchange ideas. The syllabary also gave the full-bloods a means of preserving Cherokee culture and allowed healers and religious leaders to keep their knowledge and to pass it on to initiates.[46] Preserving the traditional myths, rituals, and practices in this way undermined the religious project of the missionaries. At the time the syllabary was introduced in the early 1820s, a gap was widening between the 20 to 25 percent of mixed-bloods who knew only English and the full-bloods. Now, the majority full-bloods had a system of their own for self-expression, which helped them overcome feelings of inferiority to those Cherokees who could read and write English.[47] These feelings of inferiority had been fed by many of the missionaries, who saw themselves as "civilizers" and denigrated all things Cherokee, the people's language and culture. This strategy was aimed at making full-bloods ashamed of their heritage and the mixed-bloods proud of their education and their distinctiveness from the more "backward" members of the tribe. The ploy had worked, mainly because in Cherokee culture shame and ridicule were major means of expressing disapproval. But when the syllabary came into widespread use, the tables were turned. The people could learn to read and write using a system that was exclusively theirs but was closed to outsiders unless they devoted the time and energy necessary to learn to speak the language.

The Cherokee full-bloods took to the syllabary almost universally. Learning the system in two or three days, they began to write letters and even to erect signage along the roads. These signs, scratched on trees or fence posts, were the first indication many of the missionaries had of the syllabary's existence. But they soon sat up and took notice. "The knowledge of Mr. Guess's Alphabet is spreading through the nation like fire among the leaves," said one.[48] By early 1825, Isaac Proctor felt obliged to report to the ABCFM secretary that "letters in Cherokee are passing in all directions" and that "pens, ink, and paper [are] in great demand."[49] Daniel S. Butrick, who had labored hard and long to produce a Cherokee script, reported, "They can generally learn it in one day and in a week become writing masters and transact their business and communicate their thoughts freely and fully on religious and political subjects by writing."[50] So much for the lack of ability in the language to express abstract thought. Butrick went on to predict that the whole nation would be reading and writing within a year. Convinced of the effectiveness of the syllabary, he had already prepared a copy of the characters for his colleague Isaac Proctor.[51] Butrick also reported that the next step was to transliterate the New Testament into the Sequoyan syllabary, beginning with the book of Matthew. The work on this project began in September 1825.[52]

The Cherokees quickly put the syllabary to use. "A regular stream of correspondence was established between people in Wills Valley in the eastern nation and their countrymen beyond the Mississippi, five hundred miles to the west," reported the *Missionary Herald*.[53] Interest increased steadily, the account continues, until young Cherokees traveled "great distances to be instructed in this easy method of writing and reading." Pupils of the system generally could write letters within "three days and return home to teach others." The process of instruction in the Sequoyan syllabary seems to have been entirely unofficial, with individuals, mostly full-bloods, learning the system and then quietly passing it on to two or three others. Within a year of its introduction in 1821, Cherokee full-bloods were using it to communicate privately with one another; in 1824, William Chamberlin pointed out from Willstown that "a great part of the Cherokee people can read and write in their own language."[54] At first, it seemed to escape the notice even of prominent mixed-bloods in the nation. Elias Boudinot, for example, heard about it in the winter of 1822–23 from John Ross, who seemed to be unfamiliar with the details at the time. They were not enlightened fully on the system and its potential until a General Council meeting in 1824 at New Echota.[55]

The results of this homegrown literacy explosion were staggering. Stephen Foreman reports that by 1828, "almost all" the young and middle-aged men could read the syllabary, as well as many old men, women, and children. Cherokee symbols were painted or cut on trees by the road, on fences, on houses, and "often on pieces of bark or board, lying about the houses." Writing implements, ink, and paper continued to be in great demand.[56] Because of the informal way in which literacy in Cherokee spread, estimates of the numbers of readers involved vary widely. Willard Walker put the figure at 90 percent in the 1830s, while James Mooney said that in 1838, 75 percent could read. Elias Boudinot reported that in 1830, over 50 percent were literate. A modern linguist says that the data are too vague to ascertain an accurate figure.[57] William G. McLoughlin and Walter H. Conser, Jr., in their analysis of Cherokee census data, say that 33 to 47 percent of the population could read Cherokee in 1835; however, they go on to say that 53 to 64 percent were literate in either English or Cherokee at that time.[58] The Cherokee census of 1835 puts the number of Cherokees at 16,535, the number of readers of Cherokee at 2,714 (about 16.4 percent), and the number of readers of English at 1,071 (about 6.5 percent).[59] Whatever the exact figure is, there is no doubt that the Cherokee literacy explosion of the early 1820s was a phenomenal event, all the more incredible because of its grassroots nature; the impetus for it came from the people themselves rather than from the outside. It happened without funding, schools, or formal teachers; its effects had immense implications for the people and their future. Althea Bass's comments on the syllabary bear repeating: "Among the Cherokees, the question of a native literature was taken out of the control of the mission, by one of the most remarkable events in the history of the mind."[60] Ellen Cushman is of like mind. She writes that the Sequoyan syllabary allowed the Cherokees "to mediate and distribute knowledge in their own language using a writing system foreign to outsiders."[61]

Once the missionary societies had fully digested the news and realized the implications of Sequoyah's invention for their own work, they set out to oppose it. They realized that it would be difficult and expensive to translate texts, especially the scriptures, using this method; more important, it threatened to keep the Cherokee language alive, and they wanted it dead.[62] Although many of the whites in the Cherokee Nation did not learn the syllabary because to do so required learning the Cherokee language, many whites were sticking to the ideal of an English education for these "benighted" people. John Gambold, the veteran Moravian missionary, expressed the idea with a certainty that many in the missionary movement would agree with: "It is indispensably necessary for their preservation that they should learn our language and adopt our laws and Holy Religion," he pronounced. "The study of their language would in a great measure prove but time and labor lost . . . It seems desirable that their Language, Customs, Manner of Thinking, etc., should be forgotten."[63]

The argument of those who opposed use of the syllabary was expressed succinctly by the editor of the *Missionary Herald* in 1826. He defended the Pickering alphabet fervently, making the inaccurate point that it took "longer" to express the sounds of the Cherokee language with the syllabary than with the alphabet. He offered the example of Pickering's success with the Hawaiian language and asserted that once the alphabet was learned, a student could read "almost as soon as if it were a syllabic alphabet." It is clear that the decision to make Pickering's alphabet universally accepted for writing Native languages, whatever the clime or circumstances, had been made in the boardroom of the Prudential Committee. Another objection the editor made was the unique nature of the syllabary: "By the general use of this alphabet [sic], so unlike to every other, they will cut themselves off from that respect and sympathy from the intelligent of other nations, which they might expect should they make advances in literary acquisitions and should those advances become extensively known," because few outside the Cherokee Nation would make the effort to learn the system. He went on to say that the cost of matrices and types for printing would be great, and "printing will be a perplexing and laborious business." Additionally, there would be so few customers for printed books in Cherokee that publishers could not recoup their costs from such meager sales and so would not, in all likelihood, embark on publication in the first place. The editor's final point, which would also be made by prominent Cherokees in the post-Removal period, was that to use the Cherokee language and the syllabary to the exclusion of English would deprive the people of many of the excellent works written and printed in that language. The editor's thoughts on the matter were very similar to those of the ABCFM, as well as those of the other missionary societies and sponsors.[64]

As time went on, however, the missionaries in the Cherokee country changed their minds. One of the reasons for this was that there seemed to be an immediate effect in the mission schools. Isaac

Proctor, who lived in a traditionalist part of the Cherokee Nation, was one of the first to report on the new literacy's effect on his school. He commented on conditions in July 1825: "All the scholars, as well as all of the neighborhood, have become conversant in this new way of writing . . . This, more than anything else, has operated against English schools."[65] Proctor's view that the Cherokees did not need the schools to achieve literacy, an idea that was reinforced by a drop in attendance, especially among the full-bloods, in time got the notice of missionaries and the societies alike. In fact, the percentage of full-bloods in mission schools schools peaked in 1821, the year in which Sequoyah introduced his system to his people.[66] The missionaries in the nation were the first to regard Sequoyah's system as a way to reach the Cherokees in a way in which the "English" school system could not. Charles Hicks, the mixed-blood champion of education and Christianity, saw literacy in Cherokee as a means to increase a desire for learning among the "lower" classes (meaning full-bloods) and a way to bring them eventually to knowledge and appreciation of literature written in English. Missionary Ard Hoyt had begun to express similar views among his colleagues in 1824.[67]

William Chamberlin, another missionary, related the story of a ride he had taken with several Native youths who had become literate in Cherokee. During their discussion, the young men told Chamberlin that it was "vastly important" that the New Testament be translated and printed in the syllabary "immediately" because "a great part" of the people could now read and write. Cherokee literacy, they went on, could not be stopped and would continue to spread until everyone in the nation could read and write their native tongue. Chamberlin agreed and suggested to the ABCFM secretary that some young Cherokee men be hired to work with Ard Hoyt to translate the scriptures. A knowledge of English, he wrote, would not be required.[68]

The idea of translating the scriptures into the syllabary quickly gained support, as well as the idea of printing and distributing the finished product. Even those who had worked hard to develop a script for Cherokee based on the roman alphabet became adherents of the new system. One of these, Daniel S. Butrick, was quick to point out that the missionaries had little choice in the matter. Although he knew that the Prudential Committee of the American

Board would rather translate using the Pickering alphabet that it had helped develop and was adapting to other Native languages, Butrick pressed his superiors for use of the syllabary. Cherokees could learn it in "one day and in a week become writing masters," he wrote. In the year's time that it would take to translate the New Testament, the Cherokees would be fully proficient in the system and so could read the New Testament and other books "without any trouble on our part."[69] As the theoretical debate continued, practical-minded missionaries adopted the syllabary with the full blessing of their congregations. Butrick, never one to wait for permission from Boston to do what he saw as his duty, learned the syllabary and began to translate using that medium. Because he had done work in translating the Scriptures into the Cherokee language, he added the step of expressing his translations in the new system. It is telling that Butrick and Jones deserted the roman-based alphabet they had worked so hard to develop in favor of the syllabary. They set to work converting their manuscript translations of the Scriptures into Sequoyah's syllabary. The manuscripts copied from their work were passed from hand to hand as the Christian Cherokees eagerly devoured whatever materials were at hand in their own language, especially because they were expressed in a system from the hand of one of their own. Missionary Isaac Proctor testified to the ease of learning the syllabary when he told of "a little scholar" who could not form an English letter writing out a sentence in Cherokee that could be read by all at the mission who were literate in the Sequoyan system. Proctor was enthusiastic about the new writing and reported to Evarts that if the board could distribute five hundred Bibles printed in the syllabary to five hundred Cherokee families, all could read it within one month.[70] Later, the process would become more efficient when the King James phrases were transformed directly into Sequoyah's characters. Other religious tracts were rendered into the Sequoyan syllabary as time went on, including such standards as *The Dairy-man's Daughter* by Leigh Richmond and a work of Elias Boudinot's, a rendering of the days from Passion Week to the Ascension. By late 1826, the Cherokee National Council had gotten involved in the translation effort, appointing Major Lowery and David Brown to continue their work.[71] In a few months, Brown was working with

Samuel A. Worcester because the Cherokee was recognized as the foremost linguist among all the principals.[72]

Two figures who were to have a substantial influence on Cherokee literacy, translation, and printing were in the Cherokee Nation around the time at which the debate on adoption of Sequoyah's syllabary was going on in missionary circles. The first of these was Evan Jones, the Baptist minister who had arrived in the Valley Towns, a predominantly full-blood section of the nation, in 1821 and was an early advocate of teaching in the Cherokee Nation. Jones and his colleague, Thomas Roberts, had allied themselves with Butrick to produce a script based on the roman alphabet at the same time at which Pickering was working on his alphabet to be able to translate the scriptures and other materials into Cherokee. When Jones found out about Sequoyah's invention in early 1826, however, he adopted it "immediately"[73] and abandoned his earlier work. When Samuel Austin Worcester, an ABCFM missionary as well as a linguist with a background in printing, discovered the syllabary shortly after his arrival at Brainerd, he joined with Jones, Butrick, and other missionaries who were convinced that the syllabary could be used as a means of spreading the gospel, as well as an effective teaching tool. Jones's journal entry for March 3, 1830, succinctly states the case: "The syllabic writing, which has been frequently learned in a day, is exerting an influence almost miraculous, and if this instrument were wisely and vigorously directed, its effects [would] . . . exceed all calculations."[74] Worcester and Jones were to play significant roles in Cherokee history in subsequent years, not least in the evolution of translation and publishing.

The Baptists had been slow in initiating their missionary efforts among the Cherokees. After they founded four small schools in 1818, they abandoned their efforts because of the confusion surrounding attempts to remove the Cherokees to Arkansas at that time. In the following year, they were able to negotiate with the National Council and with local chiefs in present-day North Carolina and Alabama to establish a school and mission in the Valley Towns. The American Baptist Foreign Mission Society, parent organization of the Baptist Board of Foreign Missions, had its headquarters in Philadelphia until 1826, when it moved to Boston, where wealthy patrons were interested in the missionary effort among the Indians. Boston was also the home of the ABCFM, and many of the New Englanders who backed that group supported the Baptists as well. The result was an agreement on how the missions among the Indians should be run, including accord on issues of language and translation. It quickly became clear to missionaries such as Jones, Butrick, and Worcester that it was in their interest to pool resources and present a united front to their respective societies.

Samuel Worcester was the junior missionary in the group most concerned with language issues at the time, but he soon was in the forefront. Worcester, one in a long line of clergymen, was born on January 19, 1798, in Worcester, Massachusetts, the son of Leonard Worcester, who had begun his adult life as a printer but later became a minister, and Elizabeth Hopkins, daughter of Samuel Hopkins, D.D., of Hadley, Massachusetts. In a few years, the elder Worcester moved his family to Peacham, Vermont, where he became pastor of the Congregational Church there. Samuel began his education in the Academy of Peacham, then under the direction of Jeremiah Evarts, who later became the secretary of the ABCFM. Later, he entered the University of Vermont, where his uncle, Dr. Samuel Austin, was president. He graduated with honors in 1819 after having "experienced religion." He entered the Theological Seminary at Andover, where he showed a decided penchant for learning languages, even beyond the usual Greek, Latin, and Hebrew expected from clergymen at the time.[75] When he was ordained on August 25, 1825, the newly married Worcester set out with his wife, Ann, for the Cherokee Nation as a missionary for the ABCFM. He remained with the Cherokees for the rest of his life as missionary and teacher; like Evan Jones, he was a figure in the political history of the tribe as well. Worcester was a principal in an important Supreme Court case, *Worcester v. Georgia*, in 1832 that pitted the treaty rights of the Cherokees against the jurisdiction of the state of Georgia. John Marshall and a majority of the court sustained the position of the Cherokees and the missionary, but both the state government and the federal administration of Andrew Jackson refused to honor the decision. Worcester and fellow missionary Elizur Butler languished in a Georgia penitentiary for a year before being released. Worcester removed with the Cherokees to Indian Territory and set up his mission in Park

Hill, just outside Tahlequah, the Cherokee capital, where he remained until his death. At Park Hill, he continued the translation and publishing work he had started in the eastern nation.

From his arrival in the nation in 1825, Worcester recognized the importance and potential of the syllabary, and he wrote to convince the Prudential Committee of his opinions. For its part, the committee listened to him because of his reputation as a linguist, one of the major reasons he had been sent to the nation. Worcester not only advocated translating scriptures into and teaching in the Cherokee language but also urged his superiors to provide a printing press that would disseminate religious and other "useful" information to the people who could read the syllabary.[76] The printing press was a topic in the letters that flowed between Cherokees in Arkansas and those in the East even before Worcester made his way to the nation. As it turned out, the Cherokee leadership agreed to finance the venture when its time came.[77] Worcester answered the arguments of board members in Boston that use of the syllabary would lead to a disinterest in learning English and thus deprive the Cherokees of the joys of reading the scriptures by asserting that translation of the Bible into the syllabary would make Christian literature available to the full-bloods almost immediately. Besides, he argued, the Cherokees would stand for nothing else; "national feeling" and pride in Sequoyah's accomplishment were too strong to be ignored, he astutely reported in early 1826.[78] In correspondence with the *Missionary Herald* around the same time, Worcester reported the widespread and easily acquired employment of the syllabary, adding, "That it will prevail over every other method of writing the language, there is no doubt. If a book were printed in that character, there are those in every part of the nation, who could read it at once; and many others would only have to obtain a few hours' instruction from some friend, to enable them to do so."[79] Reading a book in English, on the other hand, would require a lengthy period in school to learn the language, and even then, readership would be restricted to children for years to come. He estimated that "at least twenty, perhaps fifty, times as many would read a book printed with Guyst's [sic] characters as would read one printed with the English alphabet."

A year later, in 1827, the ABCFM was still promoting the Pickering alphabet it had commissioned, but Worcester was still preaching his original sermon. The difference in learning the Pickering alphabet or the syllabary was small. The "grand consideration" was that "if books are printed in Guess's characters, they will be read," because the Cherokees considered the syllabary superior. Their enthusiasm for reading in it had been "kindled"; to force Pickering on them at this stage was to "throw water on fire." Once again, he pointed out that the people were circulating manuscripts and writing letters in Sequoyan, so it was too late to stanch the enthusiasm for the syllabary. Print in the Sequoyan syllabary, he told the readers of the *Missionary Herald*, and hundreds would read it immediately.[80] This correspondence perhaps marks the turning point for the mission societies' acceptance of the syllabary in the Cherokee missions because by late 1827, they had agreed that Jones, Worcester, Butrick, and others working in the nation were right. They were accepting a fait accompli. The editor of the *Missionary Herald* changed his tune to reflect those of the governing boards of the missionary societies. He reported with amazement that "in some places and in the tribe at large, more than one half are actually capable of reading their own language in their own peculiar character, having learned from small manuscripts, and without ever having become acquainted with any other alphabet, or possessed a single page of a printed book in any language." Peculiar it might be, Samuel Worcester had pointed out in the same publication previously, but the nature of the syllabary was the very reason for its success; "When an English scholar recollects the tedious months occupied in the spelling book, he regards it as a matter of astonishment, and nearly incredible, that an active Cherokee boy can learn to read his own language in a day."[81] Worcester and Jones, having convinced their superiors of the efficacy of using Sequoyah's system, now turned their attention to the next step, printing in the syllabary.

The Cherokees' decision to acquire education and literacy was part of a larger historical process. Since before the turn of the nineteenth century, the Cherokees had debated how to react to the continuing and increasing pressure from the white society closing in around them. There was little doubt that the white culture was affecting their own. Decades earlier they had acquired trade goods such as guns, iron traps, farm implements, and other metal utensils. They had watched as fellow tribesmen became addicted to the alcohol that was pressed on them. Many well-to-do Cherokees lived like white men, keeping African American slaves, using horse-drawn vehicles, and living in large houses instead of traditional cabins. Perceptive and thoughtful Cherokees saw their culture being eroded and their lifeways and customs being replaced by those of the larger society; these thinkers and leaders knew that the Cherokees as a nation needed to be heedful of these changes and to take control of the situation as best they could. They debated what appeared to be the three choices open to them: reject the white man's way and return to the traditional culture while they still could; take what they considered valuable from the white society and reject those things they regarded as evil or of no use; or adopt the white man's ways wholeheartedly, accepting the settler's culture as superior.

The Cherokee leaders chose the middle course, which led to their inviting missionaries to their country with the stipulation that the whites would build schools and bring education and literacy to the nation. Others, especially many of the full-bloods, disagreed with this policy and favored preserving the traditional lifeways, including the language. Many of the mixed-bloods, especially intermarried whites, wanted to accept the white man's ways totally. Not surprisingly, these differences of opinion led to conflict among the leaders, as well as among the rest of the populace. Whatever their convictions on the matter, however, the Cherokees were in agreement that they should take charge of their own affairs. Accordingly, the National Council passed a law during 1811–12 requiring all whites who entered Cherokee country to acquire a license from the council that limited their stay to a specific period. It also requested that the federal agent, Return J. Meigs, remove those without such permission.[82]

Around the same time, an event occurred that was to influence the Cherokees greatly. In late January 1811, a man and two women reported a vision they had seen at Rocky Mountain in present-day northern Georgia. News of the vision traveled quickly among the people, causing a sensation and eventually leading to a cultural revival. The three said that ghostly riders and a drummer had appeared to them and told them to return to the old religion. They had been told to act slowly and to reflect on what they were doing when they had to make decisions about adopting the white man's ways. The speakers did not call for armed conflict against the whites or instruct the Cherokees to reject totally what the whites dictated. Rather, the people should decide for themselves which path to take rather than have their culture abandoned or destroyed from the outside. The licensing law was in harmony with this message and, in effect, served notice that the Cherokees were in charge of their own affairs. The end of the vision held particular significance for the course the Cherokee Nation was to take for the next decades. The three were told to look to the sky, where they beheld a heavenly light and four houses. The drummer said that the houses were for James Blair and for other white men who could be useful to the nation with writing and other things.[83] The message was culturally ambivalent, but the fact that writing was specifically mentioned was not lost on the Cherokees.[84] Ten months or so later, when the earthquakes of late 1811 and early 1812 were felt, they were seen as vindication of the vision. New visions and prophecies were reported, and there was a revival of dances and ceremonies. Even mixed-bloods, well on their chosen path of acculturation, began to reconsider their adoption of white dress and American-style dances featuring fiddles and other white instruments. Meigs and other white men, unaware of the vision at Rocky Mountain, attributed the activities to the earthquakes. The agent and the Moravian missionaries maintained that the revival simmered down after 1812, but with the exception of Charles Hicks's conversion to Christianity in 1813, the missionaries recorded no converts between 1810 and 1818. The end of the revival, if not its influence, may be marked more precisely by the Battle of Horseshoe Bend in 1814. After this victory of the Cherokees over the Red Stick Muscogees, the people were left with a sense of national pride and power that further contributed to their resolve to determine their own destiny. An important part of that destiny was to be achieved through knowledge arrived at through education and literacy.

Soon, though, pressure from the whites increased and this time threatened to split the nation by sending a great many of its citizens west of the Mississippi River. The old threat of Removal was clearer and closer, causing great consternation and forcing the Cherokees to make some hard decisions. The so-called 1817 treaty, ratified in

March 1819, ceded 4 million acres to insatiable settlers and land speculators, nearly one-third of the remaining Cherokee ancestral lands. In return, the Cherokees were given a grant between the Arkansas and White Rivers in Arkansas Territory, land occupied by the Osages. An estimated two thousand to three thousand Cherokees emigrated to the new territory, hoping to preserve their traditional way of life and to remove themselves from white influence. At this same time, missionaries were entering the nation, and the federal government was pursuing its schizoid policy through the Civilization Act of 1819, increasing the pressure to acculturate on those who remained in the East. As time went on, many of the full-bloods objected to what they saw as the National Council's acquiescence to this pressure.

The threat of Removal was not new. During the winter of 1808–1809, a Cherokee delegation had met with President Thomas Jefferson in an attempt to ascertain the federal government's plans for the Indians of the Southeast. Andrew Jackson assumed that Jefferson had informed the delegation that the Cherokees were expected to cede their lands in exchange for a homeland in the West because some 1,100 to 1,500 Cherokee citizens had already emigrated to Arkansas. Jackson was mistaken, however, because the government had failed to provide land either for those who were being enticed to remove or those who had already gone. But Jackson was not satisfied, especially because he and his colleague John Coffee were speculating in land as the Georgia and South Carolina cotton growers were looking for new areas to cultivate. Jackson and Coffee planned to provide that land at the expense of the southeastern tribes. Accordingly, when Jackson made peace with the Red Stick (Muscogee) Creeks in 1814, he included within the boundaries of the area that was given to the Creeks land that had been settled by the Cherokees, Jackson's allies in the Red Stick War. The Cherokees, naturally, complained to the federal government, and in 1816, the land was ceded back to the Cherokees by treaty. A further stipulation of the March 1816 treaty, however, was the relinquishment by the Cherokees of claims to all land in South Carolina. Jackson tried to undo this settlement when in September and October of the same year, he treated with "a tiny minority" of Cherokee leaders to regain for the United States (and the land speculators) the 2.2 million acres of land that had been in dispute originally between the Creeks and Cherokees. The tireless Jackson then made a treaty with the Cherokees in 1817 that provided for the removal of the tribe to Arkansas, a treaty opposed by the majority of the people. During all the time these manuevers were going on, individual Cherokee citizens were fed a constant line from white agents urging them to remove on the grounds that it was a certain eventuality. The people were in turmoil, and many families left for the West, bringing the total there to 3,000 or 3,500. Officials in Washington then took action to try to bring some order out of the chaos Jackson had created and signed the 1819 treaty, by which the Cherokee Nation ceded 4 million acres in the East in return for a tract in Arkansas to accommodate those who had emigrated. The remainder of the tribe was allowed to stay in the East. At that point, recognizing that the populace was becoming scattered, the National Council passed an act making it illegal for any Cherokee citizen to emigrate.

Andrew Jackson had risen to power in large part because of his Indian policy. Jackson's position was that Indians were not advanced enough to use the land in the East properly, so the savages must be moved west of the Mississippi, where they would have ample hunting land and would be out of the way of settlers who would husband the land the way God intended. The mixed-blood Cherokee leaders were cognizant of Jackson's views and his rising power. Their counterview was that to resist Removal, they must move the nation quickly toward acculturation. A group of educated, churchgoing farmers, they reasoned, would not fit the white man's definition of "savage," and they would thus be allowed to stay on their land, living much as their white neighbors lived. The missionaries shared these ideas and supported the steps the mixed-blood-dominated National Council was taking toward this end, including a series of modernizing laws passed between 1823 and 1827. A Cherokee middle class that embraced white culture was gaining power in the nation's government. Already, many of the mixed-blood leaders were widening the gap between themselves and the full-blood majority of the nation. This Cherokee bourgeoisie had undertaken extensive farming practices using black slaves, had engaged in commerce through purchase of goods from white settlements for resale to Cherokees, had established and maintained ferries and turnpikes, and owned the mills that ground the Cherokee grain. These mixed-bloods cooperated with the missionaries and the government agents and embraced "English" education. Few, even leaders like Principal Chief John Ross, knew the Cherokee language well enough to address the people and were forced to communicate with the full-bloods through interpreters. They promoted the idea of the Cherokees as a "civilized" people because they saw this as their bulwark against Removal. This Cherokee "bourgeoisie," as historian William G. McLoughlin terms it, was never very large in numbers, but it was very influential, especially with the missionaries and government officials. Basing their figures on the 1835 Cherokee census, McLoughlin and Walter H. Conser, Jr. put their number at from 8 to 10 percent of the total population. This figure roughly correlates with the number of slaveholders, 7.4 percent.[85] However, a sizable number of full-bloods and others viewed the civilization strategy with alarm because they feared that it would bring about the collapse of traditional Cherokee culture and play into the hands of the whites advocating Removal. The culmination of this fundamental difference of opinion was the White Path "Rebellion" of 1827.

Ironically, Sequoyah's syllabary played an important part in the "rebel" movement. Although the Christian missionaries had come around to regarding the syllabary as a tool for "civilizing" the Cherokees at this time, the system was a source of pride to the full-bloods; it fostered national identity and contributed to the antimissionary sentiments that were being expressed by the traditionalists. These Cherokees saw the syllabary as an integral part of their culture, and they used it to oppose the speedy acculturation that the mixed-bloods promoted, as well as the proselytizing of the missionaries. White Path and his followers believed that the Cherokees had their own religion and laws that were firmly based in their traditional culture and had no need of adopting those of the white people. They had their own language, which heretofore had existed in its oral form, but which now was written as well. Furthermore, as Stephen Brandon points out, literacy in their own language was proof to the traditionalists of the equality of Cherokees to the whites.[86] It also demonstrated that they were intellectually equal to the "progressive" mixed-bloods. This attitude helped foster the continued use of the syllabary and the language and ensure their survival, along with all their cultural accoutrements. With these basic under-pinnings, the traditionalists believed, the nation could advance when and how its collective will dictated, with no help needed from the federal government or missionaries. The movement was diametrically opposed to what John Ross, Major Ridge, a long-time leader of the Cherokees, his son John Ridge, Charles Hicks, and others were promoting. What both sides held in common in the late 1820s, however, was opposition to Removal and a belief that literacy could help them achieve their ends.

In spite of all the activity by people—missionaries, wives, blacksmiths, farmers—sent out by mission societies, the proliferation of missions and schools in the early decades of the nineteenth century did not translate into the provision of an "English" education across the Cherokee population. According to McLoughlin, the mission movement among the Cherokees was at its height between 1828 and 1832; during that interval, however, among all the schools of all denominations, no more than 200 to 250 school-age children were enrolled.[87] Further, we know from missionary correspondence that the teachers were concerned that the schools' enrollees were largely mixed-blood children (many of whom spoke English at home or had at least one English-speaking parent), and that they were failing to teach English to many full-blood children. Even so, although the joint Cherokee Nation–missionary effort to teach the English language to the Cherokees languished in the East, the seed of literacy was planted and has continued to flourish among the people until the present day. However, the goal of English literacy would not be pursued enthusiastically again among the Cherokees until the 1840s in Indian Territory.

CHAPTER 3

THE *CHEROKEE PHOENIX*

One of the major intellectual achievements of Cherokees in the nineteenth century was the establishment of a national press and the founding of the first Native American newspaper in 1828. Although some would credit the missionaries for this effort, as I show in this chapter, the press and its publications were the brainchild of Cherokee citizens. The missionaries served as facilitators, but the idea came from the Indians; indeed, the newspaper's expressions were those of the Cherokee editor and other citizens of the Cherokee Nation.

Samuel A. Worcester published the first five chapters of Genesis in the Sequoyan syllabary in the *Missionary Herald* in December 1827, probably the first time the Cherokee language was seen in print. These verses antedated by a couple of months the first number of the *Cherokee Phoenix*. John Hicks reports that Worcester had gone to Boston to oversee the casting of type for the newspaper, authorized by a resolution of the Cherokee National Council in October 1827.[1] The year before, the National Council had sent Elias Boudinot on a fundraising campaign to cities in the Northeast—a campaign that was as much to spread the word among mission-minded people that their support of efforts to civilize the Cherokees was successful as it was to raise money. Here he gave his "Address to the Whites," later published as a pamphlet, in which he enumerated the ways in which the Cherokee Nation had "progressed" from aboriginal status to imitation of white lifeways. Boudinot gave statistics outlining the numbers of livestock and acres under cultivation and the numbers of looms and spinning wheels to produce cloth, as well as how road building and ferry construction had improved commerce in the area. The tour, the "Address," the planned newspaper, and the orator all spoke the same message of a nation well on its way toward civilization and touted the intellectual achievements of the Cherokees. Upon Boudinot's return in the fall of 1826, the National Council appropriated $250 for the construction of a building and furnishings in New Echota that would serve as the printing office. It also approved a salary of $400 per year for the printer, $300 for his assistant, and $300 for editor Boudinot. Later, Boudinot's salary was raised to match the printer's.

Once the council had approved the casting of type, Worcester arranged with the American Board of Commissioners for Foreign Missions (ABCFM) for the casting to be done in Boston at the Baker and Greene Print Shop and set out for that city to supervise the work. Although the missionary group paid for the font and the press, it was reimbursed by the Cherokee Nation, at least partially with funds raised by Elias Boudinot while he was on his tour. The press was a Union model, small royal size. When the syllabary font was finished, Worcester took it to the *Missionary Herald* and printed the Genesis passages. Then the type, along with fonts of the roman alphabet and the press, was sent to Augustine, Georgia, two hundred miles from New Echota, where the cargo was loaded on wagons for the rest of the journey.

Elias Boudinot issued a broadside prospectus for the paper in October 1827 that he sent to papers in the Northeast, whence much support for missionary work was forthcoming. "Prospectus for Publishing at New Echota, in the Cherokee Nation, a Weekly Newspaper, to Be Called the Cherokee Phoenix" begins by saying that "friends to the civilization" of American Indians have long thought that a newspaper published for the Natives' "benefit and under their direction" would "add great force" to the efforts of "many true friends" in the larger society who wish to see them "civilized." In the second paragraph, the editor mentions the syllabary and how it will be used in the *Phoenix* to reach "those Cherokees who are unacquainted with the English language." The Cherokee language section was to be an important part of the paper. One of the council's charges to the *Phoenix*'s editors was to print translations in Cherokee of important news and official notices from the National Council and the principal chief, an indication that at the time, some of the tribal government's business, at least, was being carried on in English. This is not surprising, given the large number of mixed-bloods who were serving in important posts at the time. Thus Boudinot (or Boudinott, as he spells his name in the prospectus and on the masthead of the paper until 1832) identifies the main segments of his audience as not only the Cherokees themselves but also those patrons of the missionary efforts to "civilize" the Natives by bringing them instruction in the ways of the whites, especially the Christian religion. Boudinot then lists the subjects to be taken up by his journal:

1. The laws and public documents of the Nation.
2. Account of the manners and customs of the Cherokees, and their progress in Education, Religion, and arts of civilized life; with such notices of other Indian tribes as our limited means of information will allow.
3. The principal interesting news of the day.
4. Miscellaneous articles, calculated to promote "Literature, Civilization, and Religion among the Cherokees."

The editor ends his prospectus with a plea for support and a paragraph outlining subscription terms. Scholars have discussed how successful Boudinot and the other editors were in covering the four topics set out in the prospectus and how the newspapermen achieved some of their unstated aims.[2]

Boudinot's reasons for publishing the *Cherokee Phoenix* are fairly clear and are in line with the objectives of both the Cherokees and of their main supporter in this enterprise, the ABCFM. First, he was repeating the message that he had put forth in his "Address to the Whites," namely, that the Cherokees were well on their way to becoming a civilized nation and, as such, should be allowed to stay on their lands, even as the drums of Removal beat louder and louder. Proof of such "progress" was, of course, the very fact of a readable weekly resembling in nearly every way the newspapers published in progressive white communities across the Union. Second, he was trying to secure an audience for the newspaper outside the Cherokee Nation and thus ensure a measure of ongoing financial support for the publishing enterprise and a means of keeping events among the Cherokees in the public eye. Third, he was planning to use the paper as a vehicle to arouse whites from the Northeast to oppose those southerners and westerners who were clamoring for government action to rid the Indians from their land. How could a benevolent government oust a civilized people from their farms and villages and force their removal to a distant land? Removing "warlike" tribes from white contact was one thing; persecuting like-minded neighbors was quite another. The Cherokees and the ABCFM wanted the newspaper to inform their supporters in the East of the ongoing Removal situation and, more important, to arm them with arguments to be used in the halls of government to thwart the wishes of the Jacksonians in Congress, the Georgia state government, land speculators, settlers, planters, and others demanding Indian Removal. Publication of the *Phoenix* is proof that the Cherokees were fully cognizant of the power of language to persuade and to focus public opinion, even in the face of such long odds.

John Foster Wheeler, a white printer who was the first to set type in the Cherokee characters for the newspaper, gives an account of the founding of the *Phoenix* in which he comments on the meteoric adoption of Sequoyah's syllabary and the National Council's intent in establishing a newspaper that would use it.[3] When Worcester was in Boston seeing to the casting of the type, Isaac N. Harris, a printer from Tennessee, secured the position of printer from the council. He then engaged Wheeler, who lived in Huntsville, Alabama, and had just finished his apprenticeship, to assist him, and the pair left for New Echota, arriving there just before Christmas in 1827. Although Worcester had returned from Boston, the press and type had not yet arrived. With little to do, the printers were put to work learning the syllabary by Worcester, who had systematically arranged the characters in the familiar grid pattern with the Cherokee vowels at the head of each line. Try as they might, Wheeler and Harris had a difficult time with the characters, a predictable occurrence because neither knew the language. While the white men were struggling with the syllabary, someone realized that they had no paper, so Harris was dispatched to Knoxville with a wagon and team to secure a supply from a paper mill there.

Apparently, the building in which the press was to be housed had already been built when the printers arrived in New Echota. Wheeler describes it as being "of hewed logs, about 30 feet long and 20 wide. The builders had cut out a log on each side 15 or 16 feet long and about two and a half feet above the floor, in which they had made a sash to fit." However, when the printers worked on arrangements inside the office, they saw that the window was too low, emitting light below the place where the type cases needed to be. They therefore raised the window and set about designing and building the accommodations for the type and press. "Stands had to be made, a bank, and cases for the Cherokee type," Wheeler says. The design for the English type cases was fairly standard, but Wheeler had to start from scratch in building trays for the Cherokee characters. These cases, each three by three and a half feet, consisted of over one hundred boxes, one for each character and miscellaneous pieces of type. Wheeler states that the Cherokee font contained no capitals and was cast on a small pica body.

When the press and fonts arrived in late January, Wheeler eagerly inspected the press, which was "like none I ever saw before or since." It was made of cast iron, with spiral springs to hold up the platen, an arrangement newly invented. The printing operation employed three men, Harris, Wheeler, and John Candy, a mixed-blood Cherokee who knew the language and proved to be of great service to the two white men, who were still baffled by the language and the syllabary. Wheeler was put in charge of setting Cherokee type and correcting proof, which apparently was a very difficult job for two reasons: first, because Wheeler was setting the Sequoyan type without knowledge of the language, the proof was fouler than usual; second, the printers did not have an impression stone, so they had to compose each page on a sled galley, run proofs on slips of paper, and make corrections on the press. It was, according to Wheeler, "a slow business," accounting somewhat for the small ratio of Cherokee copy to English that appeared in the newspaper. Although Wheeler soon became proficient in setting the Sequoyan type, the paper still had relatively fewer columns of copy in the syllabary's characters, mainly because translation from English was a difficult task that was performed almost entirely by Boudinot alone.[4] This appears to have been a continuing problem because Boudinot urged readers to send him items of interest in the syllabary to be printed and even asked for an assistant for this job. Wheeler's first experience with the syllabary was the book of Matthew as translated by George Lowery, aided by his son-in-law David Brown; however, Worcester deemed it incorrect in several places, so the final version was revised by the missionary and Elias Boudinot. The errors appear to have been theological rather than linguistic. Throughout its run, translations of the scriptures were to be a staple of the third page of the *Phoenix*.

The first issue of the *Cherokee Phoenix Tsa-la-ge Tsi-le-hi-sa-ni-hi* came off the press on February 21, 1828, the first newspaper published by an Indian nation. Physically, the four-page paper had five columns, fourteen picas wide and twenty-two inches long. Set in ten-point body type with most heads in fourteen-point blackface caps, it was sent out through the mail to subscribers and to "the leading papers of the country"[5] to reach Boudinot's readers in and beyond the Cherokee Nation. The prospectus had mentioned several agents who handled sales and subscriptions in Boston; New York City; Utica, New York; Richmond, Virginia; Nashville, Tennessee; Mobile, Alabama; Beaufort and Charleston, South Carolina; and the "Western Territory," presumably Arkansas, so the editor expected his paper to be circulated widely.

Content in English was organized generally into several departments: "Communications," letters, "New Echota," "Poetry," "Religious," "Miscellaneous," "Indians," "Gen'l Council," editorials, and synopses of local, national, and international news. The Cherokee Constitution appeared in the first three issues, followed in subsequent numbers by laws and resolutions passed by the National Council and proclamations by the principal chief. Local news was limited to obituaries and marriage notices, as well as items from the New Echota Academy. News from Washington, especially that dealing with Indian affairs, was prominent, as well as news of the Georgia governor and legislature. In the "Indians" department, Boudinot published stories about other tribes, including descriptions of their cultures, as well as their dealings with the federal government. Especially interesting was news from the Great Lakes and New York tribes, which were undergoing the same pressures to remove as the Cherokees.[6] By its second year of publication, the editor deemed the *Phoenix* the defender of all Indians; this widening scope was reflected in the paper's new subtitle, *Indians' Advocate*, which was first printed on the banner along with the slogan "Printed under the Patronage, and for the Benefit of the Cherokee Nation, and Devoted to the Cause of Indians" on February 11, 1829.

Boudinot's first editorial column was printed on page 3 of the first edition under the title "New Echota." In it, he acknowledged the support of those working for the good of the Indians, but he made it clear that the newspaper was not a charity supported by white people but rather was the property of the Cherokee Nation. Boudinot defined his relationship with the Cherokee National Council as one of editor to publisher, scotching rumors that the ABCFM had financed the paper and that Worcester was its editor.[7] Boudinot also promised that the *Phoenix* would be an active foe of Removal, but that he would not "intermeddle with politics and affairs of our neighbors" and would refrain from abusive language. He further promised that he would "invariably and faithfully state the feelings of the majority" of Cherokees. In a few years, he would have to rescind this promise when he found that his views on Removal were opposed to those of many of the Cherokee leaders and of the majority of the people.

Cherokee content was important to the editor and the publisher. The amount of Cherokee-language content varied from issue to issue; the early numbers carried the constitution and laws of the nation in both languages, so even though the syllabary-based Cherokee took up less space than the alphabet-based English, significant Native content appeared. Other homegrown content in Cherokee appeared, but there was a problem with generating enough copy because until Wheeler learned enough of the language to become somewhat fluent, typesetting in the syllabary had to be done by one of two men, Boudinot or John Candy. Isaac Harris never did learn the language, and, in any event, Boudinot dismissed him in December 1829. Some Cherokee was handwritten by persons not directly connected to the publication and then typeset, but most of the Cherokee content was prepared by Boudinot with Candy's and Worcester's assistance. The early numbers included instructions for the use of the Sequoyan syllabary, as well as a guide to pronouncing the various syllables. Boudinot probably did this not for his Cherokee readers, who knew the symbols and could pronounce the language, but to demonstrate to non-Cherokee readers that the writing system was viable and practical and was an intellectual feat equal to the attempts by academic linguists to create writing in Native languages. In one way, the syllabary was an assertion of Cherokee independence; in another, it was a demonstration of the "civilized" nature of the people that was manifested by a recognition of the importance of written communication.

But in many ways, the content of the *Cherokee Phoenix* was similar to that of other nineteenth-century American weeklies. Informative pieces of historical and educational interest and general international news appeared in its pages, such as commentaries on ancient civilizations in Europe, Africa, and the Middle East. Biographical sketches of famous historical figures were published, as well as news of conflicts in Europe and news from foreign capitals concerning politics and royalty. News reports from England and France seemed especially popular. Other educational fare included practical articles on farming or household topics, such as food preservation.

Temperance and other moralistic prose pieces were featured, often reprinted from mainly religious publications, such as *Christian Philosophy* and *Missionary Herald*. Temperance tracts were printed because of the influence in the nation of illegal whiskey peddlers, whom the missionaries fought tooth and nail. Some of the moralistic pieces were aimed at the younger generations, with such subjects as building character and maintaining one's honesty and chastity. Morals and religion were closely allied in the pages of the *Phoenix*; biblical stories, especially the cautionary tales, were a regular feature. Although Boudinot claimed to avoid sectarianism, apparently this meant espousing Protestant Christian views.

Poetry and verse had a prominent place in the *Phoenix*. Some of this was religious verse in both languages; one such feature printed the Lord's Prayer in English, followed by a version in Cherokee verse that was followed in turn by a translation into English of the verse. Bible passages, prayers, and hymns appeared regularly. Much of the English poetry was reprinted from other publications, but some original work appeared as well. The poetry and prose that Boudinot published helped foster the growing literacy rate in both languages. It set standards of writing for those who were inclined to compose in words and demonstrated various genres and forms to emulate. These examples of creative writing helped make *Phoenix* readers literate in ways that grammar books and school readers could not.

As in other newspapers, correspondence from readers was of great interest and appeared in both languages. The editor published repeated requests for more correspondence in the Cherokee language as time went on. At one point, the editor addresses his Cherokee readers: "We have a heavy task, & unless relieved by Cherokee correspondents, a greater amount of Cherokee matter cannot reasonably be expected. We hope those of our correspondents, who take a lively interest in the diffusion of intelligence in their mother language, will lend us aid in this department . . . the most arduous part of our labors."[8] The correspondence was a good gauge of what readers were thinking about the major issues of the day, especially Removal. In the days leading up to and following the passage of the Indian Removal Act in 1830, many arguments were advanced in the newspaper's pages against Cherokee Removal. In the early 1830s, other Indian nations were being forced out of their homelands because resistance to the federal government was futile. However, enough Cherokees apparently believed in the power of the written word to hold out hope that the fate of the Tsa-la-ghi, the Cherokee people, would be different. Trust in the ability of a good writer to sway the events of history was evident, too, in the many memorials the Cherokees addressed in written form to government bodies and figures. This kind of manipulation of language for political ends is truly the mark of a literate people.

Although it may be difficult to gauge the effectiveness of the *Cherokee Phoenix,* one incident suggests that by the end of its first year, it had become an irritant to the state of Georgia. In 1828 and 1829, Georgia had begun to make good its threat to extend its laws over the Cherokee Nation, having been made bold in this endeavor by the election of Andrew Jackson to the presidency in 1828. The publication in the *Phoenix* of the Cherokee Constitution and laws no doubt served to alarm those in favor of Indian Removal both in Washington and in Milledgeville, the Georgia capital. Even before its publication, a copy of the new constitution had been sent to President John Quincy Adams, who reacted by sending a message to Chiefs Hicks and Ross that such a document did not change the essential relationship between the United States and the tribe. In fact, written Cherokee law dated from 1808, when the National Council established a police force for protection of property; the constitution was written in 1827. Publication of the newspaper itself had its intended effect among those in the seaboard cities who either were against Removal or had not yet made up their minds. The *Phoenix* was at once the vehicle by which anti-Removal arguments were expressed and a demonstration of the civilized nature of its publishers.

Clearly, the federal government viewed the written Cherokee legal codes as being an important development in the debate concerning Removal, one that for the time being needed to be closely monitored. The Georgians acted more precipitously. In December 1829, the legislature enacted a law extending the jurisdiction of the state over all that portion of the Cherokee country lying within its limits and declaring that after June 1830, all Cherokee laws would be null and void. State officials sought to erase the written codes by declaring that their own laws superseded those of the Indians. Earlier that year, gold had been discovered in the nation, and white miners had flooded into the area. Pleas to the federal government for help to expel the intruders produced few results. The legislature followed its extension of jurisdiction with an even more onerous act on December 22, 1830, the caption of which reads, "An act to prevent the exercise of assumed and arbitrary power by all persons under pretext of authority from the Cherokee Indians and their laws, and to prevent white persons from residing within that part of the chartered limits of Georgia occupied by the Cherokee Indians, and to provide a guard for the protection of the gold mines and to enforce the laws of the state within the aforesaid territory."[9] The first two sections of the act forbade the convening of the National Council, and the next two denied the authority of officers of the Cherokee Nation. Section 5 forbade the selling of land in the nation, and section 6 allowed the Cherokees to continue negotiations with federal officers.

The seventh and eighth sections, however, dealt with the white men living among the tribe. These sections were doubtless spawned by general animosity toward the missionaries, but more specifically, the Georgians were disturbed by the white men's attempts to "civilize" Cherokees and, even more particularly, by those persons who worked with the written word by teaching literacy and by raising the Cherokee syllabary to the status of a printed language. The seventh and eighth sections, respectively, made it illegal for any white person to live among the Cherokees after April 30, 1831, unless that person obtained a license from the state of Georgia. The license would be issued only after the white person took an oath pledging allegiance to the state and "uprightly demean[ing] myself as a citizen thereof."[10] One of the final sections of the law established the Georgia Guard, the enforcement arm of the new law.

The Georgia Guard arrested John F. Wheeler in early March 1831 at his brother-in-law Boudinot's house. He was held in New Echota overnight and was soon joined by Samuel Worcester and Henry Gunn, a farmer and intermarried white man. Wheeler and his wife, Nancy Watie, sister of Boudinot and Stand Watie, Elias Boudinot's brother, had originally thought to leave Georgia but were persuaded to stay. By this time, the Cherokees, along with their allies in Boston, had formed a plan for a legal defense, certain that the federal government would come to their assistance. Two prominent lawyers, William Wirt, a former U.S. attorney general, and John Sergeant, sought to bring the case to the U.S. Supreme Court. Worcester and Wheeler, probably the only white man who could set type in the syllabary, were arrested along with nine others, including missionaries. In an interesting sidelight, Isaac Harris, the first printer of the *Phoenix*, had been relieved of his position by Elias Boudinot for spreading rumors that Worcester was most responsible for putting out the newspaper, as noted earlier. Wheeler had succeeded Harris. Many at the time attributed Harris's actions to the fact that he was a Methodist and Worcester was a Congregationalist, but nothing reported about Harris identifies him as a religious enthusiast. Boudinot's decisive response to the rumors (Harris's term of employment extended to December 28, 1828, but Boudinot requested a replacement in July)[11] indicates more than hurt feelings over the possible diminishment of his role; the major point of the publication in the first place was to demonstrate the civilized nature of the Indians, not the white men who aided them. Boudinot was so incensed by Harris's continued defiance after the editor had given the printer notice of termination of employment that Boudinot felt obliged to call the tribal marshal to remove him.[12] Harris's accusation was regarded as a serious threat to the image the Cherokees were working to project; news of Harris's statement was probably pounced on by the powers in Milledgeville, who saw the two white men, especially Worcester, as key figures in the Cherokees' propaganda campaign against Removal. Even the Jackson administration in Washington jumped on the bandwagon, spreading the rumor that Worcester was the de facto editor because Elias Boudinot and other Cherokees were deemed incapable of such work. The *U.S. Telegraph*, a Jackson newspaper and mouthpiece for administration ideas, put forth the rumor in its columns, only to be chastised by the *New York Journal of Commerce*, whose editors came to Boudinot and the *Phoenix*'s defense.[13]

Worcester and the other missionaries were released by a Georgia judge, however, when the point was made that the missionaries were there at the behest of the U.S. government to work in the "civilizing" process, and that a portion of their pay, in fact, was paid by the government. The fact that Worcester had been serving as postmaster at New Echota was further evidence of federal acceptance of their presence among the Cherokees. Under these circumstances, Judge Clayton released the missionaries but bound over the other white men for trial, including Wheeler. In his verdict, the judge recognized the right of the Cherokees to their land, but he also recognized the jurisdiction of Georgia over those lands, a decision that satisfied no one.

News of the legal battle in the Cherokee Nation reached the East very quickly through letters to the ABCFM headquarters and through the pages of the *Cherokee Phoenix*. Eastern newspapers, including the *New York Observer* and the *Boston Courier*, voiced their dismay at Georgia's actions. With Wheeler's arrest, Boudinot had turned over printing duties to John Candy, who proved to be a competent craftsman, and had covered the details of each move in what was developing into a complicated chess game. The missionary board met on the matter and decided that the best course was to bring legal proceedings against Georgia to the U.S. Supreme Court, where it was reasonably certain of victory. Meanwhile, as the depredations of miners and other intruders continued, many of the white missionaries, their families, and their employees within the area claimed by Georgia fled to other areas of the Cherokee Nation in Tennessee, North Carolina, and Alabama. Their homes, farms, and other improvements were immediately taken over by the Georgia authorities and rented to white people from the state. Pleas to President

Jackson were fruitless; the only advice forthcoming from his office was for the Indians to remove to an area west of Arkansas, where they would be safe in perpetuity. The executive branch's only other action was to replace Worcester as postmaster with a Georgian and to declare that missionaries were not agents of the United States, thus removing both of the legal objections to Georgia's case raised by Judge Clayton. The Georgia Guard continued to harass Cherokees and whites in the nation to the extent that the Cherokee leaders John Ross, John Ridge, and William J. Coody, a nephew of Ross's, felt compelled to move the National Council to Red Clay, Tennessee. On July 7, Worcester was arrested again. When he arrived at Camp Gilmer, the former headquarters of U.S. troops sent to the Cherokee Nation to expel intruders, but now ironically under the control of the Georgia Guard, he found missionaries Isaac Proctor, Daniel S. Butrick, John Thompson, and Elizur Butler under arrest as well. They were released temporarily on a writ of habeas corpus but were under bond to appear for trial. Worcester and Wheeler traveled to Brainerd, in Tennessee, to meet their families and avoid further persecution from the Georgia Guard. The white men and those like Wheeler released under bond earlier were tried on September 16, found guilty, and sentenced the next day to four years at hard labor in the Georgia penitentiary. However, only two of the eleven prisoners entered the prison. All were interviewed privately by the inspector of the penitentiary, who told them that they would be pardoned if they would take the oath of allegiance to Georgia. No records were kept, so it is difficult to know what their answers were; however, nine men were released after Worcester and Elizur Butler testified to their good character. The testators were imprisoned, while the others went free.

There is little doubt that Worcester and Butler's refusal to cooperate with the Georgia governor's terms for a pardon was a matter of principle, but there was another reason as well. The Cherokee National Council and the ABCFM had planned almost from the beginning to take legal recourse if the executive branch of the federal government did not step in to stop Georgia's extension of jurisdiction over the Cherokee lands. Accordingly, when the two missionaries entered the penitentiary, William Wirt and John Sergeant entered a writ of error before the U.S. Supreme Court, which was argued from February 20 to February 22, 1832. On March 3, Chief

Justice John Marshall gave his historic opinion that the Georgia law was repugnant to the laws and treaties of the United States and thus null and void.[14] President Jackson, however, refused to execute the Court's decision, so the victory for the Cherokees and their friends was moral but hollow. Worcester and Butler stayed in prison. Their confinement was serving no purpose for either side, and both Worcester and Butler's superiors and the Georgia politicians recognized this. In the end, a compromise was reached by which the missionaries would be released if they dropped all legal proceedings against the state. Worcester and Butler, after some persuasion by parties on both sides, agreed and were released on January 14, 1833.

From the beginning of the crisis, it was clear that Samuel Worcester was the prime target of the Georgians' malice. From the Georgia authorities' racist point of view, Worcester was the architect of Cherokee literacy, Sequoyah's contribution no doubt being regarded as one would view a precocious child's code for messages to her friends. The missionary, after all, had convinced the ABCFM of the desirability of a press in the Cherokee Nation and worse, a newspaper to be circulated in the cities of the power brokers. Worcester, too, was in the van of those "civilizers" who regarded the Indians as being capable of "progressing" to the point of living adjacent to and competing with white society. As we have seen, in the minds of all concerned, the great enabling force that drove progress was literacy. Cherokee literacy and print culture were evidence that the Indians were human beings who were capable of being educated and civilized.[15] The Georgia leaders were determined to wipe out this evidence and the conclusions that might be drawn from it, however belatedly.

In 1831, Elias Boudinot had gone on a fund-raising trip to the East, leaving his brother, Stand Watie, in charge of the *Phoenix*. When he returned, his views on the Cherokee's chances of resisting Removal had changed; he was nearly convinced that further opposition to Jackson's policy was futile. In the following year, when Andrew Jackson was reelected, the matter was largely settled in the minds of most observers. Although the Indians and others had hoped that a victory by Henry Clay might bring respite from pressure to remove, this was probably a false hope. Clay, speaking as a member of the cabinet in 1825, had voiced the opinion that for Indians, civilization "is not in their nature. They are destined for extinction. . . . I do not think they are, as a race, worth preserving."[16] However, John Ross and a majority of the full-bloods were determined to resist. When Boudinot attempted to print some of his views in the *Phoenix*, Ross forbade him, and Boudinot therefore resigned as editor in August 1832. Elijah Hicks, son of Charles R. Hicks and Ross's brother-in-law, succeeded him. Hicks published news and editorials relating to the clash with Georgia, including the details of a Georgia man's assault on a Cherokee woman. The accused man sued Hicks for libel and asked for $10,000 in damages. Hicks was arrested but was released on bond; he published several more issues before distributing the last *Cherokee Phoenix* on May 31, 1834. By that time, the paper was under duress. Hicks was unable to generate copy the way Boudinot and Worcester had done, for one thing. For another, he could not circulate the *Phoenix* through the mails because the new postmaster who had replaced Worcester was a Georgian who withheld mail privileges. Support funds from the Cherokee national treasury were no longer forthcoming because federal annuities were now being paid to individuals, so supplies ran out, to say nothing of salaries.[17]

Meanwhile, Boudinot was in Washington, meeting with federal officials in an attempt to negotiate an agreement for Removal. The bargaining sessions were lively, with Boudinot asking at first for $20 million; the government's first counteroffer was only $5 million. Ross, aware of what Boudinot was doing, became alarmed, according to the erstwhile editor, who wrote to his brother, Stand Watie, "Proceedings have finally so frightened Mr. Ross that he made several propositions lately, all of which have been rejected promptly."[18] The negotiations went on, but Ross became more and more convinced that resistance to the government was the better course of action; hostilities between the Boudinot-Ridge-Watie faction—known as the Treaty Party—and the Ross faction intensified. In March 1835, Boudinot again wrote to his brother, urging him to seize the printing press at New Echota for the purpose of printing handbills to circulate among the people carrying the Treaty Party's message. Watie did not take action at once, but in August, he received word that Ross was about to move the press to Red Clay, Tennessee, where he planned to resume publication of the *Phoenix* and use its pages to rally the people against Removal. To prevent Ross from using this powerful weapon, Watie contacted officers of the Georgia Guard, and together they went to Elijah Hicks's home and demanded the press, type, and furnishings. Watie's argument was that these items belonged to his brother because they had been purchased with funds he had raised in the East. Faced with the presence of the armed guards, Mrs. Hicks had no choice but to comply, turning over the press, type, and some books and articles that had been removed from Boudinot's house in New Echota.[19] According to historian Kenny Franks, the press was used to print arguments for the Treaty Party's position and thus to help it persuade some Cherokees to sign the New Echota Removal Treaty in late 1835. However, the vast majority of Cherokees were not persuaded. There is no evidence about what happened to the press after Removal, but one thing is certain: it did not make the journey to Indian Territory. Earlier, John F. Wheeler and his wife, Nancy Watie, had left to join the Cherokees in the West, and Samuel A. Worcester was not far behind.

The history of the *Cherokee Phoenix* is rich in irony. The newspaper was established in large measure to support the idea that Indians were capable of, and had indeed achieved, a key competence that has been considered a benchmark of a civilized society. A large percentage of the population could demonstrate literacy in Cherokee, and although fewer Cherokees had mastered English, a significant number of its leaders had done so, enough that the nation's constitution and other statutes were formulated and published in that language. The Cherokees, as well as their white advisers, had hoped that this competency would establish their credentials among the civilized nations so that their borders would be secure, and their communities could live in peace and mutual respect among those of their white neighbors. As we have seen, this strategy was successful among some quarters of the white population but ironically caused an opposite reaction in others. The missionary societies and their supporters greeted this demonstration of literacy as a great achievement and took a great deal of credit for it, no matter how little deserved; on the other hand, the pro-Removal forces, including segments of the federal government, the state of Georgia, and lobbyists from the cotton and land-speculation interests, regarded the Cherokees' achievements with alarm. If anything, the publication of the *Phoenix* strengthened their resolve and helped convince them that quick action was needed. Together with all the other pressures for

Removal—intruders, Georgia's earlier deals with the federal government concerning Indian Removal, the burgeoning cotton trade, the clamor of settlers for more land, the discovery of gold in the Cherokee Nation, and, most of all, Andrew Jackson's determination to rid the Southeast of its Native population—the *Phoenix*'s appearance only brought the dreaded day of Removal that much closer.

When the Cherokees did remove, it was under the terms of the 1830 Indian Removal Act, a statute enacted by the U.S. government. But a heavy hand from Georgia was felt in the process, that of Wilson Lumpkin. Lumpkin was the governor of Georgia during the time the U.S. Army was rounding up the main body of the tribe, but his role in the affair goes back to an earlier time when he was serving in the U.S. House of Representatives. The former surveyor and Indian commissioner was elected to the House in 1826, the same year Elias Boudinot was on his speaking tour of the East extolling the advances of his people. As a representative, Lumpkin had much to do with the formulation of Indian policy and offered to his colleagues two bills providing for Indian Removal that led to the Removal Act. Later, when the Cherokees had left his state, he applied for and received disbursement funds from the federal government for his state's "losses" incurred by their removal.

CHAPTER 4

Education after Removal

In an editorial titled "The Public Schools" in the May 27, 1847, issue of the *Cherokee Advocate,* William Potter Ross wrote that education was the only hope for the Cherokee Nation. With relatively few people and no army or navy, the tribe must rely on truth and reason, he said. These were nurtured by education. It is clear, then, that for the Cherokees, education was not only desirable, but a matter of survival.[1]

One of the great pillars of Cherokee intellectual life was the Cherokee Nation's dedication to education for all its citizens. The path to the goal of universal education was difficult to follow, and for the Cherokees it was full of meanderings and false trails. But as the nation grew in wealth and stature, its educational system expanded from a few missionary schools to a public school network that introduced the schoolhouse into every Cherokee community of any size in the new country in Indian Territory. Only tribal dissolution and Oklahoma statehood in the early twentieth century brought an end to the ambitious complex of primary and secondary schools where students were taught in two languages.[2]

The Cherokee school system did more to advance literacy and literary activity than merely teaching the people to read and write. It created an ethos in which the written word became an important part of the mostly rural and largely agricultural Cherokee Nation. Once students learned to read and write, they were encouraged to expand their literary horizons through participation in literary, debating, and dramatic societies, first in the schools as extracurricular activities and later in the communities where these clubs and groups flourished, especially in the larger towns. These, in turn, were supported by the Indian-produced reading materials available to most citizens, primarily the many newspapers published in the Cherokee Nation during the second half of the nineteenth century.

Cherokee leaders had recognized the value of a national educational system early. In treaty negotiations from 1805 through 1835, they sought to include a clause that would exchange land for an education fund. In this spirit, the treaty of 1819 specified that four tracts of land totaling fifteen square miles would be sold by the federal government, and the proceeds of the sale would be used to establish a national academy at New Echota. However, as the principal chiefs noted in 1828, this clause was never put into effect.

Even after the missionaries began their educational efforts in the 1820s, the Cherokee leaders did not abandon their ambition for independent schools. With the establishment of ABCFM and Baptist schools in the nation, the leadership recognized the need for educational assistance from the missionaries but sought to create a fund for school support as a way of maintaining Cherokee control. The leaders also sought to establish a "visiting committee" for the inspection of examinations and as a means of reporting on the state of the schools to the nation on a regular basis. Although the missionaries had been invited into the nation to establish schools and not to proselytize, it was clear to all except the most naive that the church people were working to convert the Cherokees to Christianity. As Daniel S. Butrick stated to ABCFM secretary Jeremiah Evarts, their plan in the early 1820s was to "educate" the older people in the Christian religion while bringing an "English" education to the "rising" generation.[3] The white missionaries' religion was a large part of the curriculum for young people as well, and the subversive nature of this system was not lost on the Indian leaders. Many of them, such as John Ross, longtime principal chief, sought to take control of the education process in order to preserve the tribe's independence. In their view, the schools belonged to the Cherokees, and the teachers' roles were to be defined by the nation. In any event, the Cherokee dream of a school system independent from the federal government and the missionaries was not codified until the 1835 Treaty of New Echota, in which a provision for an annual stipend of $16,000 was included in the tribe's annuity to be used for Cherokee-controlled public schools.[4] When the tribe reached Indian Territory and John Ross revived the dream in the 1840s, this sum was found to be too small, but the plan for a permanent fund to support public education had been established.

The idea of a "national free school" was broached to Brainerd superintendent Ard Hoyt in August 1823 by Cherokee Charles R. Hicks, who wanted the ABCFM to provide a director at "national expense."[5] Hicks was a Christian convert and, as such, often sided with those in the nation who sought assimilation and "civilization" against those who argued that imitation of white lifeways had already gone too far toward destroying Cherokee culture and religion. Hicks was not alone among the Cherokee leaders. Elias Boudinot in his "Address to the Whites" (1826) asserted the Cherokee Nation's determination to acquire both a printing press and a national "seminary," by which he meant an institution of learning beyond the elementary-school level. Although many Cherokees favored the idea of a national school, there was some debate about whether it should be an instrument for higher education, admitting only graduates of the elementary schools, or should admit students with no previous school experience. Earlier, Hicks had worked with Baptist Humphrey Posey in the Valley towns to establish a "missionary seminary" that would train Indians as preachers and had advocated for this purpose in the National Council. (This "preacher academy" idea was later adopted in the West by Evan Jones.) In 1819, the council had agreed to allow the Baptist Board of Foreign Missions to bring in "a blacksmith, millers, and a sufficient number of persons to conduct the school and farm of the establishment." For its part, the council "promised all the aid in the power of the nation to promote the interest of the school."[6]

At this time, many Cherokees believed that the schools were theirs because they were on tribal land, and that the missionaries were there to do what the Cherokees thought best concerning the education of their children. Friction often resulted between the Indians and the individual missionaries and especially between the Cherokee leadership and the officers of the missionary societies, who regarded themselves as the most competent judges of what was best for their benighted charges. Groups such as the American

Board of Commissioners for Foreign Missions and the Baptist Board of Foreign Missions had been established to proselytize their particular brand of Christianity; insofar as education promoted conversion, it was deemed worthy of support, but it never became the major aim of their endeavors. Among the Cherokees, however, the desire for education was keen; as Abraham Steiner reported in 1820, "Indeed, in every direction of the country the eagerness to have school establishments is truly great." But he lamented that there were not enough "hands" to make each school a success, and of those who come to teach, some were lazy or greedy and generally failed.[7] The problem of recruiting and retaining competent teachers in the Cherokee Nation was chronic and determined the direction of educational policy for many decades.

For several years before the events just described, Cherokees had been leaving their country in the East and migrating west in response to white encroachment. Some of these people settled in Louisiana, then under Spanish rule, but between 1780 and 1811–12, many of the immigrants entered eastern Arkansas and made their homes in the St. Francis River watershed and in the Crowley's Ridge area. There they were able to farm, hunt, and fish with little contact with whites. In time, more and more Cherokees took this step as whites stepped up their campaign to usurp the homeland in Georgia, southern Tennessee, and western North Carolina. Then came the New Madrid earthquakes of 1811–12. Although the epicenters were fifty miles or more north of the Cherokee settlements, the quakes were so powerful that they had devastating effects on the alluvial soils of the delta. The Cherokees, fearing a return of the quakes, made their way west of Little Rock into the Arkansas River valley, between the Ozark plateau and the Ouachita Mountains, an area largely unaffected by the quakes. Although this landscape was similar to that of the Cherokee Nation in the East, they now had to contend with the Osages. The Osages claimed northwest Arkansas for themselves, and a series of clashes broke out between the two nations. The Cherokees stayed there, however, and were soon joined by other immigrants. The federal government had kept an eye on these developments, and as pressure from the southern states to remove the tribes grew, Arkansas became an increasingly attractive option as a destination for removed Cherokees.

Accordingly, the United States and the Cherokee Nation entered into a treaty on July 17, 1817, in which a large portion of northwest Arkansas was set aside as Cherokee land in exchange for land in the East. From that time forward, the standard response to complaints from the Indians about mistreatment and usurpation by southern whites was that if they were displeased, they should move to their new land in Arkansas. Although the Cherokee Nation discouraged immigration, the U.S. government sought to make it more attractive. The tribal government eventually imposed strict penalties on those seeking to leave the nation, but many did so, both individually and in organized parties. Estimates of the number of Cherokees who moved to Arkansas before Removal in the 1830s vary, but most agree that the total was around four thousand.[8]

The Western Cherokees, as they became known, cleared land, established farms, planted crops, and raised livestock, mostly on the north side of the Arkansas River. They lived as they had in the East, organized into traditional towns and along matrilineal kinship lines. In time, they built salt works and mills and traded goods and services among themselves. After 1818, they moved toward a more centralized government when John Jolly became principal chief of the Cherokees in the West. The central leadership then began to make decisions governing the people's future, including those having to do with education.

The Western Cherokees shared the interest in education held by their people in the East, were eager to bring education to their children, and were especially attracted to teaching them to read and write. The first school established among the Cherokees in Arkansas was at Dwight Mission in the Arkansas River Valley. Revs. Cephas Washburn and Alfred Finney were invited to establish a boarding school there; when it opened in 1819, prospective students had to be turned away because of the large number of applicants. The first class had thirty-four male students and twenty-six females. English was taught, but apparently in a more intense fashion on the boys' side than on the girls'.[9] A second school was opened in 1828 but lasted only one term because in that year, the Western Cherokees signed a treaty ceding their country in Arkansas for lands across the border in what came to be called Indian Territory. Dwight Mission was moved in the following year to Sallisaw Creek, twelve miles from its junction with the Arkansas River, twenty-six miles west of Fort Smith. A second school was opened on the forks of the Illinois River in 1830 with thirty-one students, and in 1831, a third school was founded at Fairfield, twenty miles northwest of Dwight Mission, with ten students. These schools were supported by the ABCFM. The Moravians established a school on the Illinois River in 1830, while the Baptists built theirs in 1832 in present-day Delaware City under Duncan O'Brien. The Methodists opened Adair School in 1832, presided over by Rev. Thomas Bertholf, who in 1833 moved to Keys School, two miles south of Tahlequah.[10] The missionaries, like their counterparts in Georgia and North Carolina, experimented with teaching English and with the language of instruction for other subjects. At one point, Sequoyah was employed to teach his syllabary to some of the children, and this met with some success. However, teaching the syllabary was not a widespread practice because the missionary teachers were not fluent in Cherokee and thus were unable to provide that instruction. After Removal of the main body of Cherokees to Indian Territory, the educational system established by the Old Settlers was thrown into disarray, and the reunited Cherokee Nation sought to reorganize its educational system.

A major failure of federal Removal policy involved the avowed purpose of resettling the southeastern tribes far from the "contagion" of white frontier settlements. However, the territory to the west of Arkansas set aside for this purpose was already surrounded by areas well populated by whites when the Indians arrived. Arkansas became a state in 1836, two years before the main body of Cherokees removed from the East. The federal government had not seen fit to provide for any kind of buffer between the white and the Native populations, so the Indians encountered many of the same problems in the new land that they had had previously. Pressure to acculturate increased as more whites settled in the West, problems with whiskey traders and intruders were exacerbated by jurisdictional disputes between Indian and white justice systems, and white-controlled railroads and land companies cast covetous glances on Indian farming areas and grasslands. Further, the federal fort system imbued potential settlers with a sense of security and allayed their fears of being beset by "savages." For education, this meant that David Brown's admonition to the students at Creek Path in 1827 was as true in Indian Territory as it had been in the old nation: educate yourself or be prepared to be cheated and marginalized.

By the time of Removal, the Cherokees had experienced two decades of schools operated by the missionaries, in spite of their efforts to control the educational process among their own people. The Cherokees had much to be dissatisfied with in the missionary-controlled educational system. First, the missionary boarding schools had proved unpopular with Cherokee parents because they removed the children from the family and also because the children were made to work. Second, it was not lost on the Cherokees that the very business of the missionaries was to replace Cherokee culture with a white Christian one. Third, Removal had proved that demonstrating a high degree of "civilization" did not protect the nation from the onslaught of greedy Georgians or from anti-Indian federal policy. Emulating the whites had been a tactic encouraged by the ABCFM. Fourth, missionaries educated only a small percentage of the population, in spite of the early hopes. Finally, some of the missionaries had openly advocated Removal as being in the best interests of the tribe. This perception was reinforced by the federal government's appointment of Rev. John F. Schermerhorn as chief negotiator of the New Echota Treaty and by Samuel A. Worcester's obvious connections with the Treaty Party. By the time the Cherokees arrived in the West, they were determined to continue their educational efforts, but this time on their own terms.

The constitution of 1839 clearly asserted the nation's authority in pedagogical matters. Article 6, section 9, of that document stated that control of all aspects of schools that "may be, and are now in operation" in the nation would be subject to the "supervision and control" of the National Council. The next section provided that in the future, no missionary school was to be established without permission of the National Council, and that if a school was allowed, it was to be regulated by the nation. Finally, the constitution provided that a plan for a system of general education was to be presented to the principal chief by the next annual meeting of the council. These pronouncements, deemed important enough to be included in the constitution, demonstrate the Cherokees' determination to take control of the educational process and to limit the influence of the missionaries on that increasingly important aspect of national life.

Principal Chief John Ross was in a unique position to advance Cherokee efforts in this direction after Removal. He had strong political power, even though his domineering and ruthless behavior immediately after Removal had alienated many of the Old Settlers and all adherents of the Treaty Party. For most issues, though, Ross had the support of the majority full-bloods of the nation and many mixed-bloods. After Removal, the Cherokees found themselves in relatively close proximity to whites on three sides in their Indian Territory lands, and although these people did not constitute the immediate threat to the nation that the Georgians had, Ross was wary of his Euro-American neighbors and their motives. Above all, Ross wanted independence for the nation, an existence free from unwanted interference. As his 1840 annual message to the Cherokee legislature makes clear, he saw education as leading to this state of independence.[11] The message calls for legislation for a system of free public schools, developing the ideas of the 1839 constitution.

However, there can be little doubt that the mixed-blood leaders of the nation, including Principal Chief John Ross himself, saw education as a means of bringing "progress" to the Cherokees; for most of these leaders, that meant acculturation, in which Cherokees, primarily mixed-bloods, adopted white practices that they deemed advantageous to them and their families. Ross's ideas on the matter seem to center on the urgent need for Cherokee independence. He saw that a nation that was not educated to American standards was a people vulnerable to the same bullying tactics by the dominant society that the Cherokees had suffered since the formation of the United States. Even if the educational opportunities did not extend to all the people, this line of logic went, at least the leadership and those who were rising to acquire that status should be supported in getting the best "English" education they could. Acquiring fluency in the English language, then as today, was an integral part of this process.

For their part, the missionaries who had followed the Cherokees from the East remained active in building new churches and ancillary schools. Some, such as the tireless Evan Jones, worked hard to continue converting the tribal people to Christianity, especially the full-bloods. Many of the Cherokees who had inhabited the Valley Towns in North Carolina maintained community affiliations based on relationships in the East, and the Baptist preacher, who had been among those communities earlier, sought them out after Removal. Once he settled at Breadtown, a small settlement just west of the Arkansas border that boasted a store and a blacksmith shop, Jones turned his attention to what he saw as the major undertaking of the missions: training Cherokee speakers to preach the gospel to the full-bloods. Jones had astutely perceived shortly after his arrival in the Cherokee Nation that to convert the full-bloods, it was necessary to approach them in their own language. Accordingly, he set up an academy along the lines of a theological seminary to train Cherokee aspirants to the clergy. Using some buildings that Jesse Bushyhead had built in 1839, he established his beachhead, and soon he added churches and meeting places that he and his growing corps of Cherokee preachers used. As Breadtown grew in size and influence, its name was changed, first to Cherokee and then to Baptist Mission (sometimes shortened to Baptist), which it remained.[12]

Jones's efforts centered on religious rather than secular education, and although some of the other missionaries opened schools in the West, a general trend developed in which the missions concerned themselves with religious matters rather than education. Several missionary societies asked for permission to build schools after enactment of the 1839 constitution, but none contributed significantly to the education of children, with the exception of the Joneses. As a group, the missionaries applauded the nation's determination to establish a public school system, but they, like the Cherokees, saw that there would be a problem in recruiting teachers. Jones proposed an academy for training Cherokee teachers along the lines of his establishment for training preachers, but the idea failed to materialize because it was viewed as too expensive. The missionaries also worried about where the money to support the schools would come from, and they continued to struggle financially themselves. The missionary societies did contribute to the Cherokee educational cause by using their contacts and various publications to recruit teachers for the fledgling system. Although the efforts of Jones and his son continued beyond the Civil War and constituted an important contribution to Cherokee education, the ABCFM closed its mission schools in 1860 with the declaration that the Cherokees were now a Christian nation.[13]

In 1841, the National Council followed Ross's lead and passed the Public Education Act, providing for the appointment of a superintendent of schools to oversee the national system; this person would appoint three school directors from each community to build and maintain school buildings. The superintendent's duties included visiting the schools at least twice a year and reporting annually on their condition to the National Council. Together, the superintendent and the directors were responsible for hiring teachers, who were paid from the annuity fund. The directors and the superintendent determined the curriculum and the kinds of books to be used, the length of the teaching day, and the number and duration of vacations during the year. A requirement that at least twenty-five pupils were to be registered in each school meant that the schools would operate efficiently; a limit of sixty-five ensured that the teacher would not be overburdened. Initially, eleven schools were to be built, with two each in Delaware, Going Snake, and Flint districts and one each in the remaining five, Skin Bayou, Illinois, Canadian, Tahlequah, and Saline, with plans for further expansion until each Cherokee child had a local school. Cherokee parents were not to be charged for tuition, and attendance was voluntary. The plan called for each child between the ages of six and sixteen to receive a "common school education," including reading, writing, spelling, geography, arithmetic, and history. Teachers were encouraged also to provide Protestant moral training. Orphans were to be "taken up" and placed with families close to the schools, with money for board and clothing to be supplied by the nation.[14] Ross's plan was an ambitious one, but he clearly saw it as essential for the survival of the Cherokee Nation.

Looking ahead, Cherokee leaders also envisioned more advanced schools that would be added eventually to provide Cherokee teachers for the elementary schools. In the beginning, however, teachers were imported into the nation. Their annual salary was $525, which was competitive with salaries in New England schools. Some issues that retarded teacher recruitment included the relatively remote location of the Cherokee Nation, eastern whites' unfamiliarity with Cherokee culture, and the perceived uncertainty of tribal finances. Those who were recruited signed on for two semesters of twenty weeks each from September 1 to July 30, equivalent to terms set for schools in the East.

Although school finances were always tight in the Cherokee Nation, the school fund, first established in the 1835 Removal treaty, was probably the most solvent of tribal finances. It was supplemented by interest payments on funds held in deposit by the U.S. government for the sale of Cherokee lands in the East that were specifically targeted for education. In 1845, $7,200 was appropriated for eighteen schools and $3,600 for the care and education of orphans. The goal was to provide free education for all Cherokee children, in contrast to the missionary schools, which had charged parents for tuition and pupils' support at boarding schools.[15] After the Civil War, the treaties of 1866 and 1868 (which amended the 1866 pact) called for funds from land sales or otherwise due to the nation to be invested in stocks by the secretary of the interior. Interest from these investments was to be prorated according to the following formula: 35 percent to the school fund, 15 percent to the orphan fund, and 50 percent to the general fund.[16] After 1867, African-descended freedmen were provided schools because they were Cherokee citizens; these segregated schools were included in the appropriations.

By 1843, eight schools were operating; at that point the National Council increased their number to eighteen and in 1846 added three more. By 1860, thirty public schools were teaching around 1,500 students, an increase from the 200 pupils in 1842.[17] By 1876, 63 percent of Cherokee children were in school, and the annual per pupil expenditure was $42.80. By comparison, only 7 percent of Arkansas children and only 6 percent of Kansas children attended schools. Arkansas's annual per pupil expenditure was $7.45, and Kansas's was $8.28.[18]

Rev. Stephen Foreman was appointed the first school superintendent of the Cherokee Nation in 1841. Like any other major enterprise, this one experienced growing pains, and Foreman had his hands full. A primary requisite for the establishment of a school is a physical plant, in this case a building suitable for use during the winter months. Because many of the districts were poor, especially those with large full-blood populations that had not recovered from Removal, sometimes construction was slow. This was disheartening to Foreman, teachers, parents, and pupils. Another issue confronting the fledgling Cherokee educational system was the presence of competing mission schools; although the societies cooperated with

Foreman in his recruiting efforts, some individual missions continued to operate schools in conjunction with their religious functions,
although their impact diminished over time. Moreover, there was
more than enough work to go around. Moravians, Congregationalists, and Baptists conducted ten schools before 1852. At first, these
mission schools competed with the nation's schools for teachers as
well; those graduates of eastern schools who contemplated work in
the West were faced with a choice between living in isolated communities with a different culture and taking a position at a mission,
where at least one was in the company of people with similar backgrounds and aims. Some difficulties arose among the denominations as they aided the Cherokees in furnishing teachers for their
schools. Each denomination was eager to get members of its own
sect to teach in the Cherokee schools in the hope that they would
influence pupils to take up that particular faith. Foreman and the
Cherokee leaders also faced an even more difficult challenge: attendance was often spotty. Parents were blamed for not supporting
education, but more often absenteeism was caused by children being needed at home to work on the farms, to help around the house,
and to provide care for younger children.

Although Foreman was bilingual in Cherokee and English, he
was unable to hire bilingual teachers in the nation. He turned to the
protestant mission agencies for help in recruiting white teachers
from the East, many of whom regarded teaching in Indian Territory
as a missionary duty. Foreman's reliance on the mission societies
ensured that denominational issues would be an undercurrent in
Cherokee affairs for some time. When his recruitment efforts seemed
to be failing in 1843, he was replaced by James M. Payne, who
promptly pressed the National Council to raise teachers' pay to en-
tice teachers from the East to the Cherokee Nation. By 1847, Payne's
teachers numbered twenty-one, five of whom were Congregationalists, three Baptists, and two Methodists. Sixteen were white, and
nineteen were men. The twenty-one schools were situated according to population, a policy designed to reach all students. The budget for 1846–47 was $7,000, $200 of which went to buy books.[19]

The decision to staff the schools with imported white teachers
had long-term implications for Cherokee education, for the schools'
clientele, and for literacy. Importing white teachers meant that the

instructional language would be English; not only would the teachers address their pupils in that language, but students would be taught how to read, write, and spell English. Further, instructional materials, such as readers, arithmetics, and history books, would be in the white man's language. Although this was advantageous in that texts were readily available, it handicapped those pupils whose only language was Cherokee. To compound the problem, few Cherokees who spoke their native language were sufficiently trained to teach in the public schools, so the superintendent had little choice but to employ white people who, to a person, knew little or no Cherokee. There can be little doubt that those involved in planning the school system debated the wisdom of the choice of languages because the issues that had arisen in this regard in the eastern nation were still fresh and remained unsolved. The missionary schools, as discussed earlier, tried to find ways around the problem; both Worcester and Evan Jones experimented with Cherokee-language schools and writing in the syllabary. Even the Old Settlers had wrestled with this dilemma in schools they had set up before Removal, providing Cherokee-language instruction, with Sequoyah teaching the system he had invented. Now, however, the nation's leaders determined to forge ahead with English-only instruction, leaving use of the syllabary to informal venues.[20] The Cherokees were following the lead of American educational reformers like Horace Mann who saw assimilation of immigrant groups and others as a very important function of the public educational system, but they viewed learning English as a matter of practical survival. Some saw the difficulties in this approach, notably Evan Jones, who recognized that the way to approach the full-bloods was through their own language and their own syllabary.

Over time, it became increasingly clear to everyone that a significant reason for the reluctance of full-bloods to send their children to school, either the Cherokee Nation or the mission varieties, was that instruction was given in English. Thus full-blood children whose language was Cherokee were at a distinct disadvantage compared with mixed-blood pupils who spoke English in the home. The problem with English-only mission schools in the eastern Cherokee Nation before Removal was repeated: full-bloods dropped out at high rates, while mixed-blood children for the most part continued their education. This state of affairs had several long-term consequences. First, among the full-bloods, it eventually eroded support for the schools and produced reluctance on the part of many to spend tribal annuities to fund them because they were not serving the entire tribe. Second, it exacerbated an already-festering social problem, the schism between full-bloods and mixed-bloods. Full-bloods felt external prejudice from the white communities around them, but as the English educational gap widened between the two groups, they also felt internal prejudice from the mixed-blood members of their tribe. In addition, an important socioeconomic disparity between the groups that had its roots in the old nation became more clearly defined. With English education more widely available, the mixed-bloods went through a progressively more rapid rate of acculturation as time went on. Mixed-bloods, as they had done before Removal, were measuring their progress by the degree to which they resembled the white middle class. In general, they embraced a competitive market economy, and when they invested in privately owned "improvements" such as farms and ranches on tribal lands, they realized profits denied to full-blood subsistence farmers. At the same time, the full-bloods tied their identity to traditional cultural mores and practices. The nation before Removal had a two-class economic system that began shortly after white contact. Certain families, for example, the Vanns, the Rosses, and the Ridges, became capitalists to the extent that they built ferries and turnpikes from which they derived income; they also placed "improvements" on large acreages of tribal land. Using African American slave labor, they raised crops and stock and planted fruit orchards whose surplus produce they sold for cash. Thus a middle class developed in the old Cherokee Nation that was separated from the majority of the people, who were subsistence farmers. The social split in the old nation was largely driven by economics. After Removal, the class dichotomy was largely based on language and literacy.

Even though two-thirds to three-quarters of Cherokee citizens were full-bloods, the practice of English-only education remained national until the 1870s. In 1854, Marcus Palmer reported to the ABCFM that 1,200 pupils were enrolled in the national school system; of these, 120 were full-bloods.[21] In the same year, Samuel A. Worcester complained that many full-bloods resented the fact that the school system did not satisfy the needs of the majority of the population. The missionary saw a great danger in the resentment felt by the full-bloods and the prejudice against unschooled "Indian" children held by the mixed-bloods.[22] Although these reporters had agendas that often differed from that of the National Council and had reasons for opposing the public schools, the educational friction was apparent to everyone. Missionary John Beeson, for example, complained to a U.S. Senate committee that the rift between full-bloods and mixed-bloods was widening, and that those full-bloods who went to school used English while they were there but did not speak it at home. His conclusion was that they really did not learn English at all. Beeson ignored the question of whom the full-blood students were to converse with in English at home, but his concern was shared by others.[23]

After the Civil War, the Cherokee Nation was reorganized, and one of its first acts was to reopen the schools, three in each of the eight districts except Going Snake, which had four. Five orphans were to be "maintained and educated," according to Emmet Starr, and two segregated schools were opened for African-descended pupils.[24] In 1869, the number of schools increased by ten, and by 1871 there were fifty-nine schools in the Cherokee Nation. Because of the number of far-flung schools operating, some concern was raised among the Cherokee leadership about the quality of instruction. Many were afraid that the teachers, many of whom now were Cherokees with educational backgrounds in the tribal schools, not white people educated in the East, were not as well prepared to teach as those they replaced. Accordingly, Cherokee educational officials established summer teaching institutes designed to refresh teachers in the subjects they were teaching. At first, the institutes were voluntary; as time went on, they became a requirement for a teaching position in the nation. Typically, the topics were classroom organization, grammar, debate, arithmetic, geography, penmanship, and history. Information on the institutes was published in the *Cherokee Advocate*, including times, venues, and the topics to be discussed. These notices also were a way for the schools to be held accountable to parents and tribal officials.[25] Later, teachers who were not graduates of the Cherokee seminaries were required to pass an examination based on John Ogden's *Art of Teaching*.[26]

In the postwar Cherokee Nation, the full-bloods reasserted themselves politically in a way the Cherokees had not seen since pre-Removal days. This was demonstrated by the 1875 election of Charles Thompson as principal chief over William P. Ross, long a power in the national hierarchy. Thompson, known to the full-bloods as Oochalata, was elected when the full-bloods became disenchanted with the compromise government of Lewis Downing, who had sought to unite the slaveholding mixed-bloods with the majority full-bloods. With Oochalata's victory, the full-bloods were in control; one of the major ways they asserted this power was to revisit the question of which language was to be used in the public schools.

When the Cherokee public schools reopened after the Civil War, the National Council appropriated $200 to Evan and John Buttrick Jones to publish books in both English and the Sequoyan syllabary.[27] John B. Jones not only was determined to use the syllabary as the language of instruction in schools for full-bloods but also proposed teaching English through the syllabary. His method was based on the work of German linguist Heinrich G. Ollendorff, whose work John Jones became aware of while he was at Madison University. Ollendorff called his system "empirical," as opposed to the older "classical" method; the major difference between the two was that the empirical system deemphasized the abstract rules of grammar and syntax and paid more attention to learning everyday words and phrases by memorization and repetition. Ollendorff and his followers likened this system to the way in which children learn a language. When Jones described his plan to adopt these methods for his new textbooks to the Cherokee National Council in 1866, the members were convinced and authorized him to produce a book following this format. John B. Jones's textbook for elementary schools employed pictures and words, for example, using the image of a horse along with the Cherokee word for that animal printed in the syllabary under it, with the word spelled out in English below.[28] One small problem delayed his plan for a series of such publications, however: the lack of a printing press.

The *Cherokee Advocate* had ceased publication in 1853, and during the Civil War, the nation's printing press was stored at Fort Gibson for safekeeping. After the war, in which his facilities at Baptist

Mission had been destroyed, Evan Jones first settled in new quarters at Fort Gibson but later moved to Tahlequah. Once he was there, he petitioned his new overseers, the Home Mission Board, for a printing press with English and Sequoyan type. The board concurred, and the new equipment was procured in 1868; however, the board refused to furnish funds for paper, ink, and other printing supplies and demanded that the press be self-supporting. Jones was able to agree because of sales of religious texts, but more important, he persuaded the Cherokees to fund the publication of all the nation's extant treaties in the Sequoyan syllabary so they could be read by all citizens. By itself, this action served to demonstrate the growing political assertion of the full-blood majority. However, funds from these sources were not enough to sustain the press, so Jones went back to the council with an offer to sell it to the nation. Because the Cherokees were anxious to resume the publication of their national newspaper, the *Cherokee Advocate*, they agreed. They further agreed to allow the Joneses to use the press whenever it was not printing the *Advocate* or other official business of the nation.

Plans for Cherokee textbooks were interrupted, however, in 1870 when Ulysses S. Grant began his "Indian Peace Policy." With the change in administration came a change in personnel, especially in the federal agencies responsible for dealing with the Native population. When John B. Jones was appointed Indian agent, he left his immediate task of publishing schoolbooks but entered a position from which he was able to influence educational policy. For example, in his report of 1871, Jones recommended that the government aid the Cherokee Nation in reinstituting the two seminaries, if for no other reason than to train teachers for the public schools. He pointed out that the schools had closed before the Civil War and now needed extensive repairs to damaged buildings and a new crop of teachers as staff. The nation's finances had suffered such losses as a result of the war that the Cherokee treasury was unable to take on this added expense in the face of other needs.[29] The federal government did not respond to Jones's proposal, but he continued to press for Cherokee-language education for full-bloods. His report to the commissioner of Indian affairs for 1872 spelled out the difficulties full-blood children faced in trying to learn English and other subjects at the same time, and he again promoted the solution of using

Cherokee as the language of instruction, at least in those schools that were predominantly full-blood.[30] Jones realized that this was an expensive proposition; it required Cherokee teachers who knew English and their subject areas, as well as textbooks and other educational materials in the syllabary. Knowing that the Cherokee Nation lacked the resources to fund this enterprise, he thought it incumbent on the federal government to do so.

Jones's plan to revamp the Cherokee schools soon became a topic of discussion in the nation. John L. Adair, editor of the *Cherokee Advocate*, addressed the issue in the newspaper's pages. Adair began his discussion by pointing out the low average attendance—around five students—of the full-blood schools. In light of this seemingly meager interest in education, Adair argued, the cost-benefit ratio must be addressed; his point was that the nation could ill afford to support schools with so few students. Adair readily agreed with Jones that the cause of this lack of attendance was that the language of instruction was English, which, he asserted, the full-blood children neither understood nor wanted to understand. "The Cause of education among the full Cherokees is dead, without the hope of resurrection under the present system," Adair wrote. In the best case, all Cherokee children should learn the English language, and Adair gave all the reasons why this was necessary in the modern world. He then laid out three options. First, full-bloods should acquire a knowledge of the English language through books written in English, an option that he knew was prohibitively expensive. Second, they must learn English through "continual intercourse" with those who spoke that language. This option, Adair knew, was impractical, given the remote locations in which most full-bloods lived unless the children were removed from their homes and enrolled in boarding schools. His third option was to "teach them in their own language and give them all possible intelligence [that is, knowledge of subject areas]" in schools that used only the Cherokee language. Adair was a mixed-blood and shared the view of that group, perhaps instilled by missionaries, that the Cherokee language was incapable of expressing complex, abstract thought.[31] This final option, then, would have the effect of continuing and exacerbating the bi-level social and economic class system that was already solidifying in the Cherokee Nation.

Adair's comments, along with Jones's pronouncements, led to a debate that in many ways followed the lines of previous ones. William P. Ross, using the pen name "Native," published an article in the *Advocate* that reflected the views of a number of the mixed-bloods who considered themselves "progressive."[32] The plan Ross presented also mirrored a policy he had put into effect as superintendent of the Orphan Asylum. He argued that Cherokee children from English-speaking families should be placed in schools where they would be taught English and the other traditional subjects that a public school pupil could expect to learn, such as arithmetic, spelling, penmanship, history, and geography. The full-blood children from Cherokee-speaking families would be placed in manual training schools, in which the teachers would speak and teach in English (a practical measure having more to do with teacher recruitment than with pedagogy), while the children would be free to speak Cherokee as they worked at the tasks assigned. Ross claimed the support of the "leading men" of the nation, including the principal chief, and called the arrangement "the family or boarding industrial school plan." The plan, of course, was based on the old model of the mission boarding school that had been ineffective as a means of educating full-bloods in the eastern Cherokee Nation during the second decade of the century.

Although the response of full-blood parents was muted—the fact that their children could read and write in the syllabary of their own language seemed sufficient education to them—one of the more vocal opponents of Ross's ideas was John B. Jones. In his article, Ross had alluded to the Ollendorff method espoused by Jones and had dismissed it as good for textbook publishers but ineffective as a teaching tool. For his part, Jones saw the bilevel social and economic system that Ross's plan perpetuated and was incensed that the full-bloods were thus to be written off as lower caste. Jones eventually took himself out of the debate when he proposed in his report of 1873 that the schools of all the Indian Territory tribes be put under the control of the federal Bureau of Education.[33] Although Jones's reasoning for the prospective takeover was economic, the threat of Ross's plan was surely a factor. However, the citizens of the Cherokee Nation resoundingly rejected Jones's proposal. Emmet Starr later commented, "The progress of the Cherokees was due to their excessive pride in their schools, which were never allowed to be under the supervision in any way of the educational authorities of the United States, and none of their schools were ever visited by officers or agents of the department of education at Washington, until after June 30, 1898."[34]

The political changes the nation was undergoing in the 1870s affected the educational system, however, in that schools in predominantly full-blood areas began to employ Cherokee as the language of instruction. The practice was so entrenched by 1884 that the Cherokee Board of Education included in its rules for teachers the stipulation that "in Cherokee speaking schools, two hours per day were to be devoted to the study of English."[35] By 1892, the education of full-bloods beyond that of the manual training school was deemed so important that section 561 of the new Cherokee Constitution provided that non-English-speaking Cherokee students were to be given priority for admission to the primary departments of the seminaries.[36]

By 1847, another educational issue had arisen, the fact that wealthier Cherokees were sending their children who had graduated from the national schools to institutions of higher learning outside the nation. A few chose to send their children to some of the older colleges in the East, but this was too expensive for most Cherokees. However, alternatives were very close. Miss Sophie Sawyer, formerly a teacher at New Echota in the old nation and tutor to John Ridge's children, had fled the Cherokee Nation for Arkansas after the assassinations of John and Major Ridge and now had opened a Female Academy for young women in Fayetteville. Most of the Cherokees knew her, so her school was a natural place to send their children, especially because Fayetteville was close to the nation. Even closer was the Cane Hill Classical and English School, situated on the military road just inside the Arkansas line. As its name implied, it featured a curriculum dominated by Greek and Latin studies. Both schools offered the educational "finishing" many well-to-do Cherokee parents sought. Another northwestern Arkansas institution of higher learning was the Far West Seminary, whose headmaster, Rev. Cephas Washburn, had been an early missionary and teacher among the Old Settler Cherokees before removal. Some children of the expatriate Treaty Party attended this school, including John Rollin Ridge, the eldest son of John Ridge. In July 1847, the

Cherokee Advocate reported that Washburn had approached the National Council with a proposal for a Cherokee professorship at the academy. However, because he requested $15,000 from the nation to finance the chair, the council did not accept his offer. But these new academies on the Cherokee border were clearly attractive to the parents of children who had gotten all the education available from the national school system.

The tribal leadership recognized the problem and, fearing what today would be called a brain drain, determined to head off the difficulty by establishing high schools in the nation. This action also served to quiet the full-bloods' clamor for more Cherokee teachers. The seminaries, as they were to be called, would serve as teacher-training facilities that would swell the instructor pool open to the public schools. Provisions for the seminaries were included in an act passed by the National Council in November 1847.[37] The act provided for a board of directors that was "to consist of five men" nominated by the principal chief and confirmed by the National Committee; the principal chief would be the ex officio president and would convene meetings. The board was to employ a principal teacher for each seminary, who would employ one or more assistants and hire teachers "capable of teaching all the branches of literature and science commonly taught in the academies of the United States." Teachers at the male seminary were to be men, teachers at the female seminary women; each was expected to be of good character and "a believer in the christian religion." Prospective students were expected to be able to pass an examination in reading and spelling in the English language, arithmetic, English grammar, and geography. Twenty-five students were to be admitted initially, with an additional twenty-five added each year for four years. At that time, the senior class was expected to graduate, and a new class was to be added, thus placing the upper enrollment at one hundred for each seminary. These students were to attend tuition free, with on-campus room and board provided by the nation. However, Cherokee citizens would be able to enroll their children as day students at the discretion of the board, provided that the parents would furnish room and board at home or make private arrangements. The act stipulated that students were to be examined at the end of each term, and that the principal teacher would report the results of these examinations to the board. Thus the Male and Female Seminaries of the Cherokees were established, the first at Tahlequah and the second at Park Hill. These institutions, says Cherokee historian Emmet Starr, were "the two distinctive tribal schools that were henceforth to be the pride of the nation and its most important factors in producing solidarity and patriotic instinct. Large sums were diverted for their maintenance, instead of being used for enervating payments."[38] Starr is referring to the use of tribal funds to support schools rather than to disburse annual payments to individuals.

Starr reports that building began immediately, and that the workers used brick that was manufactured near the site of each school. The Female Seminary was erected three miles southeast of Tahlequah, while its male counterpart was located a mile and a half southwest of town. Both buildings were built on the same plan: 185 feet long and 109 feet wide, with verandas supported by Doric columns, which became emblematic of the institutions. Part of each building was two stories and part three stories; they were thus imposing structures for the time and place. Construction began in 1847, with Principal Chief John Ross dedicating the cornerstone of the Female Seminary on June 21.

The Cherokees were determined to imbue the seminaries with excellence so that they would rival the better schools in the East. Toward this end, in 1851 they sent David Vann and William P. Ross to Mount Holyoke Seminary in South Hadley, Massachusetts, to observe and recruit. Seminary planners had already decided to use that school as a model for their own and had designed the curriculum to mirror Mount Holyoke's. This was largely due to the influence of the missionaries in the nation and of the teachers already in the Cherokee school system, most of whom had come from New England. Vann and Ross wanted to see this design in operation to be sure that it would be appropriate for young people in the Cherokee Nation. They also intended to interview prospective teachers for the new institutions and to furnish them with information on the nation, the region, and the students there. They returned with positive impressions of the eastern school.[39] Samuel A. Worcester's wife, Ann Orr Worcester, had been a classmate there of Mary Lyon, a founder of the eastern academy. Ellen Whitmore, a twenty-two-year-old graduate of Mount Holyoke, became the first principal of the Female Seminary and applied many of Lyon's ideas to the new school. The Worcesters' daughter Sarah, a Mount Holyoke graduate as well, became the assistant principal.

Both schools opened in May 1851. Financing for the Cherokee education fund, which provided money for buildings, came from investments in registered stocks from money acquired through the sale of land to the United States. Only the interest was drawn and used to fund the schools. In keeping with Chief Ross's ideas about keeping the schools independent of outside interference, the federal government gave no support other than paying interest on money it borrowed from the nation, according to Starr in his *History of the Cherokee Indians*.

A steward was appointed for each institution who was responsible for maintenance and operation of the physical plant. In this, he was assisted by a domestic superintendent who was in charge of bedding, laundry, clothing, and supplies, as well as by a medical superintendent who was responsible for the infirmary and sanitation. Matrons were employed for many of the daily housekeeping chores, although in the Female Seminary, the students were responsible for much of this.

A strict regimen was enforced on all male students. The daily schedule began at 5:30 A.M., and activities were carried out with military precision until the retiring bell at 9:15 P.M. Chapel was a daily affair, as was "military drill." Although it is not certain what occurred in actual practice, the plan called for each minute of a student's time to be regulated.

Applicants for admission early in the seminaries' history had to demonstrate proficiency in reading and spelling in English, English grammar, arithmetic, and geography.[40] Two courses of study were available, the Preparatory Department and the Seminary Proper. The former consisted of three years and prepared students for the rigors of the latter. Typically, students were drilled in penmanship, reading (including phonetics), composition, grammar, geography, and arithmetic. To bolster their moral education and logic skills, a course called Object Lessons was included in all three years. The curriculum for the Seminary Proper was similar to that of the finer white schools in the eastern states. Freshmen took two ancient languages, Latin and Greek, and studied modern English grammar.

They also engaged in learning American history, science, arithmetic, algebra, physical geography, and physiology. The sophomore curriculum included the ancient languages and English rhetoric, English history, algebra, geometry, chemistry, and natural philosophy. Juniors advanced in the ancient languages by studying Cicero, Ovid, and Thucydides and beginning the modern foreign languages, French and German. They studied English and American literature, mental science, political economy, moral philosophy, trigonometry, analytic geometry, botany, and geology. Seniors were expected to read Virgil, Livy, and Homer in the original, as well as Molière and Goethe in the modern languages. They also took literary criticism, mental science, mental philosophy, and logic. Mathematical subjects for seniors were surveying and calculus; they also learned astronomy, and their knowledge of the natural world increased through the study of zoology. Although very few records of the first years of the Male Seminary are extant, the curriculum was similar to that of its female counterpart, although languages, mathematics, and science may have been emphasized to a greater degree. If the level of an education may be inferred from a school's curriculum, graduates of the Cherokee Male and Female Seminaries received an excellent education, relevant to the day.

By May 1852, the Female Seminary boasted over fifty students and was regarded as a success by both tribal and educational officials. After her first year as principal, Ellen Whitmore left the Female Seminary to be married and was replaced by two Mount Holyoke graduates in succession. However, keeping the schools open and supplied with teachers and materials was a daunting task. Delivery of textbooks and other supplies depended on water levels in the Arkansas River, on which they were shipped. Families often found it financially difficult to send a child to high school, even though much of the cost was provided by the nation. Teachers recruited from the East had to travel two thousand miles away from their homes and they were either reluctant to do so or felt they would become homesick after a while. Finally, the U.S. economy slumped in the 1850s; the downturn was exacerbated by a drought in 1854 and affected the Cherokees' finances as well.[41]

In spite of the seminaries' success and promise for the future, lack of funds forced the Cherokee Nation to close them in 1856. The Male

Seminary was closed on October 20, and its female counterpart at the end of the fall term. The schools might have reopened as soon as the financial situation improved, but the Cherokees' entry into the Civil War on both sides made that impossible. During the war, education, like everything else in the Cherokee Nation, was disrupted by marauding troops and outlaws on both sides, Indian and non-Indian. The buildings were pressed into military service. The Female Seminary became a storehouse for weapons and ordnance. The sheer weight of cannon ammunition caused classroom floors to collapse, and the library was gutted and books were destroyed. The Male Seminary building was treated similarly, pressed into service as a hospital for a time and used as barracks.

The Cherokee Nation was slow to recover from the Civil War. Money was short or just not available, and bartering and scrip systems substituted. Animosities healed very slowly among former combatants and their families because farms and improvements had been destroyed by Cherokees on both sides. The nation was called to account for the fact that some of its citizens had joined the Confederate cause, and the resulting treaties of 1866 and 1868 forced many changes. Nonetheless, the nation's leaders knew that the educational system needed to be restored if the Cherokees were to survive in the postwar world. Accordingly, in the early 1870s, they deliberated on how to bring about the revival of learning. By 1871, a renovated Female Seminary had reopened, and the Male Seminary followed in 1875, both using the original curriculum. The schools continued without incident until April 1887, when the Female Seminary at Park Hill burned to the ground. The National Council met shortly after and appropriated $60,000 to build a new building, this time at Tahlequah rather than at Park Hill. The Park Hill site was a bit remote, it was argued, and there were difficulties with the water supply. Accordingly, a forty-acre site was chosen north of the city adjacent to a large spring. Construction began in the fall of 1887, and in August 1889, the school reopened. The institution was so popular that prospective students had to be turned away.[42] The building still stands as part of Northeastern Oklahoma University. The schools continued until after the Native Nations of Indian Territory were dissolved with Oklahoma statehood in 1907. The first governor, Charles N. Haskell, asked the state legislature to establish a state training school for teachers at Tahlequah; as a result, the Female Seminary was sold to the state for this purpose. When the Cherokee Seminary opened in the fall of 1909, it was as a coeducational facility that absorbed many of the Female Seminary's former students. However, the seminary building caught fire in the spring of 1910, and it too burned to the ground, thus ending the tenures of both institutions.

The Cherokee Male and Female Seminaries did more than educate an elite group of Cherokees following eastern standards. Activities at both schools included literary discussions and debates, the staging of plays, including Shakespeare's tragedies, and the publishing of student creative writing. Reading, writing, and dramatic skills and interests continued after the students left school through social societies that emphasized the ongoing study of literature and history. Adults read and discussed literature and made presentations on their readings to their fellows. Dramatic societies not only read drama but also planned, produced, and acted in plays, providing much-desired entertainment in the days before radio, television, and film. Some larger communities, like Muscogee, boasted opera houses where itinerant dramatic and musical companies performed in front of educated and delighted audiences, many of whose members were Cherokees who traveled to take in the performances. Musicales, amateur theater, and dramatic readings were a staple of life in the larger towns. The literary and dramatic societies seemed to appeal not only to the upper crust of society but to many others as well, judging from the publicity they received from the newspapers of the day.[43] These groups fostered a love of literature and also provided outlets for budding poets and other writers, many of whom were encouraged by their peers to publish their works.

The seminaries also recognized young creative writers outside the classroom through student publications. The first number of *A Wreath of Cherokee Rose Buds*, published by the Cherokee Female Seminary, was distributed to readers in 1854; its first column carried an original poem by "Corinne" titled "Our Wreath of Rose Buds." *A Wreath* was published in both the Cherokee syllabary and English, following the custom of many Cherokee newspapers. Devoted to "The Good, the Beautiful and the True," this little publication carried prose as well as poetry. *A Wreath* was followed the next year by *The Sequoyah Memorial*, published by the Cherokee Male Seminary.

In its pages appeared poetry written by students, all signed with a single initial. These early published literary efforts encouraged others with similar ambitions, and these literary collections were the precursors of later literary publications, such as *Twin Territories*. They were also used by proud national officials to show off the talents of their young people and the products of their educational system. Cherokee Nation newspapers also published the work of creative writers, young and old, throughout the rest of the century.

The Cherokee Orphans Asylum was another institution established by the nation after Removal to care for those children who had lost their parents and were not being adequately cared for, presumably, by their extended families. The need for this facility signals a significant change in post-Removal Cherokee society: the breakdown of the clan structure.[44] Although the collapse of this age-old framework with all its religious and mythic trappings was not total, especially among the full-bloods, it was nevertheless a major part of the transformation of the national identity and says a great deal about the changing conception of the family among the Cherokees. The number of orphans requiring care increased dramatically after the Civil War, which brought devastation and bloodshed to both sides, breaking up and impoverishing families and slaughtering adults who would otherwise have been able to provide for the children. The orphan issue was recognized shortly after Removal, and in 1842 the National Council appropriated $2,200 for support of orphan children admitted to the public schools. These children were cared for by relatives or adopted into families where they were expected to be treated as members of the family. The nation provided some cash assistance to these families for their outlays for food and clothing. This support, administered by the individual schools, continued for as long as the child remained in the educational system.

In the early 1840s, the council considered the formation of a separate institution for orphans, but because of lack of funds, it tabled this decision until 1848, when it formed a committee to negotiate with the Methodist Episcopal Church South's Missionary Society to collaborate on orphanages for boys and girls. The Methodists had a history of caring for orphans in schools and homes they had established in many parts of the world, so this was the logical organization to consult on the matter. The council enacted a law that called for building schools on separate campuses, as well as residence halls for staff and children. Under this law, the buildings would be erected by the nation, using money from the Orphan Fund, which would also furnish the buildings, supply the farms with stock and equipment, and provide payments for food, clothing, and medical expenses for the children. The Methodists were to furnish a superintendent and teachers and pay their wages and support up to $1,000 annually. A board of trustees, made up of three persons appointed by the nation and three from the Methodists, would oversee the operation. The bill was signed into law by George Lowery, who was acting principal chief at the time.[45]

The original name of the institution was the Orphan Manual Labor School, and its curriculum consisted of a general English education plus occupational training. Boys were to be instructed in the use of tools and were expected to work on the farm, which was in turn to be relied on for the support of the unit. The farm produced food, and any surplus crops were to be sold, with the proceeds going to the benefit of the school. The girl pupils were instructed in spinning, weaving, knitting, sewing, dairying, and "all that pertains to household and domestic economy." This arrangement was in operation in other schools in the East and was employed in many of the Methodist institutions for orphans across the country. Orphans between the ages of four and fourteen were to be admitted, and total enrollment was to be between fifty and one hundred. The trustees were to try to maintain a balance between boys and girls admitted.

For reasons Emmet Starr does not report, this plan was never put into operation, and orphans, five to each school in the system, continued to attend the public schools.[46] The difficulty, most likely, was a lack of funds for this enterprise, coupled with the orphans' lack of political clout. Another attempt was made in 1871, when the National Council, concerned with the sheer numbers of children orphaned by the Civil War and bolstered by funds paid under the postwar treaties, produced an act to provide for the "Cherokee Orphan Asylum." This institution was temporarily housed in the Female Seminary building but then moved to the Male Seminary structure because the former school building was dilapidated. When the Male Seminary was renovated for the return of its students, the Orphans' Asylum was housed with the Asylum for the Insane, Deaf,

Dumb, and Blind at Fort Gibson, unsatisfactory quarters for all. To secure a permanent place for both, the council selected a site for a separate orphans' asylum on Lewis Ross's property at Grand Saline for which it paid $28,000. Other property, located five miles south of Tahlequah, was chosen for the second asylum. This tract was also owned by Lewis Ross, and his estate was paid $1,200 for it.[47] The larger purchase led to another row between John B. Jones and Chief William P. Ross, an educational argument that turned into an ugly political one.

The property purchased for the orphans was the Lewis Ross farm and that of his son Robert. The larger house on the property was to be used for Cherokee orphans, while the smaller Robert Ross dwelling was to house the African-descended children. Both men were deceased by this time, so the executor of their estates and receiver of the purchase price was the chief. Some of the African-descended Cherokees had gone to the National Council to complain that orphans of their group were being denied aid, although the postwar treaties stipulated that the former slaves were now full citizens of the nation. When Jones took up their cause, the chief replied that there was neither room for all the orphans in the asylum nor funds to support them, and that at any rate, aid was based on need, not race or color. When Jones demanded that a share of the orphan fund be given to the African-descended group to support those children, Ross refused, saying that this would lead to further demands, perhaps from the Delawares and Shawnees, for their shares. The issue went to court, with Jones's supporters charging malfeasance. The judge, an ally of Ross's, threw the case out on a technicality. Still, most people in the nation knew that the $28,000 Ross received was too high a price for the properties.

In 1874, Jones, the former agent, was appointed to the Cherokee delegation to Washington to defend the nation on a number of important issues, such as a proposed scheme to allot tribal lands, Cherokee Outlet grazing rights, the North Carolina Cherokee claims, and transfer of the federal district court from Arkansas to the Cherokee Nation. The Outlet, sometimes erroneously referred to as the Strip, was a long piece of land running along the southern border of Kansas and north of Oklahoma territory. Its original purpose was to give the Cherokees an outlet to the west to hunting grounds there.

Jones worked with the delegation on these and other topics, but then he approached the commissioner of Indian affairs on his own and proposed that educational and orphan-fund payments be stopped until the Cherokee Nation agreed to build a new orphans' asylum, and that Cherokee education be managed in the future by the commissioner of education and the Bureau of Indian Affairs. The reaction in the nation was tumultuous; Jones was condemned as a traitor, and his life was threatened.[48] Jones wisely withdrew his petition before leaving Washington; upon reentering the Cherokee Nation in June 1874, however, he helped organize the Downing Party convention, which met in August to decide best how to attack W. P. Ross.

When the Orphans' Asylum opened at the Ross farm, it had seventy-six students.[49] A larger building was built because the original Ross buildings were inadequate for the purposes of the school or the numbers of orphans requiring its services. Once in the larger building, the school operated with a curriculum nearly identical to that of the seminaries at the high-school level. The school, however, had three lower departments, primary (with two divisions), intermediate, and grammar. The primary and intermediate sections served by far the bulk of the student body, which consisted of slightly more girls than boys.[50]

The school continued in this fashion until the late 1880s, when another controversy arose, this time concerning the curriculum. The principals were Principal Chief Joel B. Mayes and W. A. Thompson, supervisor of the asylum. The argument was succinctly reported in the Cherokee newspaper the *Telephone* of December 19, 1889, where Thompson replied to an address by Mayes. Mayes's address, which had been reprinted in the *Cherokee Advocate* and issued as a pamphlet as well, called for the Orphans' Asylum to abandon its classical curriculum—which he called a failure in no uncertain terms—in favor of a manual-training-school format. The orphans thus taught, Mayes reasoned, would have the skills to support themselves when they left school. Thompson agreed that there was merit in training students for trades or crafts, but he disagreed that the place for such instruction was the asylum. Putting Mayes's plan in place would limit manual training to orphans. What about the male seminarian who wished to pursue a trade but found that the only education available was a classical one he asked? The solution, according to Thompson, was to open an industrial training school independent of the other seats of instruction in which all Cherokees who chose to could avail themselves of such training. This idea proved to be beyond the reach of a nation with so many other responsibilities; money, as always, was short for the Cherokees.

In November 1903, the Orphan Asylum at Salina burned, leaving 149 students homeless. Although they were temporarily given shelter by nearby residents, a new home needed to be found almost immediately. On December 1, the National Council passed an appropriation bill that called for the Insane Asylum to be converted to the Orphans' Asylum and the inmates of the former facility to be transferred to a building housing the National Prison.[51] The bill made no mention of what was to become of the prisoners.

By July 1906, the federal government had taken control of the Cherokee educational system. On July 31 of that year, the superintendent of schools for Indian Territory, John D. Benedict, wrote to Cherokee principal chief W. C. Rogers that physical control of the schools was being assumed by the U.S. Indian Service.[52] This act, in effect, ended sixty-five years of the independent Cherokee school system.

Among the responsibilities that fell to the Cherokee Nation was the founding and operation of a high school for freedmen. Although mandated by the post–Civil War treaties, the education of Cherokee freedmen and their children had been spotty at best. The school had its roots in the treaties, but the Cherokees were never quick to bestow what they considered privileges on their former slaves, the wishes of the federal government notwithstanding. Primary schools for African-descended children had been in operation since the 1870s, but it was understood that when these children left the lower schools, they were not welcome to apply to the seminaries. The founding of the first secondary school for the children of former slaves was not the result of altruism or adherence to the law of the land but a political tactic in a hotly contested election. The election of 1887 was a bitter one, featuring Joel B. Mayes as the Downing Party candidate and Rabbit Bunch for the Nationalist Party, which had been in power with Dennis W. Bushyhead as principal chief. Mayes and his supporters made the establishment of a "colored" high school a prominent plank in their platform, hoping to lure the votes of the freedmen. The tactic worked, regardless of its sincerity, and Mayes was elected.[53] Accordingly, in 1888, the Cherokee National Council authorized $10,000 for the erection of a suitable building on a site at Double Springs, about six miles northwest of Tahlequah. The building was of brick with a stone foundation, three stories high, as were the seminaries and the Orphans' Asylum, and contained about twenty rooms.

Although the school was called a high school, it was more than that. As was the case in the other Cherokee schools set up for secondary education, many of the children came unprepared for a higher level of study. Therefore, primary and intermediate classes were also held in the building so that pupils could progress until they were ready for the rigors of a high-school curriculum and could pass an examination to prove it. At the secondary level, the freedmens' school offered a daunting course of study that included astronomy, algebra, literature, physical geography, physics, history, botany, and physiology, among other subjects. Some of the teachers were of African descent, some were white, and some were Cherokee.

After the takeover of the Cherokee school system, the U.S. Congress in 1908 ordered the secretary of the interior to appraise and sell all the buildings, including schools, and deposit the proceeds in the U.S. Treasury to the credit of the Cherokee Nation. The freedmens' high school was sold for $1,350 to the Collate Missionary Baptist Association, a group of people of African descent. After some difficulty in raising the cash, the association took control of the property at Double Springs and rented it for whatever price it could get. A succession of families used it as a residence until July 1916, when the building burned. At that point, the association sold the land.

The Cherokee Nation's early recognition of the importance of education, the subsequent organization of a sophisticated school system for its time and locale, and the ongoing support from the national leadership were key elements in the spread of literacy among the tribe and the resulting flourishing of literary activity that was unrivalled among the tribal people of the Americas. The Cherokee educational system as a whole turned out a cadre of well-educated citizens, especially by frontier American standards, who became leaders in government, commerce, and the arts. However, these schools did not cater only to a few individuals from the elite class. The nation attempted to educate all its people, including poor full-bloods, orphans, and freedmen. An important dividend of this effort was that the schools engendered an ethos of literacy and literary activity in the communities they served. In the larger towns, especially, literary, dramatic, and debating societies were organized among adults with common interests. These helped create an environment for Cherokees who aspired to be writers. Thus the impact of education on literacy levels and literary activity was widespread and enormous. Education, along with publications by Cherokees for a Cherokee reading public, helped ensure that this ethos remained strong and vibrant.

CHAPTER 5

THE CHEROKEE LANGUAGE
AND THE SEQUOYAN SYLLABARY

The preceding chapters have surveyed the evolution of literacy in English and, to some extent, Cherokee among the Cherokees. In this chapter, I take a closer look at literacy in the Cherokee language itself and the contribution it made to the intellectual life of the nation. The syllabary was, after all, purely Cherokee in conception and development and quickly became an integral part of the group's culture. An examination of the ways the syllabary functioned throughout the nineteenth century and to the present day is important for understanding this source of national pride. I also examine the work of Cherokee linguists who invented a shorthand method for the language and who attempted to create an analysis of it using contemporary methods to make its serious study possible. These efforts alone were significant intellectual attainments, especially for individuals far from the traditional American seats of learning.

Cherokee, unlike the languages of its neighbors in the southeastern United States, is an Iroquoian tongue and thus is akin to Tuscarora, Mohawk, Oneida, Onondaga, Cayuga, and Seneca. There were three major dialects of Cherokee, but the Lower dialect died out around 1900, according to linguists, leaving the Middle or Kituhwa dialect, spoken by the modern-day North Carolina Cherokees, and the Western or Overhill form, spoken today in the Cherokee Nation of Oklahoma. Early missionaries, hoping to learn the Cherokee language in order to preach to the Cherokees, expected to find a simple language, with grammatical rules perhaps like those found in the

European and Middle Eastern languages with which they were familiar. Instead, they discovered a complex language that required long years of study to attain fluency. For example, Cherokee verbs are built on what linguists call bases, which may consist of verb roots or noun and verb roots, and they may additionally carry "derivational affixes," prefixes or suffixes. Further, Cherokee verbs have derived from five basic stem forms that distinguish different aspects or modes: present, imperfective, perfective, punctual, and infinitive. Verbs fall into up to eleven conjugation classes, which, in turn, are divided into subclasses, all denoted by affixes.[1] At times, as De Witt Clinton Duncan points out, the verb root seems to disappear altogether in the word phrase. In spite of these difficulties, the early missionaries came to understand this complexity and, with the help of native speakers, were able to translate many of their religious texts and ideas into Cherokee.[2]

When Sequoyah invented the syllabary around 1820, the Cherokees were given the means to put their spoken language into writing. The true extent to which they did so is hard to measure, given that much of their writing, like much of our own written language, was ephemeral. Accounts by whites who traveled through the Cherokee Nation before Removal tell of seeing the syllabary painted on fences and trees, and missionaries among Cherokees in the East and the Arkansas Cherokees reported to their headquarters that letters in the syllabary flowed between friends and relatives on a regular and frequent basis. Most of these written materials, however, have been lost. Similarly, the secret Keetoowah Society, whose membership was open to full-bloods only, kept its records in the syllabary. This was appropriate, given that the Cherokees did not define "full-blood" by blood quantum but by the ability to speak Cherokee and by having been raised in the traditional manner.

Some idea of the extent to which the syllabary was used comes to us through the work of ethnologist James Mooney. Mooney collected some six hundred manuscripts written in the Cherokee syllabary during his research among the eastern band in 1887–88. Among the papers he recovered were a large number of personal letters, which show that the Cherokee people used the syllabary for their own purposes beyond the more formal printed forms, newspapers, religious texts, and the like. The syllabary gave Cherokees the ability to write to and receive news from distant relatives, to send home reports from military posts during the Civil War, and to write out business agreements between colleagues, much as their white counterparts were doing in English.

More important to Mooney as an ethnologist, however, was the cache of "formulas" he was able to procure from the descendants of Cherokee "medicine men" or "shamans." He collected these and published them through the Bureau of American Ethnology under the title *The Sacred Formulas of the Cherokees*.[3] He describes some of these texts and their contents in the seventeenth annual report of the bureau. The ethnologist's initial forays to collect information from Cherokee elders followed an old methodology: The researcher poses a question, using a translator, to the subject. The subject replies, and the translator transmits the idea to the secretary, who then writes it down. In this sequence, much depends on the competency and trustworthiness of the translator and the secretary. Nuances of language, such as sarcasm or humor, may escape the inexperienced translator; the translator may be a native speaker, in which case his or her English may not be as fluent as it should be for this purpose; either the translator or the secretary may be tired or sloppy. At any rate, Mooney must have been elated when he was introduced to a number of written texts where none of these issues needed be considered.

The formulas consist of a body of material dealing with traditional Cherokee medicine and beliefs that go far beyond the identification of healing plants or the concoction of oral medicines and poultices. These materials include the words to go with the physical medicine, the chants and prayers without which the other aspects of the healing process are powerless. Mooney says in his introduction that the materials he collected cover "every subject pertaining to daily life and thought of the Indian, including medicine, love, hunting, fishing, war, self-protection, destruction of enemies, withcraft, the crops, the council, the ball play, etc." He relates that about half deal with medical matters, but the materials also include a large number of "love charms" that slightly exceed the songs and prayers involved in hunting and fishing. He explains the relatively small number of war formulas by saying that the last wars the Cherokees had been involved in antedated the American Revolution; the conflicts in which they had been involved since that time were really white man's wars in which they participated under the command of white officers. The formulas were handed down orally until the invention of the syllabary. Mooney's materials, he writes, were acquired from the writers themselves or from their surviving relatives.[4]

Among the papers Mooney retrieved was the Kanaheta Ani-Tsalagi Eti, a collection of papers written in ink that was fading or pencil that was blurring on various scraps of paper with disparate provenances. Some were fragments. Mooney determined to have these copied because he could not otherwise ensure the preservation of their content. He enlisted the aid of a young Cherokee who knew some English and had him copy what was written on the papers into a blank book of two hundred pages. The result is a record of 258 formulas and songs arranged with headings, a table of contents, and a title page. Mooney titled the volume "Ancient Cherokee Formulas" and placed it in the library of the Bureau of American Ethnology. Many of the formulas contain archaic expressions that were not widely known by Cherokee speakers in the late nineteenth century. Mooney's scribe, W. W. Long, conferred with his mother and uncle, who remembered most of this wording. The ethnographer reports that far from detracting from the texts, the older form of the language carries with it a nobility and beauty that surpasses the more modern form.

The Inali Manuscript was obtained from the daughter of Inali, or Black Fox, a prominent figure among the full-bloods, a councilor, keeper of the townhouse records, an officer in the Confederate army, and a Methodist minister, who later returned to the old Cherokee religion. The collection contains many letters to Inali, including a great number from Cherokees fighting with the Confederate forces, all written in the syllabary, with the usual Cherokee "gossipy" style, according to Mooney. Among other documents, Mooney found a manuscript book in the syllabary containing the records of the council at Wolftown, of which Inali had been secretary for several years.

The Gahuni Manuscript is likewise named for its author, although in this case, it contains materials written by younger family members after Gahuni's death. Gahuni combined his profession of "Indian

conjurer" or "shaman," in Mooney's language, with that of Methodist preacher, so although his papers contain much in the way of ancient formulas, they also include some translations from the Bible.
The Gahuni Manuscript contains about seventy pages of what seems
to be a Cherokee-English pronouncing dictionary, believed to have
been created by a son who had attended school, learned English,
and served as a copyist of some of the original material. Only eight
formulas were included, but these were a valuable section of the collection for Mooney because they were unique among those he collected and contained directions for their use.

Mooney was able to track down other informants with access to
old Cherokee texts through references from people from whom he
had already obtained materials. Once the word was out that the ethnologist was willing to pay to have the materials copied, he became
more welcome, especially because he apparently promised not to
share the secrets with "outsiders." One of the collections thus obtained was the Gatigwanasti papers. The writer's son, Wilnoti,
showed Mooney a box with a number of miscellaneaous records,
testaments, and hymnbooks, all in the syllabary. The chief artifact,
however, was a large-size book of 122 pages plus 75 or so more loose
pages filled with formulas in the Sequoyan script. When Mooney
offered to buy the papers, Wilnoti, a Christian, replied that he
wished to keep them, hoping to learn and "practice these things
himself." Later, when the ethnologist returned, he was able to buy
the manuscript from Wilnoti, although Wilnoti was able to copy as
much as he wanted to before Mooney removed it. The manuscript
was found to contain a great number of "love charms," complete
with directions and headings. These songs are written in elegant
poetry; the archaisms only add to their beauty.

One of the most famous of the manuscripts Mooney acquired is
the Swimmer. This was acquired from a man by the same name
who was known as a keeper of the old stories. When he was pressed
to share these, he was reluctant until he was told that many other
wise men had shared information with the men from Washington.
Not to be outdone, he agreed to share his knowledge. However,
when others found out what he was about to do, they argued against
it, saying that once Swimmer gave the information to the white
man, it would be locked up in Washington, and no one would be

able to use it. This worried Swimmer so much that he again refused to tell his stories. However, he produced a small book of about 240 pages, half-filled with writing in the syllabary. The writing contained songs and prescriptions for diseases; love, hunting, and fishing charms; and prayers for specific purposes, such as making the corn grow and warding off storms, and to specific spiritual entities, such as the Long Man, the Yellow Rattlesnake, and the Great Whirlwind. Mooney called it "an Indian ritual and pharmacopoeia." When Mooney asked Swimmer whether other shamans had such books, Swimmer replied that they all had them. In this way, the syllabary fulfilled its original purpose, to give the Cherokees their own writing system so that they could communicate with one another in their own language and record what was important to them.

Sequoyah's syllabary was not used only for religious texts, be they Christian or traditional Cherokee, however. It was used in as many ways as the European alphabets in creating words to transmit ideas, from the mundane to the profound. Jack Frederick Kilpatrick and Anna Gritts Kilpatrick have located, translated, and edited a series of Cherokee documents written between 1862 and 1964 on a wide range of subjects.[5] In their preface, the Kilpatricks address the issue of the present-day dearth of Cherokee materials. "Thirty years or so ago one might have obtained manuscripts in the syllabary by the truckload. Today the average Cherokee cabin is likely to be as devoid of a single scrap of Sequoyan as it is of a copy of Catullus. World War II dealt a deathblow to the way of living of an entire century." This comment, written in 1964, antedates the extensive language-preservation programs undertaken by both the Oklahoma and North Carolina Cherokees, in which the syllabary is used extensively. Nonetheless, they accurately portray the appalling loss of materials during the twentieth century. Most of the Kilpatricks' sources are, in fact, in archives and museums.

Many surviving documents concern people involved in the Civil War, which caused extensive damage—human, psychological, economic, and social—all across the Cherokee Nation and among neighboring people as well. Indian Territory was ravaged by people on opposing sides, who burned houses, businesses, barns, and other improvements. The Cherokees raised regiments of troops for both the Union and Confederate armies, and many of the soldiers became bitter enemies and remained so after the war. In the East, Cherokees enlisted in Confederate forces and served as soldiers and scouts. In both areas, the syllabaries served the native speakers well as they corresponded with people back home, requesting supplies and clothing and sometimes furnishing their families with last wills and testaments. Often, soldiers wrote to people back home struggling to raise food and livestock, giving permission for individuals to use their horses or their tools. These documents give insights into soldiers' lives, as well as those of the people back home.[6]

One example is that of a Cherokee "scout," Inoli, who wrote home about a skirmish in which he had been involved in the mountains. The Indian troops were ordered to scour the woods looking for deserters, Union spies, bushwhackers, and others, a practice that the Northern generals self-righteously denounced. The letter writer was engaged in this work. After they captured twenty-nine "Yankee pretenders," probably spies, they were ordered to attack a white house. When the occupants determined that the attackers were Indians, they deserted their house in fright. After being ordered to halt and after one of their number was wounded by a Cherokee rifle shot, the householders surrendered. Upon searching the house, the soldiers found a large cache of arms, but after questioning their prisoners, they were identified as allies, not enemies. So the incident ended happily for all, with the possible exception of the man who was wounded. The translation indicates that the letter was written with typically Cherokee self-deprecating humor, evident even in time of war and danger.

Inoli was a sergeant in William Holland Thomas's regiment of Indian soldiers fighting for the Confederacy. Thomas was a white man but was close to the Cherokees of North Carolina and was considered a "white chief." Inoli kept some records of the regiment in the syllabary, including one list on which the amounts of money Thomas spent on uniforms for some of his soldiers were recorded. Thomas expected to use this list for reimbursement from the Confederate government. Inoli also kept a list of those soldiers who succumbed to disease. Another list indicates the names of orphan children of regiment soldiers who died of wounds or disease and amounts expended for their care. More mundane matters were recorded as well, including bills of sale, receipts, and financial transactions of various kinds.

The Kilpatricks report an interesting use of the syllabary in funeral notices. "In Oklahoma, and probably in North Carolina also, when someone died during the night, it was traditional to tack a notice to the church door at sunrise and to ring the church bell so that the community might inform itself of the name of the deceased and the particulars of the forthcoming funeral. If the death occurred during the day, the notice was posted and the bell tolled at sundown." The notice was written in the syllabary, often in elaborations of the symbols, and sometimes scenes from the deceased person's life were drawn on the paper, cardboard, or whatever other material was at hand to make the notice.[7]

Issues of national importance were discussed in the syllabary as well. In Goingsnake District in 1877, the district solicitor resigned because of his difficulties in dealing with white intruders. His letter of resignation of 1877 was sent to Principal Chief Charles Thompson, a full-blood, in Sequoyan. The letter voices the official's frustration because he feels that he does not have the authority to prosecute the offenders even if he can catch them. Jurisdiction was such in Indian Territory that the Cherokee Nation's courts could try Cherokee defendants, but white ones could be tried only in federal courts. Ganenulisgi Newadv, the solicitor, in effect informed the chief that he was resigning from a job he found impossible to do well. Another national issue after the Civil War was the role of freedmen, former slaves and their descendants, in the political and economic life of the Cherokee Nation, a topic of much discussion in the twenty-first century as well. The treaty of 1866 stipulates that freedmen were to be accepted into the nation as citizens; however, especially with regard to disbursement of tribal funds, many were reluctant to share with the African-descended citizens on the grounds that they did not possess Indian blood. In the National Council election of 1881, this was a hotly debated question, and the letter writer Tsowa Ganisini Unesdala wrote to Tahlequah to find out which side won. Apparently, he had canvassed voters in his home Canadian District and had determined that the antifreedmen forces had won handily there. "There are not enough 'black ones,'" he writes, referring to those who wished to allow the freedmen to share in the funds.

The Keetoowah Society is said to have been founded by missionaries Evan and John B. Jones in 1859, but in reality, the Joneses took an ancient traditional society of Cherokee full-bloods and organized them into a political group to oppose the influence of the so-called treaty men, under the leadership of Stand Watie. A major issue here was the political situation in the United States leading up to the Civil War. The Joneses were fervent abolitionists, while Watie's faction leaned toward the Southern cause. In the Cherokee Nation, the divide was not between slaveholders and those who held no slaves; there were slaveholders on both sides. Nor was it entirely a matter of full-bloods against mixed-bloods, although this was a factor. In practical terms, the Joneses organized a group of traditional Cherokees to support Principal Chief John Ross, himself a slaveholder and a mixed-blood. On the other side was Watie's party, whose members came to be called the Southern Cherokees. The Keetoowahs, called Pin Indians because of the identifying crossed pins they wore, were dedicated to preserving traditional Cherokee values and practices. Later in the century, some Keetoowahs under Redbird Smith organized under the name "Nighthawks" to oppose tribal dissolution and allotment. Some Keetoowah documents written in the syllabary survive, even though its organization and activities were largely secret. One such text is an address of an official of the society written in 1901.

> Now! In a few words I will make plain the way our Keetoowah is organized; for we do not have anything like the law of the Apportioner that they have elsewhere.[8]
> This is what our Apportioner gave to us, the Indians: the White Pathway that leads to the House. Our Pathway, the White Pathway of the Apportioner, is all that there is to help us. If we understand and believe in the Keetoowah, it sustains us forever.
> This is the way it will be: If we do not listen, we cannot understand; if we do not listen, it will always be this way where we live. It will never be easy until we arrive There; it will be just as it is.
> But if we listen to our Apportioner when He speaks, all of us will be mingled together There; our own will arrive There.
> It is difficult for the multitude to understand. In order to appeal to them, one has to speak much. Then they will learn what to do.
> But they who do not take heed may think that elsewhere they will find help.
> Now! That is all.[9]

The society also kept more practical records. One such item reported by the Kilpatricks is a book of small pages stitched together on which contributions for food were recorded. The contributions were for food for one of the chapters, or *gahiyo*, of the Nighthawk Society in 1902. The book shows contributions ranging from two cents to fifty cents for such items as coffee, a pig, and cows; the animals, presumably, were to be slaughtered and roasted for feasts at meetings.

A number of Cherokees, including full-bloods, were Christians, and texts relating to the practice of that religion were written in the syllabary as well. The Kilpatricks recount the discovery on the packed dirt floor of a smokehouse of a manuscript book written by a Cherokee Baptist preacher, Anilageyv, who had recorded the last words of dying parishioners. Some typical declarations include the following, all written out in neat Sequoyan calligraphy: From Ali Usana, 1910: "Now I am going to my Father's Place. I have found a Beautiful Place to live, and I have found my little children, my brothers. You must love me and follow me." From Denili Tsisghwa, 1911: "I am in a hurry to go. Beloved ones, I am going to leave you. I have found the beautiful golden buildings of God." From Tsawayuga Ayohlani, a young girl, 1915: "I worked all the time, and now I have found where the Brightness is. Through the Narrow Door I am going into the Bright Lights, where there is gladness."[10]

An interesting article appeared in the *Tahlequah Arrow* in 1903 in which the editor commented on a recent letter from the Philippines by a missionary, J. B. Lawson. Lawson had requested books from which he might learn Cherokee so that he could teach it to his parishioners, so that in this way they might acquire a written language. This, the editor surmised, would lead to elimination through disuse of the "local jargon, thus advancing them along educational lines." However, he reported that Lawson's request would have to go unanswered because the Cherokees had "no text books, by which that language may be taught in schools or learned in private study as French, German or Spanish."[11] This article demonstrates the fame of the Cherokee writing system and an interest in it far from the borders of Indian Territory.

The dearth of Cherokee textbooks was noted in the Cherokee Nation. William P. Boudinot wrote in 1892:

Ever since the Cherokee Nation has had a school fund and a school system, the money and system have been used to educate less than one-half of the Cherokee people, to-wit, that fraction which understands and uses English as a medium of thought-exchange, and which class, therefore can alone be instructed by English teachers using English text books. With more than one-half of the Nation convinced to the use of the native tongue, not a single effort has been made by our national authorities to utilize that priceless invention of Sequoyah whereby knowledge may be imparted to Cherokee speaking children and adults with ten times the facility and with the same certainty it can be in English. Whatever, therefore, may be remarked about the progress made by the English speaking half, or less than half of our people, the Cherokee speaking portion have been left to shift for themselves.[12]

These are the words of a patriot who saw his countrymen unprepared for what lay ahead: private ownership of land, U.S. citizenship, cessation of any protection afforded by their tribal affiliation, and an influx of settlers who, although not necessarily antagonistic, would likely use any means short of violence to enrich themselves, even to the extent of relieving the Indians of land, improvements, and natural resources. Boudinot was not very optimistic about the outcome, and although he was confident that Cherokees of his level of education and experience with the white world would probably survive, he had real fears for those uneducated full-bloods who had little idea of what was to come and who made up half the Cherokee population.

Boudinot was not alone in his concern that the education of full-bloods was not being attended to. As discussed in Chapter 4, this issue had been debated earlier among the missionary educators in the eastern nation and the Cherokees themselves as they set up their model school system in Indian Territory around 1840. Several factors help explain the momentous decision by the Cherokee establishment to choose English-only schooling for their children instead of another form that included instruction in the Cherokee language using Sequoyah's syllabary. The first is the makeup of the Cherokee leadership at the time. One of John Ross's major aims as principal chief was to set up a school system whose philosophical underpinnings, as well as its practical methodology, were set by Cherokees. This was due in large part to disappointment with the educational efforts of the missionaries, whose schools were heavily criticized because they taught only a small percentage of the children, and most of these were drawn from English-speaking families. Ross and his associates in the Cherokee government were all more acculturated than their average constituent, and most of their business was conducted in the English language. Although Ross enjoyed the support of a majority of full-bloods during his long tenure as chief, he was not fluent in Cherokee and needed an interpreter to translate his addresses to those who spoke Cherokee only. It was probably difficult for him to separate the concept of education from that of speaking English for the simple reason that for all his life, when he met a person he considered educated, that person spoke English.

Closely related to Ross's personal views on the subject is a set of attitudes shared by the Cherokee leadership, as well as other influential citizens: the Cherokees were proud of their reputation as a "civilized" people and did everything they knew how to do to promote that image. For the Cherokees, this was a matter of survival; they reasoned that if the larger, more powerful white society did not regard them as savages, they would escape the treatment of other tribes, the derisively termed "blanket Indians." Although this strategy had not prevented Removal from the East, at least they had escaped the warfare and incarceration on reservations suffered by the western tribes. Cherokee delegates educated in the English language had negotiated the treaties of the 1820s, 1830s, and later, and educated people traveled to Washington to deal with government officials and others and to look after Cherokee affairs in general. To the Cherokee leadership, the ethos of education was founded on knowledge of and fluency in the English language.

Another consideration of the Cherokees in deciding on an English-only educational model was economic and centered on two issues: the availability of textbooks and other teaching materials and the availability of teachers. Because the only printing presses with Sequoyan type were in the Cherokee Nation and because the market was so small, the major textbook publishers did not produce Cherokee-language materials. Thus, if Cherokee textbooks were to be used, they would have to be created and printed in the local print shops. The Cherokee Nation's press published the weekly newspaper and did some job printing on the side, but it was entirely beyond its capability to produce enough books in the language to supply the schools. In order to accomplish this, the Cherokees would have to make enormous expenditures on personnel, equipment, and physical plant. The amounts necessary were not available. Further, books like *McGuffey's Reader* were readily available. Although the textbooks used by most schools were perhaps rudimentary by modern standards, they had a proven record of success; how well Cherokee-language texts would achieve their goals was a matter of conjecture, many thought. In this milieu, it is not hard to understand the decisions made when the school system was established.

This is not to say that the social and economic issues raised by English-only education were ignored. Especially after the Civil War, when the full-bloods became a stronger political voice, this policy was revisited. Although Boudinot's remarks on the subject were not published until the 1890s, others had seriously considered using Cherokee as the language of instruction in the public schools; in fact, in some heavily full-blood areas after 1875, Cherokee-language schools became a reality. By this time, the seminaries had educated Cherokee-language speakers and trained them to teach. Thus one of the major hurdles had been crossed. The second major obstacle to Cherokee-language schools was the availability of texts. As I noted in Chapter 4,[13] John B. Jones, who had been agent to the Five Civilized Tribes, and his father, missionary Evan Jones, were awarded $200 after the Civil War to publish books in English and Cherokee. The younger Jones was ambitious in this cause, determined to teach not only subject matter in Cherokee, but the English language besides in the public schools. He also petitioned the federal government in 1871 to aid the cash-strapped Cherokees in reopening the seminaries. His major rationale for reopening the schools was the need to educate Cherokee speakers to prepare them to teach in the public schools.

The immediate problem for the Joneses publishing efforts was the lack of a press. During the war, their operation at Baptist Mission had been destroyed, along with their printing equipment. Evan Jones petitioned the Home Mission Board for a replacement press, supplies, and equipment, making the argument that printing religious materials in the syllabary was the best way of reaching the full-bloods. The board agreed to furnish the equipment but stipulated that the printing operation must be self-supporting. This turned out to be difficult because most of the press's customers were poor subsistence farmers. The nation had given $200 in support, but this was not enough, so the Joneses entered into an agreement with the Cherokee Nation to sell the press to it, but reserved the right to access the press and equipment when it was not being used by the Cherokees. The nation, whose print shop also had been destroyed during the war, was ready to resume publication of the *Cherokee Advocate*, and this arrangement allowed it to do so, beginning in April 1870.

The textbook project was put on hold, however, when the new Ulysses S. Grant administration instituted its "Indian Peace Policy" and drafted John B. Jones as agent to the Five Tribes.[14] However, Jones used his position as a bully pulpit to advance his ideas, urging the federal government to support the reopening of the seminaries in his annual report for 1871 and arguing for support for teaching full-bloods using the syllabary in his report for the following year. Not everyone in the Cherokee Nation supported Jones in his campaign. John L. Adair, for example, a mixed-blood editor, writer, and educator, argued that preparation for life in the modern world required fluency in English and that using the native language to educate children would hamper their learning of English. His line of thinking presages the arguments of adherents of "English only" in the United States in later years, for example, when European immigrants were punished for speaking their native languages in the early twentieth century, Indian children in federal boarding schools were forbidden to use their languages from the end of the nineteenth century well into the second half of the twentieth, and more recently, restrictions have been applied on the official use of the Spanish and Asian languages. With the election of full-blood Charles Thompson in 1875 as principal chief, however, some schools, mostly in outlying rural areas, used Cherokee in the schools. The nation's newspaper, too, continued the tradition of publishing varying amounts of material in the syllabary, including the nation's laws and regulations.

Moreover, religious texts became a staple of publishing in the syllabary. Samuel Worcester had published the first text to be printed in the syllabary, the first five chapters of Genesis, in the December 1827 issue of the *Missionary Herald*, using type recently cast for the Cherokee Nation. The Cherokee printing press and type had been purchased under Worcester's direction in Massachusetts, and he used the type for this first printing before it was shipped to the Cherokee Nation. Thousands of pages of the Bible and other religious matter followed this small beginning.[15] In the Cherokee Nation, the process was simple: as soon as passages were translated, say, one of Paul's epistles, the text was set in the Cherokee font, and the pages were printed and distributed through the missionaries to the full-bloods and others. The texts accumulated, and in time, an entire Bible was available for Cherokee readers. The early work of Jones and Worcester produced Cherokee versions of Matthew's Gospel in 1829 and the Acts of the Apostles in 1833. "Selections from the Bible" appeared in 1831, and John's Gospel in 1838. These texts were produced at New Echota by Samuel Worcester and Elias Boudinot, often assisted in translating by George Lowery and David Brown.[16] After Removal, this work continued, with Stephen Foreman taking on many of the translation duties and John Candy printing the pages. In the 1840s, publication of New Testament texts continued: Paul's Epistle to Timothy in 1844, his First Epistle to the Thessalonians in 1847, the Epistle of Peter in 1848, Paul's Epistle to the Philippians in the same year, and Paul's Epistle to the Romans in 1849. The Old Testament began to be published in the 1850s, starting with Genesis, Exodus, Psalms, and Isaiah.

The American Bible Society, whose purpose is to make copies of the Bible available for mission work and other purposes, got involved with the Cherokee Bible around 1843 with the founding of the Cherokee Bible Society, a branch of the national organization.[17] The society, founded in 1816 by a group of Christians close to the abolitionist cause, had as its first president Elias Boudinot, a member of the Continental Congress and later director of the U.S. Mint. He had been a patron of Buck Watie, who, at Boudinot's request, took his name while at school in Cornwall, Connecticut, and who later became the first editor of the *Cherokee Phoenix*. Throughout its history, the society has been heavily involved in translating the Bible into various languages, usually in connection with foreign missionary efforts. During the nineteenth century, the group published Cherokee translations into the syllabary, thus continuing the early work done by Samuel A. Worcester and Evan Jones. Production of Cherokee Bibles continued in the twentieth century until at least 1953.

In addition to publishing the scriptures, the Cherokee presses also turned out other religious materials. Hymnals in the Cherokee language were very popular items, used from their first issuance in 1838 until today. Some contained only the words; others provided both words and music. In the pre-Removal years, a catechism also was published for use in missionary churches, but it doubtless was in less demand than the hymnbooks. Works of fiction long used by missionaries all over the world were translated into Cherokee as well. These attempted to serve as cautionary tales for the reader, but it is unlikely that aboriginal people would much identify with the main characters in *The Dairyman's Daughter, Bob the Sailor Boy,* and *The Swiss Peasant. The Swiss Peasant,* by Rev. César Malan, was subtitled *The One Thing Needful* and was published in Cherokee at Park Hill in 1848. *The Dairyman's Daughter,* written by Rev. Legh Richmond, and *Bob the Sailor Boy,* written by clergyman G. C. Smith, were often printed together, and the Cherokee version appeared this way as well.

Temperance tracts appeared regularly. In 1836, Asa Hitchcock of Dwight Mission published *Tracts in the Cherokee Language,* a broadside printed at Boston, according to the *Missionary Herald.*[18] Hitchcock translated this piece into the syllabary, and the copy was sent to Boston, where it was lithographed and printed on large sheets. This publication contained the Ten Commandments and the stories of John preaching in the wilderness, the star of the East, and the prodigal son.

The Cherokee government made use of syllabary font as well, printing laws and legal notices, *Constitution of the Cherokee Nation, Made and Established at a General Convention of Delegates, Duly Authorised for that Purpose, at New Echota, July 26, 1827,* said to be the first book published in the Cherokee syllabary, was printed and distributed in 1828. This was the beginning of a long tradition of printing important government documents in the syllabary so they could be shared by all citizens, because most records were kept in English. This was especially true when laws were revised and constitutions rewritten, as in the 1870s, when a new legal code was enacted. Proceedings of important meetings were printed in Cherokee, such as those of the Cherokee convention in 1861, when the question of participation in the Civil War was being debated. During the debates in Congress on the fate of Indian Territory and its people in the last three decades of the century, reports from delegates were printed in the syllabary so that Cherokee speakers and readers might keep abreast of the latest threats to national sovereignty. Proceedings, acts, and resolutions of the National Council were also printed in the syllabary and distributed to Cherokee citizens, as were addresses to the nation by the principal chiefs.

During the Civil War, both sides distributed documents printed in the syllabary to the Indian troops. A special order, designated Number 15, by Major General Thomas Hindman, commander of the Confederate forces in the Southwest, was published at Tahlequah in 1862 in both languages. This order concerned the regiment headed by Stand Watie that included mostly Cherokee troops but later added personnel from other tribes. Similarly, Major General James G. Blunt, commander of the U.S. Army of the Frontier, issued a message he called "Fellow Soldiers of the Indian Brigade" that was published in the Sequoyan syllabary and in the Creek language using the roman alphabet. After the war, the U.S. government published various texts in the syllabary, including *Laws of the United States Regulating Trade and Intercourse with Indian Tribes*" (1879), the Emancipation Proclamation (1863), the president's proclamation of pardon and amnesty (1864), the 1866 treaty, and *Treaties between the United States of America and the Cherokee Nation, from 1785* (1884).

Almanacs were also published regularly, the first by John F. Wheeler at the Mission Press in 1836. The material was copied from *The Temperance Almanac* and was calculated for the latitude of Charleston, South Carolina. Wheeler's next attempt, however, was calculated for the meridian of Fort Gibson, Indian Territory, and appeared in 1837. The almanacs appeared annually after that, and most of them were printed in both the Cherokee syllabary and English. This series continued until the Civil War.

After the Civil War, another figure emerges in Cherokee publishing, that of Amory Nelson Chamberlin. Born in 1821 at Brainerd Mission, Tennessee, he was the son of missionary William Chamberlin and the grandson of Ard Hoyt, who had been involved in early efforts to translate the scriptures into Cherokee and with Cherokee schools. The younger Chamberlin grew up speaking the native language and so attained a fluency rarely found in a white man. He removed with the Cherokees to Indian Territory, serving as an interpreter and a teacher. Later, he became superintendent of the Female Seminary. During the Civil War, he served in Stand Watie's regiment and fell victim to frostbite on his feet while stranded far from medical help. With a butcher knife, he proceeded to perform surgery on himself, amputating one foot back to the heel and cutting just back of the toes of the other. When Chamberlin was rescued, he traveled to New York City, where he was hospitalized and treated. When he returned to Indian Territory, he could walk with the aid of stiff boots and crutches. At that time, he became a Presbyterian minister and was pastor first at Pheasant Hill in present-day Craig County. He ministered to full-blood communities in the vicinity of Vinita and later established the first Presbyterian church in Vinita in 1883.[19]

Chamberlin's publishing ventures began around 1886, when the Presbyterian mission headquarters sent him a press and a Cherokee font after his repeated requests. His first printed text appears to have been a hymnal in Cherokee and English, but it included only the words, not the music, to the songs. More interesting, perhaps, is his *Cherokee Pictorial Book, with Catechism and Hymns,* published in 1888. The hymnal had been printed at Dwight Mission, but the later book was printed at Tahlequah by the *Advocate* shop there.

DeWitt Clinton Duncan, teacher, writer, and statesman, also was a translator for the Cherokee Nation in various capacities and, as such, was a student of his native language. As he thought about the structure of Cherokee and how it varied from the other languages he knew, English, Latin, and Greek, he began to take a series of notes that in time grew into a detailed linguistic description of Cherokee.

The atmosphere in which Duncan worked seemed to determine what he saw as the future of the Cherokee language. Apparently, he believed that it would die out with the dissolution of Cherokee tribal government and would be replaced by the language of the usurpers of Cherokee land. This way of regarding every part of Indian culture was popular at the time, not only among ordinary white citizens but among the intelligentsia as well. The Bureau of American Ethnology, after all, had been organized as a repository of all things Native American, including both physical and linguistic artifacts, in the belief that these cultures were rapidly disappearing.

Duncan created "Analysis of the Cherokee Language" with the help of his wife, Helen R. Duncan. The "Analysis" was sent to the Bureau of American Ethnology in 1882, where a sixty-two-page extract was prepared under the direction of J. O. Dorsey after his examination of the manuscript.[20] Dorsey then returned the manuscript to Duncan and retained the extract for the bureau's files. Duncan's letter of transmittal, dated August 10, indicates that it was sent from Charles City, Iowa, to Spencer F. Baird, the secretary of the Smithsonian. In the letter, Duncan indicates that he sees his work as helping preserve for posterity a dying tongue, an underlying principle of the Bureau of American Ethnology's linguistic efforts that had its roots in nineteenth-century scientific efforts to preserve vestiges of cultures that were being destroyed by what the arbiters of culture saw as the inexorable march of progress. The comments that follow are based on the extract.

Duncan's grammar notes typically consist of statements about an aspect of Cherokee grammar. The illustration gives the sentence in the syllabary; above each set of symbols denoting a word, Duncan includes the grammatical function of the word. The Cherokee dictionary is arranged so that a word is given first in the Cherokee syllabary, followed by an approximation in roman characters of its sound. Then a definition is given, followed by a citation in the New Testament in Cherokee. The citation is explained by Duncan in a note: "The New Testament printed by the American Bible Society is the best classic extant in the Cherokee language. For this reason I have taken it as authority for the rules which I have enunciated in the preceding pages." Duncan thus indicates that he is not relying on his personal command of the language alone, but checking his work with a text known to have been edited by a number of persons fluent in the language, including native speakers.

Duncan published "An Analysis of the Cherokee Language" in pamphlet form in Tahlequah in 1890. It begins with the following admonition: "Study the Cherokee language; it will be to you a means of pleasing recreation, besides an acquisition of useful knowledge." The author may have had in mind the general edification of his non-Cherokee audience, but more likely he saw it as a guide to the language for the white people streaming into Indian Territory at the time in search of land or other treasure. Because commerce with the Cherokees was necessary in these endeavors, at least for the foreseeable future, some acquaintance with their language would be very helpful.

The pamphlet was organized in a logical manner, including a guide to pronunciation, followed by lessons. The lessons dealt first with the prefixes and then with the suffixes, each of these categories being broken into component parts, for example, "The Personal Pronoun" and "The Noun." Each lesson included a vocabulary list, as well as exercises that helped the reader apply the principles taught in the lesson.

Duncan continued to refine his ideas on Cherokee linguistics. In 1888, he considered the "Analysis" incomplete. In a letter to James Constantine Pilling, the eminent linguist interested in Native American languages, he writes that it is ninety-nine pages long so far. He says that he has devoted many years to his research and writing, beginning in 1876.[21] He sketches his ideas for Pilling, writing that "what appear to be words are not words, but phrases, or sentences." These are composed of a "radical" with a number of appendages, either prefixes or suffixes. A radical seldom appears alone and in a phrase may seem to disappear to all but the most experienced Cherokee linguist.

He writes further that "language has a 'reverence for euphony,'" and that "it is between the numerous links that compose the concatenation of prefixes and suffixes, that euphonic change is wont to display its subtlest art and play its most fantastic antics." "When the student has mastered the rules by which these changes are controlled, he has but little else to do in Cherokee grammar." Because of this, Duncan devotes the first part of his "Analysis" to the investigation of rules of euphony. In this document, he uses Sequoyah's syllabary for economy of space and labor of writing. Duncan has condensed the syllabary to seventeen symbols, eleven consonants and six vowels, which "furnish an equivalent for the eighty-five (an eighty-sixth had been dropped earlier) characters of Sequaya [sic]" for the purposes of his study. This was also probably done to make it easier for non-Natives to understand the analysis.

Duncan then reports to Pilling the plan of his work. The first section is called "Euphonic Analysis" and includes Cherokee word phrases and word sentences trisected into prefixes, suffixes, and radicals. The section on prefixes is finished, he writes, and once he finishes the suffix section, the euphonic part will be finished. Next, he will take up the subject of grammar proper in a section called "Etymology and Syntax." This will be relatively short and easy because of analogies that will be made between Cherokee and other languages, much of this work has already been completed. The work will include a lexicon that will be helpful to antiquarians and scientists. Word phrases and sentences may be "regarded as a slice of honeycomb," he writes, "each letter constituting a cell sealed full with a honeyed idea." The main problem with the dictionary or lexicon is that of the Cherokee word phrases and word sentences. It is very difficult to resolve this "agglomeration into their elemental words as a preparatory step to tabulation and definition." He then gives several illustrations of what he means.

This largely technical letter to Pilling was an attempt to gain support from an authority figure and to give notice of what he was doing. By 1909, Duncan determined that his work was largely complete, so he wrote a proposal directed to W. P. Campbell of the Oklahoma Historical Society and sent from his home in Vinita on February 2. The prospectus is typewritten, with Cherokee characters entered by hand. He begins by commending the society for its work to preserve physical evidence of the Indian Territory tribes and suggests that to complement that work, the society begin "a line of work the special aim of which shall be to secure of some one, or more, of the languages now in use by the Five Civilized Tribes, the necessary scholaristic [sic] literature to save them from oblivion, that is, to place them on the footing of a living death, like the classic tongues of Greece and Rome."[22]

His prospectus proposes a Cherokee grammar and lexicon because linguistic rules from Old World languages will not function in the Cherokee language. He then discloses his "fundamental laws of Cherokee," beginning with the assertion that the verb is the most important element. He characterizes the verb as a word that "never stands alone in a sentence, but is always stationed in the midst of a long line of prefixes and suffixes, and is so thoroughly covered up, and obscured, that none but a master of the tongue can detect it." The verb is "generally diminutive, and in many instances it becomes so attenuated as to assume the form of a mere subvocal element in an English consonant." In other words, the verb almost disappears under the weight of other sentence elements attached to it.

Duncan next gives the fundamental rules for prefixes and suffixes. "The prefixes," he writes, "include the pronouns in all their cases, and numbers. A few adverbs are found among the prefixes, but they mainly gang with suffixes." As for suffixes, they "are made up of tense signs, and mode signs, with adverbial terminals."

"Probably no Cherokee ever heard the word 'judge' articulated in his own language," he asserts, "without its being, at the same time, tricked out with a fantastical array of prefixes and suffixes. He would neither recognize the word nor understand it without these inevitable trappings." These "trappings" may denote a variety of states of being, number and gender, tense, and intention. Duncan offers an illustration of a Cherokee word, *oo-gawt*, "to judge, determine, decide," with all its accoutrements. Finally, he comments on what he calls an "etymological curiosity" peculiar to the Cherokee language, that is, the verb that is "almost invisible upon the printed page and is only perceptible to the attenuated ear." He gives other examples of Cherokee grammar that might be included in the larger proposed study.

Duncan claims that his study will show that the Cherokee language may be reclaimed from "the homely condition of a barbarous tongue, and naturally, as a piece of linguistic art, worthy of a place in association with the classic tongues of antiquity." He asserts that "such a work is truly herculian in magnitude, transcending the financial, if not the intellectual, ability, or even any consideration of motive, on the part of an individual scholar; while, at the same time, the value of such a work as a component part of universal linguistic science, is absolutely inestimable." On a practical level, if he is to "domesticate the wild Cherokee tongue and bring it into the fold of cultured language as one of the most beautiful, if not the most useful treasures of linguistic research," he will need the society to ask the state legislature for appropriate funds. To bolster the prospectus, Duncan sent along individual sheets that carried the fruits of his work so far.

Duncan's linguistic work had received notice in 1889 when C. L. Webster published an article on the subject. Webster begins his essay as follows: "To classify and define the words of an Indian tongue, to ascertain and codify its mysterious laws of expression, and, by means of literary associations, so wed it to our own as to give it a guarantee of prospective existence commensurate with that of the English, has hitherto been regarded as one of the most difficult problems in the science of language." Saluting Duncan for undertaking this task, he then presents the main points of the "Analysis." In his interpretation of Duncan's findings, Webster finds many of the anthropological assumptions prevalent in the late nineteenth century, including the assertion that language developed from the grunts and "suggestive" sounds made by savage peoples to the more complex and "expressive" fully fledged languages of those more advanced on the evolutionary scale. Another concept is the dictum that American Indian languages, along with their native speakers, are disappearing and should be preserved, if for no other reason than historical interest.[23]

Other Cherokees were interested in the study of the language and the syllabary. William Eubanks developed a shorthand method for transcribing speech into the syllabary. The impetus for this invention came not only from his linguistic interests but also from his experience as a translator, lawyer, and Cherokee government official. The Cherokee Nation operated courts in each of its districts, each serving the people in a variety of ways, including trying criminal and civil cases, probating estates, and maintaining legal records.

The Cherokee judicial system could not try white people suspected of crimes in the nation. Instead, it was obliged by the terms of the postwar treaty to deliver those persons to Fort Smith, Arkansas, where they were tried in the federal court there. When full-bloods were tried in the district courts, proceedings were held in the Cherokee language and translated into English. Testimony was often given in the native language, and because of the lack of an accurate, rapid system of recording, the actual court proceedings were not recorded.[24] In courts conducted in English, this was not a problem because of the invention in 1837 of the Pitman shorthand method. Thus these courtrooms were meeting grounds for the two languages, needing the services of translators and bilingual clerks. Written records were kept in English only, so translation was necessary. When efficient shorthand methods came into use for English, it became apparent to Eubanks and others that a corresponding system could be of great use for the Cherokee language. Testimony and depositions in court cases were often in Cherokee, especially in such districts as Goingsnake and Flint, in which large numbers of full-bloods resided. Marriage and birth records, as well, depended on the translation of Cherokee statements into English.

Because the business of the Cherokee government was carried out in English and was later translated into the native language for the full-bloods' benefit, the district courts followed suit. The problem was one of providing rapid and accurate translations, especially in trials where testimony and depositions in Cherokee needed to be available in both languages before judgments could be made. Clearly, inaccurate or slow translation could result in justice not being delivered in a timely fashion or perhaps not being delivered at all. By this time, the courts' reliance on English was apparent. Forms issued by the Cherokee Nation and printed on the national press for use of the courts, such as subpoenas, were in English.

The symbols of Eubanks's system owed much to the Pitman method. His system consists of a series of straight and curved lines drawn at various angles between perpendicular and horizontal and marked with strategically positioned dots. In addition, one syllabary symbol is represented by an oval, and three are transcribed as lines with ovals, or loops, attached. To a layman's eye, some of the angles differentiating the angles seem too small for rapid transcription or reading, but perhaps with experience a practitioner would become adept at seeing these small distinctions. Eubanks's system differed from that of Pitman in that the latter is phonetically based, but its Cherokee counterpart is based on the syllabary.[25] Thus the Pitman system may be (and has been) fitted to a variety of languages, but Eubanks's method may be applied to only one.

Printed by the *Indian Arrow* at his own expense,[26] Eubanks's system rearranges the order in which the syllabary had been traditionally presented according to the format devised by Samuel A. Worcester. Eubanks's arrangement allows for the one-to-one pairing of Sequoyah's and Eubanks's symbols. However, Eubanks uses eighty-four syllables instead of eighty-five, deleting the Sequoyah symbol for "nah" because it is so close in pronunciation to the syllable "na." Further, the Sequoyan symbols are thinner than those traditionally used, although this does not impair their readability. This may have been Eubanks's innovation, but more likely it is the *Arrow*'s or the type cutter's. Similarly, some of Pitman's characters are thicker than others; thus the character for the "ch" sound is a slim right-to-left slash, while the "j" sound takes an identical line except that it is thicker. Vowels in the Pitman system consist of a series of three dashes, arranged diagonally, with a dot placed on either side of one of the dashes. Eubanks's method incorporates both vowels and consonants in the syllables, so no such distinction is needed.

Unfortunately, the Cherokee shorthand system was invented in 1891, when tribal courts were being abolished and giving way to a federal court established at Muskogee. Nonetheless, this innovation is probably unique among the Indian nations of the United States; it demonstrates the vitality of the Cherokee language, as well as the linguistic expertise of a native speaker.

The Sequoyan syllabary fulfilled its early promise. Although it is difficult to document the full extent of its use because of the loss of materials, it was clearly used in a variety of ways, for recording ceremonies and incantations used by Cherokee priests, correspondence among friends and family members, financial transactions of various sorts, and testimonies, legal and religious. It was used in newspapers, Bibles, and hymnbooks—in short, in every way in which English and other languages are written and printed. The syllabary's success depended on the thoroughness with which it was constructed; it fits the language perfectly, according to native speakers. Its success and vitality are evident today because it is used in teaching Cherokee and has even been adapted for use on modern electronic communications devices.

SE - QUO - YAH

Sequoyah

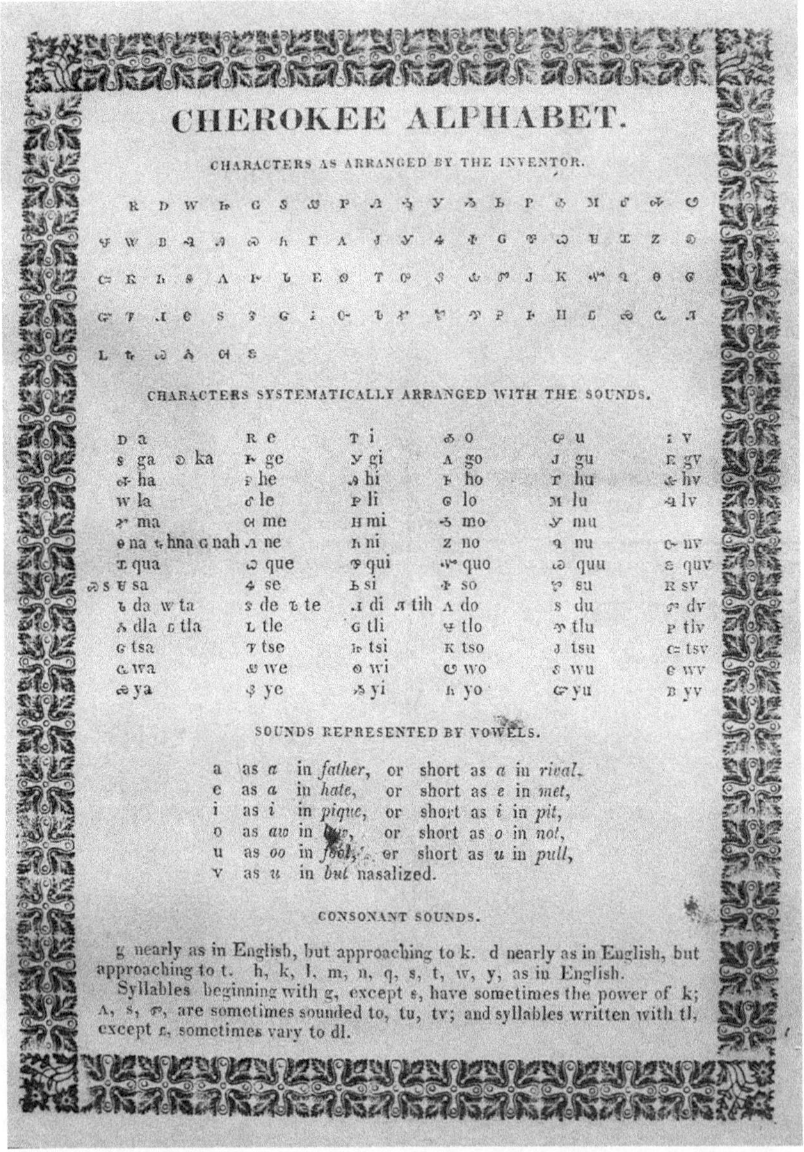

CHEROKEE ALPHABET.

CHARACTERS AS ARRANGED BY THE INVENTOR.

Ꭱ Ꭰ Ꮃ Ꮵ Ꮐ Ꮽ Ꮺ Ꮅ Ꮑ Ꮌ Ꭹ Ᏹ Ꮟ Ꮲ Ꭳ Ꮇ Ꮄ Ꭽ Ꮼ

Ꮰ Ꮤ Ᏼ Ꮈ Ꭿ Ꮝ Ᏺ Ꮁ Ꭺ Ꮷ Ꮍ Ꮞ Ꮠ Ꮆ Ꮘ Ꮗ Ꮜ Ꮖ Ꮓ Ꭷ

Ꮸ Ꮢ Ꮒ Ꭶ Ꮩ Ꭸ Ꮣ Ꭼ Ꮻ Ꭲ Ꭴ Ᏸ Ꮂ Ꮫ Ꭻ Ꮶ Ꮙ Ꮔ Ꮎ Ꮳ

Ᏻ Ꮴ Ꮧ Ꮾ Ꮪ Ꮥ Ꮯ Ꭵ Ꮕ Ꮦ Ꮉ Ꮡ Ꮱ Ꭾ Ꮀ Ꮋ Ꮭ Ꮿ Ꮹ Ꮨ

Ꮮ Ꮏ Ꮚ Ꮬ Ꮊ Ꮛ

CHARACTERS SYSTEMATICALLY ARRANGED WITH THE SOUNDS.

Ꭰ a	Ꭱ e	Ꭲ i	Ꭳ o	Ꭴ u	Ꭵ v
Ꭶ ga Ꭷ ka	Ꭸ ge	Ꭹ gi	Ꭺ go	Ꭻ gu	Ꭼ gv
Ꭽ ha	Ꭾ he	Ꭿ hi	Ꮀ ho	Ꮁ hu	Ꮂ hv
Ꮃ la	Ꮄ le	Ꮅ li	Ꮆ lo	Ꮇ lu	Ꮈ lv
Ꮉ ma	Ꮊ me	Ꮋ mi	Ꮌ mo	Ꮍ mu	
Ꮎ na Ꮏ hna Ꮐ nah	Ꮑ ne	Ꮒ ni	Ꮓ no	Ꮔ nu	Ꮕ nv
Ꮖ qua	Ꮗ que	Ꮘ qui	Ꮙ quo	Ꮚ quu	Ꮛ quv
Ꮝ s Ꮜ sa	Ꮞ se	Ꮟ si	Ꮠ so	Ꮡ su	Ꮢ sv
Ꮣ da Ꮤ ta	Ꮥ de Ꮦ te	Ꮧ di Ꮨ tih	Ꮩ do	Ꮪ du	Ꮫ dv
Ꮬ dla Ꮭ tla	Ꮮ tle	Ꮯ tli	Ꮰ tlo	Ꮱ tlu	Ꮲ tlv
Ꮳ tsa	Ꮴ tse	Ꮵ tsi	Ꮶ tso	Ꮷ tsu	Ꮸ tsv
Ꮹ wa	Ꮺ we	Ꮻ wi	Ꮼ wo	Ꮽ wu	Ꮾ wv
Ꮿ ya	Ᏸ ye	Ᏹ yi	Ᏺ yo	Ᏻ yu	Ᏼ yv

SOUNDS REPRESENTED BY VOWELS.

a as *a* in *father*, or short as *a* in *rival*.
e as *a* in *hate*, or short as *e* in *met*,
i as *i* in *pique*, or short as *i* in *pit*,
o as *aw* in *law*, or short as *o* in *not*,
u as *oo* in *fool*, or short as *u* in *pull*,
v as *u* in *but* nasalized.

CONSONANT SOUNDS.

g nearly as in English, but approaching to k. d nearly as in English, but approaching to t. h, k, l, m, n, q, s, t, w, y, as in English.

Syllables beginning with g, except Ꭷ, have sometimes the power of k; Ꭺ, Ꮪ, Ꮫ, are sometimes sounded to, tu, tv; and syllables written with tl, except Ꮭ, sometimes vary to dl.

Cherokee Syllabary

CHEROKEE

PICTORIAL BOOK.

WITH CATECHISM AND HYMNS.

COMPILED AND TRASLATED BY

REV. A. N. CHAMBERLIN.

1888.

GWY ᎠᏍᏕᏘᏍᏗᎠᎵ, ᏗᎵᎯᎠᏉᎠᎵᏃ ᎠᏓ .ᎢᎧᏃᎩᏎᏍᎢᏔᎵ.

ᎡᏂᎯᎲ ᏚᏑᏌᏬᎠ-Ꭼ.

T. W. FOREMAN, PRINTER.
TAHLEQUAH, I. T.

Title page of William Chamberlin's *Cherokee Pictorial Book, With Catechism and Hymnal*

Page from William Chamberlin's *Cherokee Pictorial Book, With Catechism and Hymnal*

Elias Boudinot

John Ross

Office of the *Cherokee Advocate*, Tahlequah, Cherokee Nation

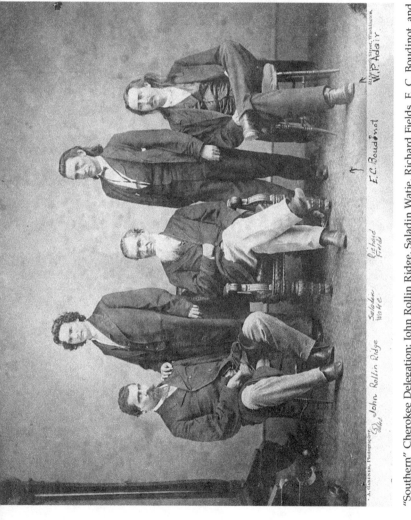

"Southern" Cherokee Delegation: John Rollin Ridge, Saladin Watie, Richard Fields, E. C. Boudinot, and William Penn Adair

DeWitt Clinton Duncan (Too Quah-stee)

William Potter Ross

EDWARD WILKERSON BUSHYHEAD
From a photograph belonging to Mrs. Carolyn McNair McSpadden, Tahlequah

Edward (Ned) Bushyhead

Ora V. Eddleman

CHAPTER 6

THE *CHEROKEE ADVOCATE* AND OTHER INDIAN NEWSPAPERS

Along with the high priority the Cherokees gave to education, another major factor supporting literacy and literary effort in the Cherokee Nation was newspaper publishing. Nowhere else in Indian country did the tribal people invest in, edit, write for, and publish their own newspapers to the extent that the Cherokees did. These publications are manifestations of the rich intellectual life among members of the group because their content went beyond that of most frontier newspapers by including a large percentage of writing by the community, with significant debates not only on current affairs but on larger philosophical and historical issues as well. Newspapers, especially the weeklies, became an important element in the fabric of daily life in the Cherokee Nation after Removal; readership of these newspapers reached every level of Cherokee society, even those who read no English, thanks to the materials printed in the Sequoyan syllabary. As the number of newspapers increased in the 1880s and 1890s, they often took opposing editorial views on a variety of issues, but especially on Cherokee politics. The resulting debates helped bolster their democracy by keeping readers informed and energized about issues important to their present and future lives.

Newspapers supported Cherokee literary efforts, too, by publishing the work of Native writers. Almost without exception, the editors were Cherokees, many of whom had been either educated in tribal schools or involved intimately in the institution and maintenance of the public educational system. Perhaps more important was the fact that many of the reporters and correspondents were Native writers; creative writers in the nation found outlets for their works in the pages of Indian weeklies, which allowed them to demonstrate their skills before an audience perhaps more critical than teachers and family. This symbiosis has not been explored fully, but it is an important element in the rise of Cherokee literature.

The *Cherokee Messenger* was the first periodical to be published in what is now Oklahoma. Published by Evan Jones at Baptist Mission near the Arkansas line, it was a religious magazine. Small in size, it was also of short duration, appearing twelve times between August 1844 and May 1846. Printed in both the English alphabet and the Cherokee syllabary, the magazine's main purpose was to bring religious literature to Cherokee readers. It did publish some temperance news, Cherokee grammar lessons, and other small items in English, but the bulk of the publication was given over to Bible translations: parts of Genesis, Luke, First Thessalonians, the Psalms, the Epistle of Jude, and First Corinthians. Sections of Bunyan's *Pilgrim's Progress* were published in Cherokee, as well as parts of Peter Parley's *Universal History*.

The newspapers that began to be published shortly after Removal of the five major southeastern Indian nations, the Cherokees, Creeks, Choctaws, Chickasaws, and Seminoles, played an important part in supporting literacy among the people and their efforts at writing. That much of the content of these Indian Territory publications was furnished by readers and other correspondents from the community contributed to their appeal. Reports from tribal governments were written by officials, oftentimes including members of delegations that seemed to be traveling perpetually to Washington, D.C., to meet with federal officials, supporters, congressmen, and senators, as well as to testify before various committees in Congress. The members were encouraged to write reports on their activities and to send news from Washington that would appear in the newspapers back home to inform the people what was transpiring on that big stage.

The value of the press had been established among the Cherokees with the publication of the *Cherokee Phoenix* in the eastern nation, so the leadership was eager to establish a newspaper soon after Removal. The press and the type had been lost in the turmoil of the days before Removal, but another press, equipment, and type were purchased at Boston with the help of the American Board of Commissioners for Foreign Missions (ABCFM) and shipped to the Cherokee Nation in 1844. For the new paper, the *Cherokee Advocate*, the National Council chose as the first editor William Potter Ross, nephew of Principal Chief John Ross. Chief Ross then selected English and Cherokee printers, typesetters, and translators. The newspaper, published at the Cherokee capital, Tahlequah, was a six-column, four-page weekly, with copy in both English and the Sequoyan syllabary.[1]

The *Phoenix*'s purpose had clearly been to promote the Cherokees as a civilized people and at the same time to inform and educate the people; the *Advocate* adopted a similar set of goals, but with more emphasis on information and education. The content printed in the syllabary was intended to inform and educate those Cherokees who did not speak English; to this end, the paper was offered at reduced rates to those non-English-speaking readers who perhaps had not regarded newspapers as sources of news or other information. That the editor and the national leadership were thinking this way is an indication of their serious intent to bring education to all citizens. This same philosophy was evident in the way the national school system was established. Because of the Cherokee Nation's location, the editor also saw the newspaper as a supplier of news concerning the border between the states and territories and Indian Territory. It also printed news of the Mexican War and the annexation of Texas.

William Potter Ross was born at Lookout Mountain in 1820 to John Golden and Eliza (Ross) Ross and was related to the principal chief through his mother. After attending schools in Alabama and Tennessee, he was sent to a preparatory school in New Jersey before entering Princeton University, at that time called the College of New Jersey, from which he graduated in 1842. Thus well educated himself, he was able to choose content intelligently so that the purposes of the newspaper were met.

The *Advocate*'s initial layout remained stable for many years. It consisted of two pages in English devoted to general Indian news, foreign news, agents' reports, laws, anecdotal matter, and items on general topics, such as agriculture, geography, societies, and organizations. Fiction, poetry, nonfiction creative writing, and inspirational articles were also staples. Another page included legal items and material in the syllabary, and another carried editorials and local news, including that from the other Indian Territory nations.

In its early years, the *Advocate* could not be described as a national or tribal newspaper. It was, especially in the turbulent 1840s, clearly on the side of the Ross faction, which was in power, and against the Treaty Party, led by Stand Watie. Editorially, it lobbied against the Treaty people, even those who had take refuge in Arkansas. The Starr family, often involved in the violence between the two factions, was a favorite editorial target, as was the very idea of tribal division, floated by Watie and others as a way of settling the rivalry that was fast escalating into a civil war. The Cherokee national government, under the firm control of John Ross, financed the publication and, in the end, determined its editorial policy. William Potter Ross expounded on other favorite topics as well during this time, including temperance, Cherokee jurisdiction over adopted or intermarried whites, the 1846 treaty that was to stop the interfactional rivalry, and a stronger judiciary and criminal code.

In 1846, when William Potter Ross was sent to Washington as a delegate, his brother, Daniel Hicks Ross, took the reins as editor and continued in general his brother's editorial policies. Upon William Potter Ross's return after the 1846 treaty had stopped the warfare between the factions, the editor began to address domestic issues in a serious way. The public school system was beginning to blossom, but there were growing pains, all of which were discussed in the *Advocate*'s pages. Discussion of the formation of institutions of higher learning in the nation was carried on and led to the building of the Male and Female Seminaries. Old Settler claims, elections, improvements to the infrastructure, such as bridges and roads, and other issues were addressed as well. As time went on, the slavery issue being debated across the United States became a topic of discussion.

In October 1848, William Potter Ross again left Tahlequah as a delegate to Washington and was replaced by James Shepherd Vann, son of Joseph ("Rich Joe") Vann, a wealthy Cherokee in the eastern nation who was later killed in a steamboat accident. Vann lasted only a short time in the editor's chair because he abruptly left for the California gold fields in April 1849. His place was taken by David Carter (Ta-wak). Carter was born in 1807, the grandson of Nathaniel

Carter, a white man who as a child had been carried off, had grown up among the Cherokees, and had married a Cherokee woman. The younger Carter attended the Cornwall Foreign Mission School in Connecticut before returning to the Cherokee Nation to take up a number of posts, including superintendent of education from 1836 to 1845. When the Cherokee Public School system got underway in 1841, Stephen Foreman took on the superintendency of that endeavor. Under Carter's editorship, a good deal of space was given to education; slavery in Indian Territory, the Intercourse Act of 1834 that was supposed to govern Indian-white relations, temperance, and news from Washington concerning the tribes were other frequent topics. Cherokee-language content was a staple component of the *Advocate* from 1844 to 1853, with translators James D. Wofford and Joseph B. Bird providing the copy. Other Cherokee speakers served as typesetters and translators. Copy in the syllabary ranged from three to five columns, the equivalent of from two to four times the space needed for the content using the alphabet.

Vann returned from California in 1851 and once again was appointed editor. He carried on much as Carter had, although he did publish more exchange material, that is, articles taken from other publications in exchange for material in the Cherokee newspapers. This was common practice in nineteenth-century journalism. In addition, many of the Cherokees who had left the nation for the California gold-mining district were now writing letters home, often filled with news, humor, and nostalgia. Vann published the most entertaining and newsworthy of these. He was also concerned with white intruders and interference from federal authorities in the nation's business and made them topics of his editorials. An auspicious event took place in November 1852 when William Penn Boudinot substituted for Vann as editor; this was the first time that a member of the Treaty Party emerged as a part of the Cherokee "establishment." Boudinot was the eldest son of Elias Boudinot, editor of the *Cherokee Phoenix*, signer and supporter of the New Echota Removal Treaty of 1835, and avowed enemy of the Ross party. The elder Boudinot had been assassinated with John and Major Ridge in 1839, allegedly by revenge seekers from the Ross faction, an event that precipitated the interfactional violence of 1839–46. Boudinot served only until April 1853, when Vann returned. At this point, funding for the newspaper had become difficult, and by September, the *Cherokee Advocate* closed its doors, to reopen only after the Civil War.

During the Civil War, the press, type, and equipment were stored at Fort Gibson for protection. In 1867, in spite of the depressed postwar economy, the National Council retrieved the press and repaired the printing office so that the business of the nation could be documented and printed for distribution to the citizens. It was not until 1870, however, that the *Advocate* rose from the ashes of war and began to publish again.

The postwar Cherokee Nation was a different place after the turmoil had died down and rebuilding had begun. The old animosities between factions were very much alive because the nation had split with the outbreak of hostilities, with the Treaty Party, for the most part, fighting on the Confederate side, while the Ross faction largely sided with the North. Immediately after the war, the federal government helped perpetuate the rift because it negotiated its peace treaty with both sides separately, playing them off against each other. In the end, the U.S. "peacemakers" in effect dictated terms to the Cherokees and imposed penalties on the entire nation even though at least half the people had fought on the Union side. Thus the bitterness continued. In addition, the Cherokees learned from this treaty-making process that the federal government was not interested in acting as their protectors, nor did it especially want to honor the previous treaties it had made with the Cherokees. It was more interested in satisfying the railroads' and homesteaders' hunger for land. So the nation now faced a whole new set of problems, and the leadership recognized that its people must be kept informed and vigilant about the dangers that confronted them. The *Cherokee Advocate* was revived to help carry out this function. The leadership knew that a literate, informed public was necessary for the nation's survival.

When the first issue of the new series came out on April 26, 1870, it was again edited by William Penn Boudinot. Boudinot was born in the eastern nation in 1830 to Elias Boudinot and Harriet Ruggles Gold Boudinot, a white woman his father had met while he was at Cornwall School. Harriet had died before Removal, and Elias had remarried, this time another white woman, Delight Sargent, who removed with the family to Indian Territory. After the assassinations, Mrs. Boudinot fled with her family to New England, where she had family. There William and his siblings were sent to school; he returned to the Cherokee Nation as a young man. As editor, he was assisted in preparing the Cherokee-language content of the *Advocate* by John Buttrick Jones, who with his father was involved in publishing texts in the syllabary. Jones was soon replaced as translator by William Eubanks, the Cherokee linguist and writer.

One of the big events of 1870 was the treaty-driven Grand Council of Tribes of the Indian Territory, which met at Okmulgee. Most likely, the whites and the Indians saw different purposes for the council. The whites hoped that Indian Territory would become a U.S. territory and thus would be placed under a set of laws and regulations that would lead to white settlement and eventually to statehood. The Indians, on the other hand, saw the council as an opportunity to consolidate Native control of Indian Territory and keep the existing tribal power structures in place. Boudinot covered council news closely and editorialized that the Indian nations needed to act together to overcome threats from without. The content of the *Advocate* during this period bolstered this idea. The editor exhorted his compatriots to use the tribal land in public domain to plant crops and graze livestock. He feared that white men, seeing empty land, would pressure the government to open it to white settlement so that it could be "used" properly. Subsequent events were to validate Boudinot's concerns. Preserving the Cherokees' title to their land became a staple of his editorials. He also included articles on modern agricultural methods as a means of demonstrating how individual Cherokees could work to occupy the outlying lands in the nation.

Connected with this set of concerns were the problems involving white intruders. Boudinot saw this as a two-pronged issue. The first concerned the intruders themselves. Some of them were illicit whiskey traders, but as time went on, more and more of them were whites who squatted on Cherokee and other tribal land and erected buildings and fences as if they owned it. The second issue was that under contemporary laws, the Cherokees were not allowed to arrest white people because they did not fall under Cherokee law. Instead, they had to rely on marshals sent from the federal court at Fort Smith. Boudinot addressed these problems again and again, but the issues never really went away. The editor was a consistent supporter of Indian rights and railed against the constant barrage of territorial bills being introduced in Congress, some of which, ironically, were supported energetically by his brother, Elias Cornelius Boudinot. William P. Boudinot was an accomplished writer who drove his arguments home with logic and an occasional touch of humor.

Boudinot was succeeded in his work by John Lynch Adair in 1873. Adair was born in the eastern nation in 1828. Orphaned early, he was reared by relatives who made sure he attended good schools. After Removal, he received further education in northeast Arkansas from Rev. Cephas Washburn, mentioned in Chapter 4 as a missionary and teacher for the Old Settler Cherokees before Removal. William Eubanks continued to serve as translator until 1874, when he was replaced by Hiram Terrell Landrum, who was himself replaced a year later by John Leaf Springston. Springston, educated in Cherokee schools, was a skilled translator, and the content in the syllabary increased to up to seven columns per issue.

Adair's editorial stance understandably followed Boudinot's because the same problems persisted. He wrote against territorial bills in Congress and, like Boudinot, called for a revision of Cherokee law to bring it more in line with that of the surrounding area and to make it stronger. He supported education because, like most Cherokees, he saw it as the only hope for the nation, and he kept a close eye on tribal finances. At this time, an issue came into prominence that has remained in the forefront of Cherokee national consciousness to the present day: Cherokee citizenship. Many white people saw acquiring citizenship as a means of acquiring land in the Cherokee Nation. Some men married Cherokee women as a way of becoming adopted citizens, but of course, avaricious motives cannot be applied to an entire class of people.

A fire struck the *Advocate's* office in February 1875, burning it to the ground and destroying the type and equipment. This was a heavy blow that ended the publication of the second series of the newspaper. It took the Cherokees an entire year to rebuild and to locate and purchase a press, equipment, and type. When the third and final series began, William P. Boudinot was once again the editor.

Boudinot and his translator, William Eubanks, took the role of their newspaper very seriously, seeing it as a necessary partner of good government at home and a means of combating hostile interests outside the nation. Specifically, Boudinot took it on himself to explain the New Code, the recently revised set of laws adopted by the Cherokees, especially concepts new to many traditional citizens, such as the need for a national jail. By this time, railroads had just been introduced into the territory, and although Boudinot understood the need for modern transportation, he set himself against the federal government's providing huge land grants to the railroad companies along the right-of-way. Much of his ink and energy was expended against the territorial bills, now introduced regularly in Congress. Although these bills differed in particulars, they all agreed on one central scheme: to repeal Indian Territory's status as an exclusive Indian enclave, to permit white settlement and exploitation of natural resources, and eventually to dissolve tribal land title. Boudinot published some of the arguments of the territorialists and then proceeded to dismantle them. In this way, he sought to inform his countrymen of the serious threat to Cherokee sovereignty. He thus demonstrated his belief in the necessity of a literate and vigilant population. In general, Boudinot's editorial policies supported the idea of "progress" among his people. For him, this meant adopting those ways of white society that he thought would equip them for survival in a world where the Cherokees were surrounded by white communities, many of whose inhabitants were casting envious looks at the Indian lands. Chief among these adopted skills was literacy for all Cherokees, and he advocated an educational system that would help bring this about.

When the election for editor took place in the National Council in 1877, George Washington Johnson, a lawyer, became editor. Johnson continued most of Boudinot's editorial policies, most of which were approved by the council, and opposed the territorial bills while seeking to inform and educate his readership. Johnson also spoke out against ethnic stereotypic language, such as "buck," "warpath," and "red devils," terms often used in the white press when it was reporting on the conflicts on the plains. He published articles supporting the Poncas, Utes, and Sioux at a time when many frontier newspapers were calling for their extermination. Under Johnson, the level of items in the syllabary increased, varying from three columns to a full page, at the instigation of the former editor, Boudinot, who as a Cherokee official continued to press for informing and educating all citizens, not only readers of English. Eubanks remained translator until 1878, when he was replaced by S. H. Downing, who served briefly before being replaced by Philip H. Israel.

After H. D. Reese substituted as editor for a short time in 1878, Elias Cornelius Boudinot, Jr., was elected in 1879. The son of W. P. Boudinot, he had been born in 1854, and he vowed to carry on the editorial traditions without engaging in partisan activities in a time of fierce factionalism in the nation. Cherokee-language content increased while the younger Boudinot was editor, rising to seven columns each issue. In 1881, the National Council decreed that a full page of Cherokee was to be published, and a banner headline in the syllabary was added on that page. Boudinot hired two Cherokee apprentices to help with the increase.

Although the content was similar to that of previous years, new issues arose that needed to be brought to the people's attention. For example, David L. Payne, ironically at the instigation of the editor's uncle, Elias Cornelius Boudinot, had tried to establish a boomer colony in Oklahoma, a direct threat to the Indian nations and an act in defiance of federal law. The *Advocate* gave the colony close coverage. The census of 1880, the citizenship controversy, and intruders' incursions were all topics of interest presented in the *Advocate*'s pages. A new issue that arose largely as a result of the railroads' coming to Indian Territory was that of preservation of the public domain. The railways made mineral extraction feasible, and some enterprising denizens of Indian Territory began to explore coal and other sorts of mining. The builders of railroads needed vast amounts of timber for ties and trestles, and this was acquired from Indian lands. Many Cherokees got involved for their own profit, which did not sit well with others who did not benefit.

In 1881, Daniel Hicks Ross became editor, a post he had held in the 1840s, and remained until 1885. New issues arose to greet the new editor, such as the leasing of the Cherokee Outlet, a broad band of land forming the northern tier of Indian Territory and Oklahoma, to white ranchers and the political emergency in the Muscogee (Creek) Nation called the Green Peach War. The citizenship question, intruders, and education remained subjects of debate. As time went on, more and more space was devoted to correspondence, both from government officials and citizens speaking out on important issues from all corners of the nation. In the citizens' letters, increased literacy among the Cherokees was evident; the epistles ranged from news from outlying areas to legal and political arguments to humor to satire, and they demonstrated sophistication in the manipulation of language for a specific purpose. This highly literate correspondence reached levels at least as elevated as those of examples from states around the territory, setting a lofty standard for aspiring Cherokee writers.

When Ross was called away to carry out delegate duties for the nation, E. C. Boudinot, Jr., once again became editor. In his previous tenure, he had been accused of partisanship, but now he was even more open about his support for the National Party, which was in power at the time, and members of which had elected him editor. The *Advocate* subsequently entered an editorial war with the *Telephone*, another Cherokee newspaper, over the hotly contested Cherokee election of 1887. As election day approached, the charges between Boudinot and B. H. Stone, editor of the *Telephone*, became more frequent and furious. After a particularly vituperative exchange in October, Boudinot marched to the opposition paper's office and "called out" Stone from the street. When he did not appear, Boudinot strode inside the office and shot Stone dead.

Ridge Paschal, nephew of John Ridge, took over from Boudinot in December and called for peace between the parties and an end to factionalism. William P. Boudinot returned to the editorship at that point, retaining Paschal as associate editor. Now that the election was over and the political situation had returned to normal, Boudinot focused on major problems facing the nation. Intruders had become an increasing difficulty, exacerbated by the opening of the Oklahoma lands in the west to white settlement. Loud voices from the surrounding states, as well as from Washington, called for the "opening" of the Indian lands to homesteaders as well. Ironically, much of the clamor for negating the treaties and doing away with Indian land claims was the result of a letter titled "Indian Territory" that William's brother, Elias Cornelius Boudinot, sent to the *Chicago Times* in February 1879. The letter claimed that the land west of the Indian nations was "unassigned" public land and thus open to homesteading. E. C. Boudinot published the letter as a pamphlet as well and traveled throughout the Midwest to speak to thousands of land-hungry settlers as confederates passed out the document. It had a huge impact, partially at least because of the speaker's assertion of Cherokee heritage. Now, the Cherokees and other Indian Territory tribes were bearing the brunt of attacks on their sovereignty. The Cherokees had no more staunch defender in this battle than W. P. Boudinot. He also was a tireless campaigner against those who were fraudulently attempting to claim citizenship in the nation, widely seen as an entrée to Cherokee land. He led discussions, too, of the practice of leasing grazing rights in the Cherokee Outlet. During Boudinot's tenure, Springston continued as translator of the Cherokee page, and the size of this material remained constant at from seven columns to a full page.

In 1891, Boudinot relinquished the editorship to Robert Fletcher Wylie, a white man who had married Mary J. Buffington. Wylie had been born in Georgia in 1827 and had moved to the Cherokee Nation in 1857. Under Wylie, Charles Tehee became translator, and the Cherokee content fell to six columns. Wylie editorialized less than his predecessors but included more local and national news.

Wylie was replaced in 1891 by Hugh Montgomery Adair, who had been born in Flint District in 1840 and educated in the Cherokee schools, including the Male Seminary. He also attended Cane Hill College in Arkansas. Adair was devoted to the welfare and happiness of his people and, as a teacher, took a keen interest in their enlightenment. With William Eubanks once again serving as translator, the Cherokee material was restored to a full page. Adair did not editorialize to any great extent but instead let his readers discuss the major issues of the day. An increasingly literate populace was contributing a large volume of correspondence to each issue of the *Advocate*, taking up subjects such as the possible sale of the Cherokee Outlet, what to do with the proceeds of such a sale, rights of the Delaware citizens, the Cherokee National debt, and the increasing threat of statehood for Indian Territory.

In 1893, George Oliver Butler became editor. A former law partner of E. C. Boudinot, Jr., and son-in-law of Daniel H. Ross, Butler was more forthcoming about voicing his personal opinions on the editorial page than the previous two editors had been. He correctly estimated that the Cherokees were in the middle of a crisis period, with national survival at stake. Much of the stress at the time was caused by the presence of the Dawes Commission in the Cherokee Nation.

A general federal policy of the allotment of land in severalty was instituted in 1887, and in 1893, a commission was organized to negotiate with the Five Civilized Tribes of Indian Territory to create a plan that would bring allotment into effect. Advocates of allotment foresaw that in a short time, tribal land titles would be extinguished, tribal members would become U.S. citizens who would receive an allotment of land for themselves, and the "surplus" lands would be sold. The commission became known as the Dawes Commission after its chairman, Senator Henry L. Dawes; it reached Muskogee in 1894, from where it was to do business.[2] Cherokee principal chief C. J. Harris then appointed a commission of five members to carry out negotiations for the nation. Harris also reacted negatively to the first demands of the Dawes Commission by calling an international council in February 1894. Here, the Cherokees found that they were not the only ones alarmed, because the Muscogees (Creeks) sent a large delegation. The council decided to resist, and a second council met in March. The *Advocate* covered these events in detail. The Dawes Commission–Cherokee Nation maneuvers continued through the next few years, and the newspaper carried accounts of each thrust and counterthrust. Along with the news, commentary was provided by the editor, corresponding citizens, and delegates reporting on developments from various venues in Arkansas and Indian Territory where the Dawes people were meeting, as well as from Washington, where Cherokee delegates fought the allotment policy. Finally, in 1898, the Curtis Act was passed, providing for the replacement of Cherokee law by federal law, effective dissolution of tribal government, and allotment of Cherokee land in severalty. By this time, the other nations of Indian Territory had succumbed to federal power and had settled the details of allotment.

Waddie Hudson, an intermarried white citizen, was editor of the *Advocate* from 1895 to 1897 and editorialized against tribal dissolution. The pages were filled with news of negotiations with the Dawes Commission, as well as the difficulties posed by people applying for citizenship because they saw it as a means of obtaining a land allotment. Hudson carried news from the other nations of Indian Territory and much exchange material. Included, too, was correspondence on crises facing the Cherokee people, much of it written by full-bloods who were in total opposition to allotment and tribal dissolution.

Hudson's tenure was followed by that of Joseph R. Sequichie, who served from 1897 to 1899. A conservative Cherokee, he was in agreement with the full-blood positions on various issues, including the Freedmen Compromise, fraud engendered by the prospective breakup of the nation, the Curtis Act, and whites who organized to find ways of getting themselves enrolled as citizens. He also editorialized against a movement involving full-blood emigration to Mexico. Sequichie reported news of the deterioration of schools as the federal government took over, intruders and other outlaws, and abolition of tribal law and the court system. He often published more than a page in Cherokee, indicating a large readership among full-bloods. When Sequichie left the editor's chair, he was replaced by the former business manager, William T. Loeser.

Loeser reported and editorialized on all the important issues of the era, including town-site development, the Cherokee Agreement of 1900, allotment, and the statehood question for Indian Territory. The *Cherokee Advocate*'s pages at this time also included many articles by Cherokee and other Indian writers, including William Eubanks, James Roane Gregory, and Walter A. Duncan. Each issue carried at least one page of Cherokee and sometimes two, as well as exchange material featuring writers from other parts of the country.

Loeser was replaced by George Oliver Butler, who was editor from 1901 to 1903. Although Butler was not fluent in Cherokee, he employed translators and typesetters who were, so the pages in the syllabary continued. He, like his predecessors, reported on the news of the day, including statehood, mineral leases, allotment, and education. He also covered full-blood movements, including the Keetoowah Society, and "Crazy Snake" uprisings in the Muscogee (Creek) Nation. Butler was followed as editor by Wiley James Melton, the last of the *Advocate*'s headmen. Melton knew that the newspaper was the sole source of printed news for many Cherokees; as a result, he published fewer editorials, two full pages in the syllabary, and more news coverage from the nation and Indian Territory. The paper published news of the Final Settlement, restrictions on the sale of allotments, and the maneuverings surrounding statehood. Melton supported the Sequoyah Constitution of 1905, the attempt to set up the state of Sequoyah to replace Indian Territory. One of Melton's last editorials was addressed to the full-bloods, whom he urged to hold on to their allotments, to accept the facts of tribal dissolution, and to face the future with resolve.

All through its run, the *Cherokee Advocate* engaged in exchanges with other publications, a standard practice then and now, in which copies of the publications were exchanged, along with permission to reprint items. In the years before the Civil War, the *Advocate* exchanged with national journals, such as *Home Journal and Citizen Soldier, Southern and Western Literary Messenger and Review, Friend of Youth, Scientific American,* the *Baptist Memorial,* and the *Saturday Evening Post.* In addition, it carried exchanges with other newspapers from the region. The reprinted items from these exchanges provided variety and substance to the reading fare of a literature-hungry public and helped the paper appear vibrant and inviting.

To aspiring writers among the Cherokee people, the exchange materials offered models for writing and in many ways developed the literary taste of writers and nonwriters alike. The *Advocate* carried a regular poetry column that published works of contemporary writers from outside Indian Territory, such as Henry Wadsworth Longfellow, John Greenleaf Whittier, William Cullen Bryant, and D. Ellen Goodman, and British poets, such as Alfred Tennyson, Barry Cornwall, Mrs. Felicia Hemans, and Robert Southey. Of special interest seemed to be Mrs. Lydia Sigourney, a prolific writer who produced many verses and sketches between 1835 and 1865. These writers became the models for literary aspirants, complementing those authors, mainly from New England and Britain, who had been part of the Cherokee schools' curricula.

Short fiction in both languages appeared in the pages of the *Advocate* as well, although this genre was not as well represented as poetry. The English-language fiction was largely reprinted and shared with the Cherokee-language stories a strong didactic flavor. Kate Sutherland published "The Unruly Member" in its pages, and "A Married Woman's Soliloquy" was another title that was sure to catch the reader's eye. The Cherokee fiction was religious and, for the most part, represented translations of stories written by churchmen from the East. *The Dairyman's Daughter* and *Bob the Sailor Boy* are examples of cautionary moral tales aimed especially at a youthful audience.

Creative nonfiction also found a place in the *Advocate.* It was not as evident in the early years, but after the Civil War, it became more plentiful. The *Advocate* (and most other nineteenth-century newspapers) often reprinted thoughts on moral behavior and Christian beliefs from other publications, but some writers in the Cherokee Nation adopted the form and used it quite well. An example from 1851 is "Sentiment," by Cherokee. "Natural things are the language of God to his children," Cherokee writes, "to teach them what they are and who he is. Flowers, trees, brooks, the seasons—all the infinite variety of material manifestations are but so many Divine Words. Unless the meaning of this is at least partially understood, the SENSES may acknowledge their existence, but the MIND will not. They can with no more reason be entitled to the majesty of Life, than the mysterious hieroglyphics of the ancient Egyptians be denominated language."[3] This excerpt gives the general tenor of much of the writing in this form, demonstrating a general interest in explaining the natural world to its inhabitants. One might speculate that this would be a natural occurrence among a people who so relatively recently had been uprooted from their homelands and had had their ancient belief systems denigrated. Cherokee also contributed a piece on the history of aboriginal people in America, beginning in the dimmest reaches of prehistory and continuing to the present, in which he or she extols the "progress" that many of the Indian nations have made. He chides those who hang on to the old ways: "Some cling with death-like tenacity to our old rites and ceremonies" and do not consider moral change. People, he goes on to write, change "progressively" as time goes on, and everyone should embrace these modifications as positive.[4]

Cherokee poetry, mostly in English, appeared in the *Cherokee Advocate* almost from the newspaper's beginning. In many ways, the *Advocate* became the standard for subsequent Indian Territory publications because the practice of publishing homegrown literary works was carried on in other Indian nations. Perhaps the first poem to be published in the *Advocate* was one in 1845 by "R. M. S.," who began a practice that the editors were soon to lament, signing one's work with initials or pseudonyms. William P. Boudinot, editor of the *Advocate* in 1850, felt compelled to publish a notice demanding that contributors furnish their full names.[5] The pseudonym "Cherokee" was especially problematic because it was used by several people over a period of years. Still, the practice continued, possibly because many of the initials or pen names were readily identified by the reading public. The pen name "Venice," for example, was widely known to be used by Elijah Hicks. As time went on, literary contributions were so numerous that the editors had problems in using all the submissions and keeping the writers satisfied, proof of the rich literary vein running through the Cherokee national community in the years soon after Removal. Some of the more prolific poets whose work appeared in the *Advocate*'s pages were Tsu-hu-o-tli, Osage Dreamer, Cherokee, Rustic Bard, and Chenango. Some representative examples of this work follow:

A SONG
    THE POLAR STAR
    AIR "TWILIGHT HUES"
When day melts off the glowing skies
    And sinks in twilight's hush,
And beaming soft heav'n's starry eyes
    Warm tremble through her blush;
While in eternal wand'ring far
    Burns on each orb at ev'n,
Has thou not seen one only star
    Still true to 'tis throne in heav'n.

Thus too my truth—while all is bright
    Unseen through noonday's glare
Should sorrow gloom thy heart in night
    Will smile love's sweetest star;
And though all else around me change,
    I like that star at ev'n,
To thee my hopes sweet throne am true,
    As he is true to heav'n.

The poem was published in the October 22, 1850, issue and was signed Gu-Tla-Ona-Wv in symbols from the syllabary. An untitled poem from the same issue was contributed by O-Kee-Cho-Tsee:

There was a tear of deep distress,
A tear which words cannot express,
When Martha first began to pray,
That God would wash her sins away.

There was an hour of sweet relief,
An hour of triumph, not of grief—

When Martha look'd by Faith above—
And triumphed in the God of love.

There was a time of holy joy—
A time of peace without alloy—
When Martha felt her sins forgiven,
And knew she was an heir of heaven.

An example of another Cherokee verse is "Sunshine and Shade."

SUNSHINE AND SHADE
Hours there are when all is fair,
When joys are sweet and hopes are bright,
When pleasure binds the brow—
And life glides on wings of light.

Hours there are when all is dark,
When joys are fled and spirits gone—
With saddened heart and aching brow,
We sigh in crowds and feel alone.
        Wigwam, Cherokee Nation, May 27, 1851

As time went on, Cherokees continued to contribute poetry and articles to the nation's newspapers. Political opinion was a rich vein of writing with a broad range of contributors, from farmers and tradesmen to lawyers and officials. Humor can often be found as well, appearing less as the major point of a piece (although some humorous pieces were published and relished by the readers) than as an inherent component of the writing. This humor was often self-deprecating or teasing in tone.

Content in the Cherokee language and syllabary was to occupy page 3 of the usual four-page format for a long time. This is not to say that the ratio of English to Cherokee was three to one: the syllabary took less space than the alphabet-based English language sections to express the same ideas because in Cherokee, it takes only one symbol to denote a syllable, while in English it may take two, three, or four. The nation employed translators because the leadership deemed it important that all laws, regulations, decrees, and messages from the government be transmitted to the people in both languages. At different times, separate typesetters were employed, most often when the typesetter of the English portion did not know the Cherokee language. Although it was more expensive and sometimes more cumbersome to print both languages, the Cherokees knew that it was important to get information to citizens who did not read English. William Eubanks was often the translator when the *Advocate* reopened in 1870, translating the Cherokee laws and tribal business so they could be presented in the paper.

After Charles Thompson was elected principal chief in the 1870s and the full-bloods were beginning to assert themselves politically, people demanded more and more Cherokee content. As a result, the National Council decreed that at least eight columns should be devoted to writing in the syllabary. In later years, and especially in the last few years of the newspaper's existence, the Cherokee content was increased, at times filling two or more pages. When former editor William P. Boudinot became executive secretary to the nation around this time, he monitored the Cherokee content relentlessly and directed that delegates to Washington submit reports to the *Advocate* in Cherokee. Boudinot was a great believer in education for all Cherokees and saw using the national newspaper in this way as a means of teaching the people, especially the full-bloods. Later editors understood that the full-bloods' only source of printed news was the section printed in the Cherokee syllabary, and that they were obligated to publish as much of the news as possible in this form during the time when tribal ownership of land was ending and dissolution of their national government was expected.

The last issue of the *Cherokee Advocate* was published on March 3, 1906. In 1911, the federal government ordered that the press and equipment be sold, and that the Cherokee type be sent to the Smithsonian Institution.

Other newspapers were published in the Cherokee Nation during the nineteenth century, indicating a literate public hungry for reading matter. One of the more important of these was the *Indian Chieftain*, published at Vinita beginning in 1882. The first issue of this four-page weekly declared it to be "devoted to the Interests of the Cherokees, Choctaws, Chickasaws, Seminoles, Creeks and Other Indians of the Indian Territory."[6] The newspaper was owned by George W. Green, a white merchant from Vinita, and was edited by Augustus E. "Gus" Ivey, a mixed-blood Cherokee who had been born in Texas in 1855 and had trained as a printer before moving to the Cherokee Nation in 1877. He was appointed publisher of the

Cherokee Advocate and briefly edited that newspaper in 1878. As publisher, Ivey was responsible for printing and distributing the paper, as well as acting as business manager. In this capacity, he was in charge of job printing and book work for the press. In 1883, Ivey left the *Chieftain* and was replaced by Robert L. Owen and William Hollingsworth, editor and associate editor, respectively. Owen was a Cherokee born at Lynchburg, Virginia, in 1856, the son of Robert Owen and Narcissa (Chisholm) Owen. He attended Washington and Lee University and received an M.A. from that institution before moving to the Cherokee Nation with his widowed mother. There he taught at the Orphans' Asylum, practiced law, and served as secretary of the Board of Education. He served as editor for only eight months before turning over the reins to William Potter Ross, who edited the editorial pages, J. W. Scroggs, who edited and wrote the local pages, and G. W. Miller, who was business manager.

By this time, W. P. Ross was one of the leaders of the Cherokee people. The first editor of the *Cherokee Advocate*, during the Civil War he served in the Confederate army, after which he was a delegate to the Okmulgee Council. He was elected principal chief in 1873 after his appointment to serve out the term after Downing's death in 1872, but retired from that office in 1875. From then on, he was engaged in newspaper work in Indian Territory, editing the *Indian Journal* and the *Indian Arrow*. The *Journal* was published at Eufaula in the Muscogee (Creek) Nation and contained considerable literary content during its long run, beginning in 1876 and continuing well into the twentieth century. The *Chieftain* was sold in 1884, and the new owner, M. E. Milford, and S. J. Thompson became editors. Milford had been an editor in Topeka and other places before coming to Vinita, where he became a leading citizen and made the newspaper a commercial success.

In December 1885, John Lynch Adair began to edit the newspaper. A writer himself, Adair brought a high literary standard to the *Chieftain*. Much national, local, and regional news was published, and from time to time, Adair wrote editorials on the big social and political issues of the day. For example, in reply to a border newspaper's assertion that Indian land should be allotted in severalty and the "balance" opened to white settlers, Adair replied that nowhere else in the United States was land taken from people because they had too much of it.

Although it was published in Arkansas, *Wheelers' Independent* was an influential newspaper in the Cherokee Nation. Owned by John Fisher Wheeler, John Carnell, and John Caldwell Wheeler, the paper was known as *Wheelers' Western Independent* between 1877 and 1879, when *Western* was removed. John F. Wheeler was a white with a long history in Indian publishing, having served as a printer for the *Cherokee Phoenix* from its beginnings to 1831. Wheeler's connection with the Cherokee Nation was strong, however, because he married Elias Boudinot's sister, Nancy Watie. Their son, John C. Wheeler, had established the *Fort Smith Picayune* in 1860 and fought in the Civil War under his uncle, Stand Watie. When Carnell left the paper in 1872, John C. became junior editor.

The *Independent* was a Democratic, anti–Radical Republican paper during Reconstruction. It carried much news from western Arkansas, true to its goal of providing a cheap family newspaper for the region. In keeping with this aim, the newspaper published recipes and household hints, agricultural information, and pieces on family medicine, as well as entertaining items by such writers as Artemus Ward and Josh Billings. It also carried news from Indian Territory, especially from the Cherokee Nation, including political reports. Of special interest was its coverage of the federal court at Fort Smith, where many cases from the territory were tried in the courtroom of Judge Isaac C. Parker. Both Wheelers died in 1880, after which the newspaper was sold. It lasted until 1883.

The *Indian Arrow,* later the *Tahlequah Arrow* and the *Tahlequah Herald* before becoming the *Cherokee County Democrat,* was one of the longest-lived newspapers in the Cherokee Nation. The weekly's first issue came out on February 10, 1888, at Vinita. It later moved to Fort Gibson and then to Tahlequah. The paper was founded as the official organ of the National Party and was owned by a company formed by National Party men, including its first editor, William Potter Ross. Ross, editor of the *Advocate* in the 1840s, served in various offices in the Cherokee Nation, twice occupying the office of principal chief. Under Ross's editorship, the newspaper endeavored to include a large amount of local news from smaller settlements in the nation.

When the *Arrow* moved to Tahlequah in 1889, a new editor, John Drew, took over from Ross. Drew was born at Webbers Falls to John and Charlotte Scales Drew and attended McKenzie College in Texas and Cane Hill College in Arkansas. In 1877, he was appointed district attorney for the Canadian District, and in the next year, he became clerk of the Cherokee Senate. In 1879, he was elected attorney general and later became a Cherokee Supreme Court judge, serving three times as chief justice. Drew was joined at the paper by Waddie Hudson, an intermarried white man who had worked as a printer for other newspapers. Hudson became editor in 1891 when Drew became national treasurer. At that time, Hudson purchased the newspaper but sold it two years later to a joint-stock company.

The *Arrow* continued to cover local news but expanded with a column titled "Territorial Things," which covered major events in other parts of Indian Territory. It also covered political news, outlaws, education, fraud, and citizenship. The Dawes Commission received much attention, as did the implementation of the Curtis Act, Cherokees emigrating to Mexico, the town-site issue, oil and mineral leases, and activities of the Keetoowah Society. During the 1890s and the early years of the twentieth century, the paper had a succession of editors. After tribal dissolution, ownership changed hands several times until the paper was consolidated with another Oklahoma publication in 1930.

The *Telephone* was first published on June 10, 1887, by an intermarried white, B. H. Stone, a Kentucky native who also worked as a photographer and attorney. Stone's intention, he wrote, was to help the young men of the nation take control after tribal dissolution. His major aim for the paper was to promote "education, progress, and advancement of all the people of the Cherokee Nation." Accordingly, he published information on home manufactures, arts and science, and agriculture.

Like other newspapers in the nation, the *Telephone* carried much local news, much of it political. Stone took a political stance opposite that of the *Cherokee Advocate*, and his editorials often drew heated rebuttals from the *Advocate*'s editor, E. C. Boudinot, Jr. This rivalry came to a head in the election of 1887 when Stone backed Joel B. Mayes, while Boudinot was a strong supporter of Rabbit Bunch; the result of this dispute was Stone's death, as reported earlier in this chapter.

After Stone's demise, his wife, Emma Stone, hired William T. Canup as editor. Canup was a Cherokee from the eastern nation who was editor for a short time before relinquishing that post to

Harvey Wirt Courtland Shelton. Shelton, born in 1864, graduated from the Male Seminary in 1882 and then attended Kimball Union Academy in New Hampshire before entering Dartmouth. When Emma Stone sold the operation in 1888 to a joint-stock company, William A. Thompson became editor, with Will Canup acting as manager. In the spring of 1889, a woman's department was added under Captola Wyly, the Cherokee daughter of Judge R. F. Wyly, publishing articles such as "Educate the Girls," "Woman's Love," and "Heroic Lives at Home." Around the same time, an educational department was added, fulfilling B. H. Stone's goal of making the newspaper a source of information rather than a mere conduit of news. The educational section, edited by Helen R. Duncan, DeWitt Clinton Duncan's wife, carried articles on academic subjects, observations of nature, support for public education, and advice to women. During this time, the *Telephone* published news, editorials, and correspondence concerning major events of the time, including leasing the Cherokee Strip, the opening of Oklahoma, federal courts and legal affairs, education, and freedmen issues, as well as local items from towns in the nation and throughout Indian Territory.

In 1890, the editorship was passed to Augustus E. Ivey, a mixed-blood mentioned earlier. Ivey spoke out on some major issues, advocating the teaching of English to all public school pupils, allotment of land, and opening the schools to noncitizen whites in the nation. When Ivey left the paper for a time, his position was filled by Will Canup, who then left the *Cherokee Telephone*, as Ivey had renamed the paper, to join William P. Boudinot in a venture that would furnish news from Indian Territory to the leading dailies in the United States. When Canup left, Ivey returned and remained as editor until 1894, when once again, the paper was sold to the Telephone Publishing Company, which named John Henry Dick as editor.

Dick was born in Flint District in 1869, the son of Charles and Margaret (Tickaneaskie) Dick. After attending Cherokee schools, he entered the Indian University in Muskogee. Later he worked as an interpreter for the National Council, taught in Cherokee Nation schools, and translated for the *Cherokee Advocate*. He also served as district attorney for Tahlequah District. In 1894, too, the newspaper merged with Waddie Hudson's *Indian Arrow* but soon separated again because of disagreements over politics. Dick supported the

Downing Party and spoke out against allotment. Dick's political pronouncements perhaps were too strong for the publishers because in 1895, he was replaced for a short time by John L. Adair, Jr., son of a leading figure in Cherokee affairs, John L. Adair, Sr.

Dick was reappointed, but this did not prove satisfactory, so he was replaced by E. C. Boudinot, Jr., who had bought the paper, and who had shot its first editor. The *Telephone* closed in 1895 but reopened as the *Weekly Capital* under the editorship of Sallie E. (Jones) Dick, Cherokee wife of John Henry Dick. The *Capital* did not last long, however, and stopped publication in 1896.

Will Canup was involved in another Cherokee Nation newspaper, the *Indian Sentinel*. Apparently, Canup's experience—he worked for the *Dallas News*, the *Fort Worth Gazette*, the *Cincinnati Post*, the *New York Sun*, the *Atlanta Constitution*, the *St. Louis Post-Dispatch*, and the *Kansas City Journal* before coming to Indian Territory—was in demand, especially with regard to founding newspapers or reviving moribund ones. Canup organized the *Sentinel* at Webbers Falls in 1890, hiring as editor Robert T. Hanks, a former clerk of the Cherokee Senate. The next year, Canup moved the paper to Tahlequah, where he sold it to the Sentinel Publishing Company, and moved to Fort Smith, Arkansas.

At Tahlequah, the *Sentinel* was edited by William Abbott Thompson, a Cherokee teacher, and supported the Downing Party. In 1892, however, Hanks again became editor; he was also a stockholder in the company. Jeter Thompson Cunningham, a Cherokee, became editor in 1895. Cunningham was educated in the Cherokee schools and in Missouri. During the Civil War, he served under Stand Watie, and after the war he farmed and ran a drug store before sitting on the National Council and on the bench as associate and chief justice of the Cherokee Supreme Court. During the editorships of Hanks, Thompson, and Cunningham, the *Sentinel* published much political news, local news from Tahlequah and other settlements in the nation, legal notices and rewards, and editorials on citizenship, outlaws and intruders, and the Cherokee Outlet.

Later, in 1895 or 1896, the editor was Jefferson Thompson Parks, who was born in 1862 to Cherokee parents, attended the Male Seminary, taught school, practiced law, and ran a general store. Under Parks, the newspaper covered the major issues important to

Cherokees, such as the Dawes Commission, the Curtis Act, the court system, freedmen matters, town sites, and activities of the Keetoowah Society. The *Sentinel* also carried items on political campaigns and U.S. news, especially surrounding events of the Spanish-American War and congressional actions having to do with Indian people. Local news concerning individuals, churches, and societies was published as well. The paper was sold to J. W. Patton and F. P. Shields in 1900 and was not published after 1902. Other newspapers published in the Cherokee Nation in the last three decades of the nineteenth century included the *Vinita Leader* (1895–1929), the *Vinita Vidette* (1878), the *Cherokee Orphan Asylum Press* (1880–81), the *Sallisaw Gazette* (1898–1907), and the *Tahlequah Courier* (1893).

The extent of newspaper publishing in the Cherokee Nation after Removal was impressive, and these newspapers provided a wealth of printed material clearly in demand by a reading public. These organs strengthened the Cherokee democracy by providing forums for debate of wide-ranging issues, many of which determined the survival of the Cherokee way of life. They also furnished models for young people who wished to write by providing examples of literary and journalistic work by American and British writers, as well as Cherokee and other Indian authors, and nurtured these new writers by providing outlets for their best work.

This examination of Cherokee newspapers is also revealing in that it has identified a great number of Cherokee literary people and editors who put out these weeklies. Many were educated in the nation's pubic schools, which gave them a solid grounding in literary conventions, rhetoric, and logical disputation, as well as literary and world history. Although these men and women came from a variety of circumstances, they were all intensely proud of their Cherokee heritage and were determined to prove to the "outside" world that their nation constituted a thinking and feeling populace that could hold its own in any part of the United States in terms of that great nineteenth-century barometer, progress.

CHAPTER 7

Four Cherokee Writers

Although it may be helpful to distinguish between creative writers, on the one hand, and nonfiction writers, on the other, most Cherokees producing literary work in the nineteenth century exhibited a certain amount of crossover. John Rollin Ridge, perhaps best known for his poetry and novel, was also a thoughtful essayist and a vociferous political writer. Too Quah-stee also wrote poetry, although his main body of work consisted of essays, often in the form of epistles to his people. Other examples abound. This chapter examines four writers and their major works, including poetry, fiction, and nonfiction prose, in an attempt to demonstrate the wide range of Cherokee writing in the period from Removal to the tribal dissolution that came with Oklahoma statehood.

The conditions made possible by the Cherokees' high regard for education and the printed word encouraged those who had ambitions for creative writing. The literary traditions begun in the nineteenth century remain strong today among Cherokee writers. The Cherokee who was best known as a writer outside Indian Territory during the period was John Rollin Ridge, the scion of an influential and tragic family, who eventually felt forced to leave the Cherokee Nation for California. There he became one of that state's best-known writers.

Ridge was both a product of and a contributor to Cherokee intellectual life. His writing in California was not ignored by Cherokees in Indian Territory, as shown by his selection as one of the Southern delegation to negotiate with the United States after the Civil War.

Clearly a member of the Cherokee intelligentsia, he was quick to point out in his writing that the Cherokees were an advanced people, using terms recognized by nineteenth-century anthropologists. He described his people as being cultured and capable of using abstract concepts in their thinking. He saw himself as a model of the intellectual and highly developed Cherokee. This position was one that many later Cherokee writers emulated, though perhaps less obviously. Ridge was born in the eastern nation to John Ridge, a leader of the Cherokees, as his father, Major Ridge, had been. John Ridge was educated in Cherokee schools, then at Cornwall Academy in Connecticut, along with his compatriot, Buck Watie, who took the name Elias Boudinot. Like Boudinot, Ridge married a Connecticut woman, Sarah Bird Northrup, and returned with her to Georgia. The couple lived quite happily on the family's plantation, where Ridge owned orchards and raised crops and animals, all tended by African-descended slaves as he engaged in negotiations and legal business for both the Cherokees and the Muscogees (Creeks) in their deliberations with the federal government. In that position, he knew firsthand how important it was to have a knowledge of white ways of doing things. His son, John Rollin Ridge, was the first of several children in the Ridge household.

The Ridge family had long been champions of education for Cherokee children. Major Ridge, Rollin's grandfather, had been raised in the traditional Cherokee manner, but his status as first a warrior (where he acquired the given name that was to follow him for his entire life) and as a peacetime leader of his people brought him to the conclusion that future generations of Cherokees must learn white American ways if they were not to be marginalized further or even annihilated. Thus he made arrangements to ensure that his children attended schools in the Cherokee Nation and later to send his son John to the Cornwall School, an institution founded to educate "aboriginal" leaders, including some Cherokees.

When Rollin became old enough, John and Sarah hired Sophia Sawyer, a teacher from New England, to guide his and his siblings' education. Sawyer had come to the Cherokee Nation as a missionary, but this strong-willed woman had no patience for the paternalistic views of the male missionaries who sought to define her role among the Cherokees. In time, Sawyer was teaching a number of children in New Echota, the Cherokee capital, even some of African descent. When the Georgia Guard visited her and demanded that she stop this illegal practice, Sawyer stood her ground, and the Georgians beat a retreat. She subsequently followed the Ridge family to Indian Territory and then to Arkansas, where she established a school for young women that became a model of such institutions on the frontier. She served the Ridge family well, providing a quality education for all the children, but especially the curious and quick-learning John Rollin.

John Ridge was one of the signers of the 1835 Treaty of New Echota, which provided for the removal of the Cherokees to Indian Territory. Because the majority of Cherokees did not agree with what they saw as surrender on the part of the treaty's signers, Ridge became the object of derision and malice. In September 1837, the Ridges left for the West, along with Elias Boudinot, his family, and some others. Traveling a northern route, crossing the Mississippi near Cape Girardeau, and continuing through Missouri and skirting the top of Arkansas, they arrived in November at Honey Creek in the northeastern corner of the Cherokee Nation, a place that was to be home for the Boudinot-Ridge-Watie clan for a long time. Sophia Sawyer joined them there and continued the children's education.

In the winter of 1838–39, the last of the Cherokees arrived in the new nation. Chief John Ross, by now the enemy of the Ridges and Boudinot, quickly consolidated his power over the people. On June 22, 1839, parties of assassins attacked John Ridge, Major Ridge, and Elias Boudinot and killed them all. John Ridge, according to his twelve-year-old son's account, was dragged from his bed into the yard of his house and, in front of his wife and children, stabbed repeatedly until he died. Major Ridge and Elias Boudinot were killed in similar fashion, but Stand Watie, Boudinot's brother and John Ridge's cousin, escaped the assassins, as did other targeted members of the Treaty Party. The terrified Ridge and Boudinot families fled to northwest Arkansas, on the edge of the Cherokee Nation, where Sarah Ridge and Sophia Sawyer set up a household. The Boudinot children, however, returned to the East, where they were taken in by relatives.

In Arkansas, Ridge's education continued, first under Cephas Washburn, a missionary to the Western Cherokees who operated the Far West Academy, one of the first institutions of higher learning in the region, where he learned languages, mathematics, history, and all the usual subjects taught in a classical curriculum. Later, he studied for the law under a Fayetteville, Arkansas, attorney, but he never reached the bar. Instead, he married Elizabeth Wilson in May 1847, and they moved to Honey Creek in the Cherokee Nation. Here the couple lived happily, and Ridge farmed and wrote. His poetry appeared in Texas and Arkansas newspapers along with prose he wrote on Cherokee history and politics. His poetry of this period was largely in a romantic vein, the kind of work he would have been reading in the newspapers and magazines of the day. Examples are "An October Morn" and "To a Mockingbird Singing in a Tree," written before he left for California.[1]

So far, the Ridges had lived an almost idyllic life at Honey Creek, and the young couple's future looked bright. The Cherokee Nation was a dangerous place in the 1840s, however, because the schism stemming from the Removal treaty was still very much alive. Violence broke out from time to time between the two sides, and some of those involved were killed. Rollin, his uncle Stand Watie, members of the Starr family, and others seemed to act as lightning rods for hotheads from the Ross side. For Rollin Ridge, the situation came to a head in 1849, when a stallion belonging to him was taken from his farm. He accosted a Ross party man, David Kell, on the latter's property, where he found his horse, still bleeding from being castrated. The pair argued, and Rollin drew a pistol and killed Kell.[2] Fearing retribution from the Ross faction, he fled to southwest Missouri, just a few miles from Honey Creek, where he tried to raise a group of armed men to attack the Ross party. His uncle Stand was able to quell this rash act, and after a time, Rollin, joined by his brother Aeneas and a slave, left for the gold fields of California in April 1850, joining a wagon train organized in Fayetteville, Arkansas.[3] His wife, Elizabeth, was left behind with the understanding that he would send for her when he could.

After a long and arduous trek across half the continent, Ridge's party reached the gold fields, only to find the richest claims already made. He had documented his journey in a series of letters to his family published in a Fort Smith newspaper.[4] He tried mining for a while but derived little reward for a lot of hard work. He then decided to travel to Sacramento, the capital of the mining area, to seek whatever fortune he could find. Advertising himself as a writer, he secured a post with the *New Orleans True Delta*, at first writing sketches of the gold fields and later becoming an agent for the publication, as well as a reporter. The *True Delta* was one of the more popular newspapers in the region, carrying, as it did, national and international news and entertaining features to the print-starved American immigrants in California. At the same time, he continued to write poetry, a practice he had started back in Indian Territory, and published two poems, "The Harp of Broken Strings" and "Yuba City Dedicate" in the *Marysville Herald* in 1850 and 1851. Thus began Ridge's career as a poet and newspaper writer.

Ridge's poems appeared mostly in newspapers during his lifetime. However, his wife published a posthumous collection in 1868, partly in tribute and partly in an attempt to raise money to support herself and the couple's daughter. His poetry falls readily into two modes, the romantic and the occasional. His occasional work often commemorates events Ridge judged to be notable or historic, the celebration of a civic anniversary, for example, or the completion of the Atlantic telegraph cable. In these works, he is the inveterate municipal booster, praising the "progressiveness" of city leadership; on a larger scale, ironically, he is the spokesman for Manifest Destiny, the spreading of the Euro-American "civilization" across North America and the gathering of other races, specifically the Hispanics and the Indians, under the canopy of this movement's revival tent.

Ridge's early romantic work in California stems from his perceived banishment from his family's bosom and the painful separation from his young wife. Rollin and Elizabeth's plan was for him to go ahead to California to make a new start and for her to join him shortly afterward, but their youthful optimism had not prepared them for the time it would take for him to make that beginning. In these early works, he sees himself as a defiant exile, "a stranger in a stranger land," cut off from his true love by sinister forces. In "The Harp of Broken Strings," where these themes appear, Ridge writes poignantly of the separated lovers, but here he takes stock of his situation. Writing "by Sacramento's stream," the poet spells out his anticipation of making his fortune in the gold fields, only to find himself in an alien environment, without money or friends and with little prospect for employment. The poem exhibits a full share of self-pity, but it portrays a man tortured by self-doubt as well. As he continued to write, his poems began to reflect not only the inner man but also the persona that Ridge was to spend the rest of his life establishing, the handsome, half-tamed Indian genius who lived with one foot in the aboriginal world and the other in white America. He cultivated this public image and half believed it himself, enjoying the air of mystery that came with it.

An almost morose poem, "The Still Small Voice," carries a refrain throughout that alludes to his personal history—especially his desire for revenge for the assassination of his father and grandfather and the perceived injustice of his being forced to shoot Kell—and how it shapes his future. "Too late! Too late! The doom is set, the die is cast," runs the repeated line, a statement designed to depict his desperation. He sees himself as a Byronic hero whose destiny is determined by what he has done and what has been done to him, and to whom fate has given special attention.

> *A raven-thought is darkly set*
> *Upon my brow—where shades are met*
> *Of grief, of pain, of toil, and care—*
> *The raven-thought of stern despair!* [Lines 33–36]

"The Stolen White Girl" is a ballad that tells the story of the young noble savage who swoops down and captures the white girl he has fallen in love with. The capture is both physical and emotional, because the girl falls for the irresistible dusky stranger, and they sweep off into, presumably, a bower of bliss. Ridge, of course, sees himself as the manly stranger, feared by men and loved by women, and cultivates this persona as he makes his way in the strange land to which he has been forced to flee.

Ridge wrote many conventionally romantic poems during his years in California, mostly for publication in the many small newspapers that sprouted in the small towns that catered to miners. They were light, often sentimental entertainment for his largely male audiences, many of whom were living lonely bachelor lives, separated from families back home and wives and girlfriends. These poems most often centered on love, with a smattering of the natural world in the mix, and in most ways were indistinguishable from similar works in eastern newspapers and magazines. Ridge knew the mass market, which explains why he was in such demand as an editor later.

His most notable occasional poems were written in the 1860s and were delivered orally by the poet before they were published. These four poems, "California," "The Atlantic Cable," and two called "Poem," are thematically related. They present the nineteenth-century view of progress in its white American version. The first "Poem," written and delivered in 1860, adds a characteristic Ridgean twist in that he extols the ancient Indian civilizations of Mexico and South America. It is an interesting point of view, but it is consistent with Ridge's views of contemporary Indian societies; he believed in the great racial ladder, in which "savage" races, such as the Australian aborigines and most African tribes, were on the bottom rung, with other tribes further up. The Five Civilized Tribes, especially the Cherokees, he asserted, were well on their way toward "civilization" and thus were near the top, just under the Europeans and Americans. Progress is made on the upward climb by emulating those peoples at the top. The journey may be chronicled, Ridge says, by examining the ways in which the various peoples make their livelihoods; hunter-gatherer nomads are at the bottom, but as cultures learn agriculture and sedentary ways, their lot improves. He uses the Aztecs and Incas as examples and contrasts their civilizations with the wanderers of the North American plains who live in teepees. He traces the progress of peoples through three stages: hunter-gatherers, keepers of flocks and herds, and finally, agriculturists.

> But came in turn the third and better state,
> With cheering omens of a higher fate.
> Then, did the restless Nomad cease to roam—
> His hardships o'er, he found at last his home. [Lines 51–54]

With settled agricultural communities, cooperation and invention lead to higher material standards of living and technological progress. Ridge uses the ancient civilizations of the Old World as further examples of this historical "truth." This is a most fitting topic for his audience, the Agricultural, Horticultural, and Mechanics' Society in

August 1860. This version of the progress theme was revisited in his poem "California," in which he praises the state's wealth of natural resources, as well as the talents of those Euro-Americans who settled there after 1849 to exploit them. The familiar theme of humans mastering their environment is in full force here, as well as in the second "Poem," given at the commencement ceremonies of Oakland College.

In probably his most widely read poem, "The Atlantic Cable," Ridge continues with these popular ideas.

> *Let all mankind rejoice! For time nor space*
> *Shall check the progress of the human race!*
> *Though Nature heaved the Continents apart,*
> *She cast in one great mould the human heart.* [Lines 3–6]

Ridge sees the linkup of the civilizations of Europe and America as a step up another rung of the ladder of progress, another example of humans controlling their world. To subdue an elementary force, such as electricity, to the human will, Ridge declares, is a feat that would stun the hunter-gatherer mind. His sentiments played well before his nineteenth-century audience, to whom their time was the great mother age that would give birth to prosperity and peace for all. The implications of such thinking for American Indians is clear; the message is that of the "progressive" elements within the Cherokee and other Indian nations: adapt to the white ways and accept their values and practices if you would join in the prosperity. To reject what the whites are offering is death for the nations, a passing into oblivion.

This is not to say that Ridge ignored the injustices that were inflicted on the minorities of midcentury California. He spoke out against the treatment of those who derogatorily were called "Digger" Indians at the time, who, it was reported, were hunted down and shot from horseback by white "sportsmen." Treated as subhuman, they were regarded by many as debris to be cleared away so that civilization could commence. Ridge also was aware of the treatment given to the earlier settlers of the area, the Hispanic people who had made California their home when it was a Spanish and then a Mexican province. They, too, were regarded by the Americans as being in the way, a detriment to progress, and hostile to the presence of the immigrants from the East. Ironically, it was this oppressed minority that furnished the material for Ridge's novel, *The Life and Adventures of Joaquín Murieta, the Celebrated California Bandit*, published in 1854 and pirated in several other versions in English and Spanish, including a relatively recent one by Pablo Neruda.

As Ridge himself claimed, the bare bones of the narrative are essentially true. At the time, as I have noted, there was animosity between the "American" and "foreign" populations. To many Californians, "Americans" included those immigrants from the United States east of the state, as well as white Europeans who had joined the gold rush from their home countries. "Foreigners" included longtime California residents, as well as Mexicans, Chileans, Peruvians, and Chinese immigrants who had arrived about the same time as most of the "Americans." With the "Americans" firmly in control, especially after California statehood in 1850, the minority "foreigners" were often treated roughly and unjustly. The situation was exacerbated by the large number of U.S. veterans of the Mexican War who flocked to the area to mine gold and had no intention of sharing that gold with people they saw as their vanquished enemies. The American authorities issued a number of oppressive regulations limiting the activities of the "foreigners," including a tax on mining gold. A series of violent events, widely reported in the press, erupted because of this social friction, especially in the mining camps. When the Hispanics were forced to leave the gold fields, some of them took to raiding ranches for cattle and horses. Vigilante whites pursued these foreign "outlaws." Joaquín Murieta, a young Hispanic man, was one of these outlaws who robbed white businesses and ranches and in time became almost legendary on both sides of the social divide. The situation came to a head when Murieta defended some Hispanic miners, was taken into custody, and was flogged. His wife was also "insulted." From then on, he became the enemy of the whites, leading a gang of men, including the notorious bandit Manuel García, or Three-Finger Jack, that raided the Americans at every opportunity. They were pursued, but between 1851 and 1853, they eluded capture. As a result, the California Rangers was established under Captain Harry Love, a decorated veteran of the Mexican War, who began to track down Murieta's band. The rangers caught up with the outlaws in 1853 and killed Murieta and García. To authenticate their deed, they preserved Murieta's head and García's hand in a keg of whiskey, for which a glass jar of alcohol was later substituted. This display drew large crowds of Americans.

The story was screamed from the headlines of newspapers around the state, and it was from these news stories that Ridge got the idea to tell the whole story in a novel. A work like this would sell very well, he thought, not only in California but also all over the United States and beyond. He was the right person for the job because by this time, he had gotten to know the topography of the area from his travels as agent for the *True Delta*, as well as the types of people he could fashion into lifelike characters. He went to work and by the spring of 1854 had produced his book. He reported in a letter to Stand Watie that the initial press run was seven thousand and that the publisher, William Cooke Company, had gone out of business and cheated him out of his royalties. He also reported to Watie that he was negotiating with an eastern publisher for a second edition. All this seems unlikely. First, the press run seems extravagant because very few copies are extant. Second, records show that the William Cooke Company did not go out of business. Third, there is no evidence of a second edition or even of negotiations for one.[5] One thing is certain: the work was widely pirated, especially after its publication in the *California Police Gazette* (San Francisco) in 1859. The *Gazette* version is probably as close as Ridge got to publishing a second edition. Three weeks after the *Gazette* version, a garbled pamphlet came out with the story, with the added panache of California artist Charles C. Nahl's illustrations. A "third" edition did come out in 1871 that may have been prepared by Ridge before his death. When Ridge published *The Life and Adventures of Joaquín Murieta*, he was not yet the businessman that he was to become, and that fact hurt his income.

A curious part of the *Murieta*-Ridge linkup is that historians of early California history used the work as a reference for their discussion not only of the Murieta figure but also of the relationships between the American and Hispanic communities at the time. Noted historians Hubert Howe Bancroft and Theodore Hittell included Ridge's version of the Murieta story in their histories of California.[6]

It is clear that Ridge considered himself an eclectic writer, not a "poet" or "novelist." He knew that he had the skills to be a journalist from his experience with the *True Delta* and as a stringer with other California publications. He had been planning, although somewhat abstractly, to publish an "Indian" newspaper from Arkansas, somewhere close to the Cherokee Nation. He and others in the family, most notably Elias Cornelius Boudinot and Josiah Woodward Washbourne, Ridge's brother-in-law, wanted to use such an organ to attack the Ross faction. They turned to Stand Watie, the Boudinot-Watie-Ridge family patriarch, for help, and although Stand seems to have been sympathetic to the idea, he was practical enough to know that the three had few resources of their own to begin such a venture. The Civil War soon put to rest any ambitions in this direction.

But Ridge's reputation as a writer grew in California, and after making some political connections within the Know-Nothing Party, he became an associate editor of the *California American* in 1856. In the following year, a group of Sacramento businessmen bought out the paper and started a new journal, the *Sacramento Daily Bee*, with John Rollin Ridge as editor. This was the beginning of a long journalistic career that included many editorships throughout northern California. Much of his newspaper writing was political; he was anti-North and virulently anti-Lincoln during the Civil War, and he supported politicians who had similar views.[7]

Ridge produced a series of articles in *Hesperian* magazine in which he addressed some general issues on American Indians. Ridge had published some verse in the magazine in the 1850s, so the publisher knew of him and his reputation. The series, "North American Indians," appeared in the March, April, and May 1862 issues and discussed Indian history and relationships with the whites, how the Civil War affected them, and the clash of cultures. The series appears to have been cut short by Ridge's move from San Francisco to Red Bluff to take on editorship of the local newspaper. After this time, he must have had little time for such reflective writing and dedicated himself to the daily grind of newspaper work.

John Rollin Ridge in many ways may be considered the first Indian professional writer. The Cherokee wrote successfully in several genres, producing poetry that was as good as most being published at the time and writing a successful, if gaudy, thriller. Although his political views may provoke dismay, he was a vital force in early California journalism, turning out reams of very readable copy that retains an originality still evident today. He is one of the giants of American Indian literature, a product of the Cherokee embrace of education and the written word.

Too Quah-stee, or DeWitt Clinton Duncan, was a lawyer and writer who often represented his nation in Washington during some of the most critical years of the Cherokees' existence. This experience informed his writing, and he often wrote directly to the people through the pages of Indian Territory newspapers to inform them of decisions being made about their lives in far-off Washington, D.C. But his writing did more than transmit the news. Time and time again, Duncan's cogent arguments against proposed federal policy provided a philosophical underpinning to the Cherokee Nation's responses to these proposals. Although in the end Cherokee resistance was swept away, like that of most other tribes, Duncan's essays provide insight into an important period when much federal policy regarding Indians was formulated. His poetry often uses the same themes that appear in his political work. He wrote fiction as well. Duncan spoke Cherokee and knew the language well. He translated from English to Cherokee and Cherokee to English. His command of his native tongue enabled him to produce the linguistic work on that language described in Chapter 5.

Born at Dahlonega, Georgia, in the eastern Cherokee Nation, DeWitt Clinton Duncan was the son of John and Elizabeth Abercrombie Duncan, who removed to the West with the tribe in 1839. Young Duncan attended mission and Cherokee national schools before going to Dartmouth College, from which he graduated in 1861. When he was ready to return home, the Cherokee Nation was beset by the Civil War; with Cherokees on both sides of the conflict, the nation was a particularly dangerous place. Furthermore, most occupations were disrupted, and schools and government offices were in disarray, so little would have been left for Duncan to do there except fight. As a result, Duncan did not return to Indian Territory at that time but found work teaching school in northern states where there was no fighting before finally settling in 1866 at Charles City, Iowa, where he practiced law, held petty political offices, and taught school. For more than a decade after 1880, Duncan divided his time

between the Cherokee Nation and Iowa, but he served the Cherokees in various capacities: as attorney for the nation; teacher of English, Latin, and Greek at the Cherokee Male Seminary; and translator of the Cherokee laws. Throughout this period and beyond, he
attempted to write a linguistic analysis of the Cherokee language. In
the early 1880s, he also began to write for Cherokee newspapers,
particularly the *Indian Chieftain* at Vinita, where he took up permanent residence in the 1890s, and the *Cherokee Advocate* at Tahlequah.

Although he became known as a poet, linguist, and fiction writer,
Duncan was best known for dozens of letters that appeared under
the pen name Too Qua-stee. The range of subjects in Too Qua-stee's
letters is great, but the predominant subject is the U.S. attack on the
sovereignty of the Cherokee Nation. Although he was a product of
assimilation, Duncan complained of the federal government's policy of forcing it on his fellow Cherokees who as yet had not accepted
white ways. Ironically, though, he believed that because the Cherokees had an intelligentsia, the nation was better equipped to understand the whites and to resist encroachment on their national sovereignty. He saw, too, that the educational system and the free press in
the Cherokee Nation allowed his people to prepare for the inevitable
outcome and escape altogether the degradation of the reservation
system to which other tribes were subjected in the last half of the
century. They escaped, as well, the resulting poverty and disease
that decimated the ranks of Native populations. But the price of the
Cherokees' escape was the dissolution of their nation and forced
citizenship in the United States, as provided for by the Curtis Act of
1898. Although Duncan saw these ironies, he raised his voice to the
last in opposition to the destruction of his nation and, after the fact,
lamented its passing and attempted to prick the United States' con-
science about its unfair dealings with the Cherokees.

Early in his career, Duncan published an article in the *Cherokee
Advocate* in which he speaks out on the Black Hills situation in 1876.[8]
Specifically, he differs with the conclusions of General William
Vandever's report on the white invasion of the Black Hills, held sa-
cred by Sioux tribes and other Plains Indians. Among other things,
Vandever decided that although the influx of white settlers and
miners into the area was illegal, they were now so numerous as to
make their removal difficult. In his report, he recommended that

they be allowed to stay, and that any remaining Indians should be removed. According to Duncan, he also recommended that the army kill as few Indians as practicable in effecting their removal. Duncan goes on to comment on an account of General George Crook's engagement with the "villainous Sioux," the term used by an Iowa newspaper. He objects to the language used to describe the character of these border conflicts and says that it is employed "to delude right-minded people into the false notion that it is a Christian warfare in behalf of civilization." He asks by what laws of Nature or Christianity the white society is entitled to inflict warfare on other people to acquire their land. Duncan claims that the motivation of the white Americans in the nineteenth century is the same as that held by Pizarro and Cortez, the Spanish conquerors of Peru and Mexico, known to have employed harsh methods to achieve their aims. The settlers are "wrong-doers," he asserts, and, as such, should be chastised at least as far as returning their ill-gotten gains to their rightful owners. But, Vandever reports, they now desire to have peace.

The federal government, Too Quah-stee says, is the protector of the Indians but has failed miserably in that role. Events have proved that the mandates of the American government may be obeyed or disobeyed by its citizens as they see fit. In this, they are likened to Goths and Vandals. Duncan concludes his article with the statement "Republican form of government is a chimera—only a league for mutual protection." He might have added to that assertion "of its strongest members."

Duncan saw it as his duty throughout his life to monitor statements about Indian-white relations, whether they were made in interviews with him or were published in newspapers and periodicals. In one such case in 1876, he responds to a statement by Jane Swisshelm published in the St. Cloud *Independent*. Swisshelm was a journalist and the editor of several Minnesota newspapers. She was an advocate of abolitionism and women's rights, and her commentaries on these topics were widely read. A resident of St. Cloud, Minnesota, during the "Sioux uprising" of 1862, Swisshelm sided with the settlers, as did most editors of frontier newspapers, and advocated a policy of clearing the land of Indians to allow more whites to settle on Indian lands. Duncan's response to her more recent comments in the *Independent* opens with a quote from the journalist:

"The central pivot of the Mosaic history is the right of a civilized nation to take from barbarians the land devoted to crime, and Christ re-echoes this principle in the parable of the talents."[9]

Duncan's comments begin with the observation that it is one thing to hear such sentiments from the illiterate, ignorant, and unscrupulous, but quite another for them to issue from the pen of a well-educated intellectual. Duncan tests Swisshelm's assertion by asking whether it is true that persons in a civilized society believe that it is their right to displace the Indians and take control of what is theirs. He agrees that this seems to be a tenet of what he calls Anglo-Saxon culture. However, this belief has no support "in moral truth." The belief, then, is attributed to "a very curious piece of human philosophy," or what today is called psychology, in which people will often do collectively what they would abhor individually. Duncan offers the following example: "Corporations are proverbially soulless and are capable of much wrong, while the individuals, of whom they are composed, all have a reputation for the fairest integrity." A civilization that carries out immoral policies against its minorities, he reasons, is "a demon whose only attribute is selfishness and whose only object is self-gratification." Although the demon has destroyed countless Native people through the years, no individuals may be found who will take responsibility for these acts of annihilation and robbery. Further, to draw authority for these acts from the tenets of Christianity is the height of blasphemy, Duncan asserts. "Certainly the idea that a civilized nation is, on account of its consistent loyalty to the King of heaven authorized to make booty of barbarians, is quite enough to perplex far better faculties than those of an Indian."

Duncan's essay continues by reviewing the history of Indian-white relations to prove the points he has made. He takes up the topic of treaties, saying that they have "accumulated upon the public records, until they are now numbered by the hundreds, yet they are nearly all defunct, and are interesting only as showing how vain it is for a weak people to rely upon the promises of a mighty nation." Citations from sections of treaties made with the Cherokees support this statement. Swisshelm's declaration that Grant's peace policy has been a failure, following the peace policies of the Quakers since William Penn in that regard, Duncan greets with chagrin, saying that it has been the only hope of the Indian in recent years. The Modoc War of 1872–73 and the Black Hills campaign and its battle of Greasy Grass (or Little Bighorn) have proved that a war policy is good for neither the majority's moral life nor the minority's well-being.

When bills began to inundate Congress for the allotment of Indian land in severalty in the early 1880s, Too Quah-stee recognized the danger to national sovereignty of the tribes in spite of the guarantees of former treaties. He spoke out against these bills, writing in the pages of Indian Territory newspapers to alert the people to the menace and to keep them informed about aspects of the bills from the Indian perspective. He considered this last point extremely important because when he looked at the history of the tribes, he saw promises broken, misrepresentations made, and treaty provisions disguised as benefiting Indian people when in fact they led to losses for them.

The 1880s also saw the intensification of an old problem related to allotment: the illegal entry of settlers into Indian lands. Of immediate concern to the Cherokees and other tribes was the Oklahoma territory, lying directly west of the Indian nations and regarded by the settlers and their supporters as "open" land owned by the government. A celebrated incident involving David L. Payne brought the question whether Oklahoma was "open" to white settlement or reserved for the future use of the Indians to a climax. Payne and a small band of followers, inspired by Elias Cornelius Boudinot's "Letter" in the *Chicago Times*, which outlined the case for settlement and which was subsequently reprinted and widely distributed, entered Oklahoma and proceeded to fence land they claimed as their own and to build homes and other buildings. Payne's band was arrested by U.S. troops and taken to the federal court in Fort Smith, where they were to stand trial for trespassing. During the interval before the trial, the question of Payne's right to settle in Oklahoma was debated in national newspapers and on the floor of the U.S. Congress. In an article published in the *Cherokee Advocate* of February 9, 1881, Duncan takes as a typical prosettler speech one delivered by George G. Vest of Missouri on the floor of the Senate. Vest, a longtime supporter of the settlers, admits that the government originally set aside Oklahoma for the use of the tribes, but he claims that it subsequently rescinded that action by purchasing the land from the tribes and prohibiting the locating of Indians there. Because the lands were ceded to the government and Indians are forbidden entry, it follows, in Vest's logic, that the Oklahoma lands are open to white settlement. This line of reasoning was the same as that used by Boudinot in his "Letter." "The Courts can never punish a single person arrested and the end will be, as it has always been, the onward march of civilization [here Duncan interjects a question mark] and the Anglo-Saxon blood," Vest thundered from the Senate podium.

Duncan refuses to swallow Vest's argument in spite of its rhetorical gusto. This line of thinking, he says, is inappropriate for a civilized society, and he draws a parallel involving two farmers and a horse. One farmer enters another's barn and takes possession of his horse. When he is questioned by the horse's owner, the thief replies that he is entitled to the horse because unlike his neighbor, he is an Anglo-Saxon and a Christian, can build big houses, is educated, has a greater need for the horse, and is stronger than the other. "I am also the offspring of a glorious civilization and as such, God has a special liking for me and wants me to kill off people not of our society much as Joshua did the Canaanites." Duncan adds, "We will wait to see what Mr. Vest will do with the horse." In the court case, Judge Isaac C. Parker ruled against Payne, forbade settlement of Oklahoma, and fined Payne $1,000.

With the passage of a rider on an appropriations bill pushed through Congress in 1897, Duncan wrote to predict the damages the bill would inflict on the Cherokee Nation. The bill stipulated that after January 1898, all legislation concerning the Cherokees was to be supervised by the president of the United States. Effectively banning the Cherokee legal system, it was a major step on the trail to tribal dissolution. The bill made federal and Arkansas law superior to Cherokee law; in effect, it severely limited the powers of the National Council and transferred the jurisdiction of Cherokee courts to federal ones. In his article, Duncan lists some of the difficulties with this arrangement, including inheritances and other examples of tort law formerly spelled out under tribal law that now has no standing. Cherokee criminal law, too, was now superseded by Arkansas statutes, but Duncan does not analyze what that means for the Cherokee people, perhaps seeing it as too daunting a task for the present. The article is another example of Too Quah-stee's campaign to inform the people of consequences and ramifications of measures taken in regard to them.

He continued in this vein with an article in September 1897, originally published in the *Vinita Chieftain* and later reprinted in the *Cherokee Advocate*. The piece is remarkable in that although the author has displayed bitterness toward the white officials and commentators who hide behind the mantle of "civilization" to veil their nefarious deeds, here he turns his guns on the Indian "treaty men," those who tried to reach an agreement with the Dawes Commission and who now agitate for the Cherokee Nation to capitulate and merge into the United States. The occasion of Duncan's writing was the impending visit of a subcommittee from the U.S. Senate Indian Committee, the aims of which visit had not been fully spelled out, according to the writer.

After describing the delegation's members as men of importance on the world stage, Duncan notes that their prominence there has little meaning to the full-blood Cherokee. The senators, Duncan asserts, are "nowhere in touch with the poor people whose interests they are commissioned to look after" and, having had no intercourse with the majority of the Indian people, have no idea of their concerns or needs. A full-blood's hens, pigs, and cow hold much more meaning to him than the actions of the federal government in foreign affairs or what are called current events in the East. He is much more interested in the threats to his way of life that the government seems determined to carry out against him and his neighbors.

However, Too Quah-stee says, the whole trouble does not lie in Washington. Those he describes as "our own native statesmen" belong to that class of humanity that may be seen as civilized, intelligent, cultured, and progressive and that the senators, too, represent. These native statesmen have minds filled with the "same grand things" as their white counterparts: the need for "change in the order of things" in Indian Territory, the abundance of natural resources, the validity of mineral leases, the importance of building cities, "the transcendent sacredness of invested capital and its acquired equities," and the prospects for a few fat positions that will become available to them when Indian Territory becomes a state. He then makes a serious charge: "These are the men, too, who are always foremost to meet accredited commissions at the threshold of our nation," meaning that they are most often the delegates of the Cherokee Nation's government and thus purport to transmit the wishes of the people as a whole. "They cheekily monopolize diplomatic attention, and by pulling themselves into the front of affairs, manage to shape negotiations to suit their own selfish purposes." Too Quah-stee has put his finger on the split in the nation, in many ways a linguistic one, that had plagued the Cherokees since the early days in the East. In an analogy he draws, the full-blood is cut off from playing in "this great, elegant, and exciting ball-play of mixed speculation and diplomacy." And yet, he is the one who always puts up the stake and pays the expenses. Duncan ends the article with the hope that in the end the full-bloods will be treated fairly, but the tone of the writing is not optimistic.

Writing in the *Indian Chieftain* of November 3, 1898, Duncan ruminates on the legal and moral nature of treaties, dwelling particularly on those broken by the United States in its dealings with the Cherokees. He points out that the United States sees it as its right to abrogate treaties when they are deemed to be of no further use to it; in fact, this idea has been codified in the U.S. Supreme Court's decision in the Cherokee Tobacco Case, in which E. C. Boudinot defended his actions under the treaty of 1866 and which the Internal Revenue Service opposed under laws passed by Congress. The Supreme Court decided that the laws enacted by Congress took precedence over the treaty. This decision, by extension, served to limit every treaty with an Indian nation to be valid only at the pleasure of one of its parties, to wit, the federal government.

Duncan's major point in this discussion is the idea that a treaty is a moral as well as a legal obligation. Thus, if it is entered on in good faith, both parties should be obliged to abide by its provisions. However, the federal government has taken the position that it has the "right" to rescind treaties or provisions of them simply because it can. Compounding this moral wrong, Too Quah-stee says, is the fact that seldom did an Indian nation enter into a treaty unless it was coerced in some way by the stronger federal government, and therefore, it is more incumbent on the coercer to take the moral path. Sadly, this is not the case, and thus the government's actions are immoral until such time as "the poles of the moral universe have been inverted, and wrong becomes right, and the united voice of mankind be that of Milton's devil: 'Evil, be thou my good.' "

Duncan provides a devastating description of the U.S. Senate chamber during the passage of the Curtis Act, which extended the allotment of tribal lands in severalty, abolished tribal courts and tribal government, established town lots, and prepared the way for statehood for Oklahoma. Despite the enormous scope of the bill, a quorum was not present, only half a dozen members, and the visitors' gallery was empty except for a few Indians. As a list of amendments was read off and declared approved by the Senate's president, the Indians looked down with feelings of "helpless contempt upon the false assumptions of fact, the hypocrisies of argument, and the injustice of conclusions, which pushed on to consummation, this most remarkable act in the great drama of civilization." They saw "the sweet angel of plighted faith taken and knifed by Christian hands, and laid upon the altar of insatiable greed, and offered up as a sacrifice to the god of mammon." And Duncan comments bitterly, "Barbarism quaked at the spectacle with a sense of insupportable horror, and with just aversion turned its swarthy face from the gleams of Calvary, as only the delusive lights of pride, power, arrogance and oppression." They also saw their homes taken and given to "unentitled strangers," while the few acres allotted to them were limited to the surface, and whatever mineral resources might lie underground were handed over to the rich. When the bill passed, the spectators left the building, where the sun greeted them with the message that "the day is coming!" "Egypt, Greece, Rome, and all other nations whose wrecks adorn the shores of time have paid the penalty of such conduct; and the United States cannot expect to escape." Duncan's chagrin and bitterness were doubtless shared by the majority of Cherokees when the news reached the nation in the *Cherokee Advocate* of November 3, 1898, of the debacle that had occurred in Washington.

Too Quah-stee expressed his diminished hopes for his people in verse, as well as prose. In iambic-pentameter couplets revealing his classical training, he published "Cherokee Memories" in the *Chieftain* for October 4, 1900, in which he invokes an idyllic past life for his people. This former peaceful existence is played off against the encroachment of white society. In other days, he writes,

> *Every man was every other's friend*
> *And the least call for aid made all attend.*
> *Then hospitality, broad as the day,*
> *Took in the weary traveler on his way;*
> *Made every home a refuge from distress.*

Thus he paints Cherokee society as a cooperative one, in which each individual acts in the community's interests, as well as in his own:

> *Whilst one man made the plow, or shaped the hoe,*
> *Another built the cart and made it go;*
> *Another turned the sod, or pushed the plane,*
> *And so life's toil was shared, and so the gain.*

The tension between that world and the white man's is almost palpable as Duncan tells civilization's tale of profit and wanton destruction, where its minions shoot birds like the passenger pigeons into extinction,

> *And brings them down to death without a cause;*
> *To reap vain glory from vast agony,*
> *Shoots down the bison just to see him die.*

The Indians, Too Quah-stee writes, cannot withstand the flood of white men into their lands or quell the destructive behavior they bring with them.

> *O civilization! The destructive hand*
> *Of God's free bounties, hath despoiled our land;*
> *Hath set starvation on the Indian's track,*
> *And no degree of force can drive him back.*

Around this same time, when the dissolution of tribal government had become apparent to all, Duncan expressed his thoughts on the subject through iambic-pentameter quatrains titled "The Dead Nation: An Elegy at the Tomb of the Cherokee Nation, by One of Her Own Sons." Published in the *Chieftain* for April 27, 1899, the poem traces the history of the fall of his people, beginning with white contact and civilization's seductive "art."

But then came Art, in rouge and ribbons dressed,
The source of awe, borne on the winged hours,
And, squat upon thine own salubrious west,
Bred pestilence and rot within thy bowers.

Art was followed by Might, its "adjutant," which

Wrenched off the hinges from the joints of truth,
And tore its system into shreds apart—
Repealed, in short, the moral code for sooth. [Chieftain, *October 11, 1900*]

Duncan touches here on a theme that he has relentlessly pursued in his prose writing, that is, the immorality of white society's actions against the Cherokees and, by extension, against all Indian peoples. He also returns here to a frequent theme, that of the white man's greed for land, obviously, but also, more insidiously, the installation of the capitalist economic system in place of the traditional Cherokee cooperative system. For Duncan, the dead nation of the title is more than the end of the political entity called the Cherokee Nation; it is the finish of a proud cultural entity as well. Fortunately, neither of these demises proved permanent.

In a truly apocalyptic poem, "A Vision of the End," published in the *Chieftain,* Duncan's main image is the terminus of time's river, a filthy sea. On this sea floats the wreckage of civilization, "government, a monstrous form," "The bodies of great syndicates / And corporations, trusts . . . all beasts of savage lusts," and "Greed— Immortal Greed— / Of all hell's hosts he took the lead, / A monarch of the slime." Even in this timeless morass, Greed lives on in Duncan's vision, devouring all that comes floating its way. And so, he pictures the end: "The years, all drifted down in slime, In filth dishonored lay." For Duncan, then, greed and the system that sustains it, unfettered capitalism, with its only end the amassing of money and materials, leads to a dark and dismal future.

Even in his lighter verse, a poem on Christmas, for example, and one on Thanksgiving, there are hints of the difficult times faced by the Indians. He also writes poems on courtesy and dignity, as if he is urging the need for these abstract qualities in perilous days. His poetic strength, however, lies in his political works. Another good example of this is the poem "The Truth Is Mortal," published in the *Chieftain* on the Muscogee (Creek) patriot Chitto Harjo, or, as he was called by the whites, Crazy Snake. Chitto Harjo led a movement of full-bloods against allotment, refusing to be entered on the allotment rolls. He wished to establish an independent Muscogee (Creek) nation and petitioned Theodore Roosevelt and addressed the U.S. Senate, asking that allotment of his people's land be rescinded. His rebellion was dubbed the Crazy Snake War by the newspapers and politicians, and in 1909 he was forced to flee into the Kiamichi Mountains after a shootout at his home. He later died of his gunshot wounds.

The poem compares Chitto Harjo to other Native fighters for independence, such as Emilio Aquinaldo, a Filipino leader who fought against Spain and later the United States for Philippine independence; Osceola, captured through the treachery of the U.S. Army; and Sitting Bull. Crazy Snake, as Duncan calls him, lives on with the souls of these men. In his final stanza, the poet sees the "truth" of these men dying with them:

> The truth that lives and laugh's a sneak,
> That crouching licks the hand of power,
> While that what's worth the name is Weak,
> And under foot dies every hour. [Chieftain, November 3, 1898]

The defeat of resistance against the all-powerful forces of the United States is inevitable, Duncan seems to say, even though truth and morality are on the side of the oppressed people. This is a most gloomy outlook, but it is the only conclusion that Too Quah-stee felt that he could draw after a careful perusal of the political facts.

Another Cherokee who wrote well and thoughtfully in the nineteenth century was William Eubanks, or Unenudi. Eubanks, the son of a white father and a Cherokee mother, was well educated and became one of the leading intellectuals of Indian Territory. The Civil War came to the nation when he was a young man, and Eubanks joined the Cherokee regiment under Stand Watie, fighting for the Confederacy. At the end of the war, he became a teacher, but because of his knowledge of both Cherokee and English, he became a translator for the *Cherokee Advocate*, a post that he occupied, except for brief interruptions, until 1906, when the paper ceased publication. He also translated the constitution and laws of the nation into Cherokee so all citizens could read them and translated for the Cherokee committee negotiating with the Dawes Commission in the 1890s. A self-taught linguist, he invented a shorthand method to be applied to the syllabary, as discussed in Chapter 5; however, it came too late to be used by court reporters in Cherokee courts, where it would have been most useful. Under the pseudonym Cornsilk, he also wrote political pieces that expressed what many Cherokees were thinking in the late nineteenth century as they watched their nation fall prey to ravenous outsiders.

Eubanks was truly an intellectual. As an essayist, he researched ancient languages, religions, and philosophies. Theosophy, a mystical set of teachings practiced by Madame Helena Blavatsky and William Butler Yeats, enjoyed popularity among thousands of Americans and Europeans in the late nineteenth century, mostly those who lived in urban settings. Eubanks, far from the crowds of the cities, became interested in the movement and wrote essays attempting to explain its tenets to the Cherokees. He also wrote on Christianity, tracing the origins of that religion to early Cherokees. In 1893, his opinions on these subjects were sought after, and he lectured on these and other topics throughout the South.

Eubanks, like most nineteenth-century thinkers, was also interested in science. He researched scientific subjects and formulated theories on various natural phenomena, with varying results. No Cherokee writing at the time could ignore politics, and Eubanks was no exception. Writing under his pseudonym Cornsilk, he fulminated against the Dawes Commission's plans for allotment and tribal dissolution. He, like Duncan, offered cogent arguments on legal and moral grounds against these federal policies. Publishing his work in Indian Territory newspapers, he found that he was in agreement with the vast majority of Cherokees, but, of course, his arguments were directed at people who were not interested in what the Indians thought or wanted. Eubanks married Eliza Thompson; among their children was another writer, Royal Roger Eubanks, who was also a teacher, a professional newspaper cartoonist, and an artist.

Eubanks wrote on serious subjects, such as scientific principles and philosophy. These articles are of interest not only because of what the writer says but also for the level of sophistication of their audience that they imply. Although they are not deeply philosophical treatises, they go beyond the level of practical tips for the farmer and homemaker, news stories, and reprinted fiction that were the meat of the newspapers of the day, especially the nonurban ones. The decision of the writer to publish in this venue, as well as the editor's decision to print these articles, implies an interest in this kind of writing among a substantial portion of the Cherokee readership. Eubanks's work helps us draw some conclusions about the education level of the population and about the kinds of subjects to which they were drawn.

Eubanks's essays on Theosophy were published in the *Cherokee Advocate* and thus were guaranteed a potentially large audience. " 'Theosophy' or Wisdom Religion and Its Opponents" appeared in the October 26, 1892, issue. He prefaces his work with a quote from "Bstan-ligsur" that sounds very much like the Golden Rule: "Hear ye all this moral maxim; and having heard it keep it well: Whatever be displeasing to yourselves never do to another." Because one of Eubanks's major ideas on religion was that all sects were related and essentially followed the same principles, the epigraph is apt. He begins his essay with a reference to the fact that articles on Theosophy have been appearing in the local press, no doubt reprinted from other publications.

In defining his subject, he provides a quote from Proverbs that he attributes to Solomon: "My son—if thou incline thine ear unto wisdom, . . . if thou criest after knowledge, . . . then shalt thou find the knowledge of God." He calls this yearning the pursuit of "universal" knowledge and identifies it as the aim of the Theosophists, who practice in various countries. "No man knows or can know anything more of his creator and Governor than what He has chosen to exhibit of Himself through His works, and what that really is, goes with men by the name of 'Truth.' " Theosophy, he says, lays "special stress" on two doctrines of truth, Karma and Reincarnation. He then goes on to define each of these.

Karma, according to Eubanks, is the idea that every human being will be rewarded or punished according to his actions. However, he points out, demonstrating his Protestant upbringing, Theosophy also teaches "justification by faith," the doctrine that belief in the deity is more important than good works. He defends what he sees as an apparent inconsistency with an analogy: "If after gathering my crop of corn, I cannot see how it is that I have reaped the results of my sowing and work, and yet would nor could have reaped any crop at all, had it not been for the soil, the atmosphere, the sunshine and the rain furnished me free—if I cannot see how both facts may be true and consistent with each other the fault may be in my seeing faculty and not in the things seen." Then he says, "So much for Karma," and turns to reincarnation.

Reincarnation is an old concept in the world at large, although a relatively new one in Indian Territory, he begins. Human individuals return to earth over and over again, taking on a new body each time, much as one would wear out a suit of clothes and replace it with another. The process continues until the soul accomplishes the purpose of living, and "then comes the end." These two central dogmas, Karma and Reincarnation, are at the heart of Theosophy, and it is through them that the soul "learns the lessons of experience" and regular growth takes place through several lifetimes until some sort of perfection is attained. These are "the golden stairs up the steps of which the learner may climb to the Temple of Divine Wisdom."

Eubanks ends his piece with some history of Theosophy in America. Tracing Theosophy as a European and American movement, as distinct from the ancient teachings, he identifies Madame Helena P. Blavatsky, who was born in Russia (as a countess), and who died in 1891. She and a couple of like-minded persons began the Theosophical Society in 1875, with branches in New York, London, and India, the supposed source of its precepts. When Blavatsky came under attack as a charlatan by scholars and journalists, she was defended by society members, and a public relations battle ensued.Here, Eubanks defends her as a friend to the human race who imparted this "secret science" to those who did not share the depth of her "spiritual perception."

Eubanks published an article provocatively titled "The Seed of the Plant and Spirit of Man" in the January 17, 1894, edition of the *Cherokee Advocate*; here, he explains the Theosophical analogy of the human being as a plant. The analogy starts with a seed. Just as a plant arises from the planting of a seed, so does a person grow from a spiritual seed or "ego," as it is called. The spiritual ego becomes "incarnated" when it becomes "clothed with flesh," just as the plant seed grows stems, branches, and leaves. The seed, then, is the first principle of life, according to Theosophy.

The second stage, or principle, is "vitality," or a life of the body. Just as a plant has life, so does the human animal, and just as a plant dies, so does the human body. At death, the spiritual ego, or seed, rests until it germinates again upon its "re-incarnation."

Eubanks is more cryptic about the third principle, the "astral body or double" of a human. His full explanation is as follows: "This paper is too short to furnish you the evidence to demonstrate the real existence of this astral man. But it is the body within the material body, and as the body is the casket in which is contained vitality, so this astral body is the casket or house in which dwells the soul of man." He is more forthcoming about the soul itself. The fourth principle is the "animal soul," which is the highest of the lower four principles and "the seat of our desires, emotions, the lower intellect and the lower reasoning faculty." Humans have this soul in common with the other animals, but ours is more developed. Many people, the Theosophists believe, never evolve beyond this animal soul, but some evolve into the three "higher principles" after shucking off the lower ones in a manner that resembles rising from the dead. Once this is achieved, "he lives for ever more."

Following close on the heels of this essay is another, "The New Age the Coming of Which This the Twentieth Century Is the Beginning," published in the *Advocate* on January 19, 1894. Here, Eubanks looks at the coming century, convinced, as many people often are, that a new century will usher in new ideas and practices and foster more "advanced" thinking, not considering that a "century" is only an arbitrary clump of contiguous years rather than any mystical entity. Eubanks's predictions for the New Age that will supposedly be initiated on January 1, 1901, are based on what he calls the Alcyonic Cycle. This, he explains, is a period of approximately 26,000 solar years, the time the universe takes to complete one rotatation around the "Alcyonic Pivot." This rotation is powered by the Pleiades, the constellation of the "seven sisters," who, presumably, are tied to the seven principles of Theosophy. Eubanks admits that the "secret of the hidden power" of the Pleiades is unknown to us because we lack the necessary understanding. One thing we do know, however, and that is that the universe is divided into four quarters, divided by a cross, and each quarter is ruled by a subordinate deity. The age that will end with the start of the twentieth century is called Kali Yuga, or the black age, and is ruled by the evil Dragon Star. The evil influence of the Dragon Star permeates every human endeavor; as proof, Eubanks points first to the East. "Look at the civilized Christian powers of today in their united efforts to dismember, loot, rob and massacre the people of the Chinese empire," he writes, referring to the nineteenth-century imperialist machinations of Western governments to take control of African, Asian, and island nations for economic and military ends. "Look at the Christian missionaries sent ostensibly to preach to the heathen Chinese the gentle gospel of Christ urging the powers to rob and loot wealthy families among the Chinese." Eubanks then strikes home: "Look at the civilized Christian intruder in the Indian Territory through the instrumentality of the statehood newspaper and the pulpit, urging, petitioning, praying and memorializing Congress of the United States to open up the lands of the Indian to white settlement, suspend the laws of the Indian nations, abolish their councils and governments, and in a manner exterminate the race in order that their lands may be inherited by the merciful, just and upright Christian of the Dragon Star." If any argument was going to persuade his Indian Territory audience of the validity of his unorthodox views, it would be this one. Something must be motivating the professedly civilized and Christian despoilers of the Indian nations, and the Dragon Star was as good as any reason given thus far.

But now, at the dawn of the New Age, it is time to take heart, Eubanks writes. He predicts what will happen in the new century: "The age of the resurrection of truth, morality, justice and uprightness is to make its appearance once more as it often has done in the past golden ages of peace and wisdom." He sees that "instead of low-minded preachers peddlng out Grecian myths for Indian land and money we will have noble sons of God teaching the truth." The seven great religions will put aside their differences and "dance in the mystic circles of moral truth," the seven sisters of the future. As for the Indians, "the remnants of the despised red races now stuggling in their weakness because they have refused to bend the knee to Belial, will be exalted in the position of truly civilized races." He sees them partaking in a new nation that will arise in which "the pulpit will wear no sanctimonious mask to cloak hypocrisy . . . there will be no chosen few—no preordained elect—no sainted patriarchs—no unctuous flatterers of men—no crime condoning sacraments." Philosophy will reign supreme and will bring with it peace and wisdom.

As the twentieth century and the impending doom of the Cherokee Nation approached, Eubanks continued to apply Theosophical concepts to the political situation. His "Measure for Measure," published in the *Advocate* for July 11, 1894, uses an Essenian text reflecting the doctrine of Karma to comment on the broken treaties. The text, "That which you measure out to other men shall be measured to you again," applies to the U.S. government in that just as it turns a blind eye to those who violate sacred treaties in their quest for Indian land and material gain, so shall the "nihilist, the anarchist, the striker, the up-rising of that foreign pauper against the capitalist of your country" cause grave injury to the United States.

Eubanks's condemnation of contemporary religion echoes Duncan's criticism of the immorality and hypocrisy inherent in the actions of the Christians seeking to destroy the Indian nations politically and economically, with little regard for the human consequences of their deeds. This bitter insight appears throughout his writing during the 1890s. In another piece, he writes that he is not a preacher, "for the word preacher is becoming synonymous with fraud. Remember also that we are not dealing with religion, for the word religion is becoming to be synonymous with the word farce."[10] As for spiritual belief, he exhorts his reader to "love the Lord thy God, and thy neighbor as thyself." Eubanks enlarges on this dictum: "For every man and woman and every responsible human being to love his own individual God, Higher Self, or Spiritual Ego, which is the only God with whom we can communicate, and with whom we can communicate only by meditation and concentration of the lower mind. As long as we are unacquainted with our own God, or refuse to keep the commandments of our Higher Self, it is absolute nonsense to address our petitions to, and expect to be heard by the Absolute Deity." Thus in Theosophy, Eubanks finds a spiritual reality to replace what he sees as the failed system of Christian religion, with all its contradictions and hypocrisies. He is able to salvage, however, certain truths from the orthodox beliefs and incorporate them into his new array of spiritual truth.

That he used his writing to persuade his fellow Cherokees to abandon the religion of the missionaries and in many cases of their parents is in many ways remarkable, especially because he wished to replace Christian orthodoxy with Theosophy, an even more unfamiliar system of thought that claimed the exotic Far East as its birthplace. Although it may be maintained that the Levant, the birthplace of Judaism and Christianity, was no less exotic to the people of Indian Territory, they at least had a nodding acquaintanceship with the area thanks to the widely circulated King James Bible and its Cherokee translations. It is hardly surprising, then, that Eubanks's attempts to influence the Cherokees to move away from Christianity did not appear to be effective.

Although Eubanks's disdain for contemporary Christianity had its roots in his observation of its adherents, especially those who expressed belief but acted counter to its basic tenets, another factor was present in his writing that supported his religious views. Eubanks was a student of the history of religion and had clearly read widely, if not deeply, in the subject. At the time Eubanks was writing, the public, as well as the scholarly community, was very interested in ancient thought. Various attempts to trace the origins of religions and philosophies were put forward, some based on scientific evidence, others based more on surmise and pseudoscience. At the same time, much attention was being given to the fledgling discipline of anthropology; here, too, various theories arose among both professionals and amateurs. Ideas on the origins of various peoples were rampant, and notions on both the similarities and the differences among the "races" were popular even among those with no training in science. At times, dubious social and political policies were formulated that were based on anthropological theses that were discredited later. Eubanks, whose scientific education was informal and selective, was one of the amateurs who delved into these subjects.

The result of this line of study was a thesis that may be summed up in the title of an article Eubanks wrote for the *Cherokee Advocate* of January 12, 1901: "The Red Race, Originators of the Ancient Apollo Worship, Now Known as the Christian Religion. As Proof We Give the Cherokee Legend of the Son of Man and U-tsa-yi." The immediate impetus for the article was a request from the *Advocate*'s editor, William T. Loeser, for a sketch of the ancient and legendary history of the Cherokees. Eubanks begins his tale with some comments on the origins of the original people of America. Modern scientists err in stating that the Indians came from Asia, he writes, and he looks to the tribes themselves for their origin. Many Indian cultures claim in their creation stories that they were placed in North America from the beginning. Those cultures that have a migration in their origin story say that they crossed no land, or that they crossed a bridge that subsequently sank into the sea.

Eubanks, with his deep interest in the Cherokee language, claims that although the Cherokee people are not "Greek, Hebrew, Egyptian, nor Hindu," words from those people's languages appear in their language. Further, Cherokee rites and religious customs resemble those of the ancient Jewish and Egyptian religions, and the original name of the people means "lights received from the sun." This evidence is offered as proof that the Cherokees are part of an "ancient Solar race." Eubanks goes on to credit the "Red Race" with "inventing or receiving from a divine source the great religions of the world, as well as building the greatest structures in the world together with discovering and formulating the grandest scientific truths of record." Eubanks is clearly taking his cue from Albert Ross Parsons (who was principally a musician, but who also considered himself an Egyptologist and a historian of religion. His book *New Light from the Great Pyramid: The Astronomico-geographical System of the Ancients Recovered and Applied to the Elucidation of History, Ceremony, Symbolism, and Religion*, published in 1893, is grounded in his study of Egyptology and religion and focuses on the concept of Adam Kadmon from the Kabbalah, a concept of original humanity or an archetype of the human soul. This concept has similarities in other ancient religions, such as Manichaeism, Gnosticism, and Sufic philosophy.

Eubanks, taking his cue from his sources, especially Parsons, introduces his main thesis with "it now appears that the red race of America, of whom the Cherokee is a direct descendant, were not only the builders of Stonehenge in England, but were the originators of the Ancient Apollo worship, known at this day and time as the Christian religion." As proof, he presents the Cherokee legend of

U-tsa-yi and the Son of Man, as well as the account of Plutarch in which he tells of the coming of Greeks to America to participate in the worship of Apollo or Saturn. Incidentally, Eubanks goes on, this accounts for the many Greek place names in the Appalachian area.

Eubanks's account of Ogyie, or the Great Gambler, coming among the Cherokees also interprets his main adversary, Son of Man, as being the youngest son of the Great Man, whom Eubanks calls the "American Jupiter." In the legend, Son of Man defeats the evil Ogyie and imprisons him in a cave on Lookout Mountain. The Cherokees call this site "Saturn Yuga," according to Eubanks, which the whites mispronounce as Chattanooga. To make the connection with Plutarch, Eubanks uses another source, C. A. King, editor of Plutarch's "*Moralia (XII): Concerning the Face Which Appears in the Orb of the Moon.*" Plutarch writes of an island far out in the Atlantic called Ogygiah, on which, the inhabitants claim, Saturn is imprisoned by Jupiter. It is from the people of Ogygiah, says Eubanks, that the Greeks adopted the worship of Saturn and, in turn, introduced it to Europe.

On the origin of Stonehenge, he points to an ancient source, Diodorus Seculus, who claims that the circle was built as a temple to Apollo. On the basis of this assertion, Eubanks makes some assumptions: "Great Britain could not have received the religion of Apollo from Greece, for it is expressly said that the religion of the Apollo of Greece came from the Isle of the Hyperborians, or Britain. To find the birth place of Apollo in America is a natural and credible explanation of the mystery of Stonehenge." Eubanks then takes his readers from Wiltshire to the Nile valley, where the "Hiddkelic race" built the great pyramid of Giza. The Hiddkels derived from the Biblical Esau, according to his source, Parsons, who bases his statement on that patriarch's "color." From there, Parsons extrapolates that "this race excels in all the branches of literary and scientific attainment that gives beauty and strength to a nation," giving it the technological expertise to build such a great edifice.

In continuing to construct his historical edifice, Eubanks next turns to another linguist-anthropologist, Augustus Le Plongeon, an early student of the Mayan language, who believed that Egyptian hieroglyphics and Mayan writing were similar.[11] Eubanks, and presumably Parsons, conclude from this that the Indians built the pyramids, and that both the Mayan and Egyptian pyramids derive from the Ohio River mounds. Further, Eubanks conjectures that the name Tahlequah comes from the Telchines, Egyptian priests who escaped to Mauritania when Atlantis was destroyed and who gave their names to the Tellegewi, or Muscogees.

In addition to these delvings into the ancient origins of the Cherokees, Eubanks's writing touched on the realm of science in an earlier series of articles published in the *Cherokee Advocate* in the 1880s. Although some of his scientific ideas are pure conjecture with little basis in fact, his arguments are so constructed as to seem plausible. Many important experiments in electromagnetism were conducted around this time and were being reported in the news media, including advances in telecommunications. The public read about what scientists were doing and eagerly awaited the next advance in science and technology. Magnetism and electricity were still mysterious forces, especially to the lay population. Perhaps in response to this public curiosity, Eubanks published a piece titled "Magnetism— What Is it?" in the *Advocate*'s January 19, 1883, issue in which he attempts to answer the question posed by the title. He begins with comments on the Chinese, who gave the compass to the Europeans. Eubanks writes that one could go to Chinese scientists and inquire about the nature of magnetism, but "it would be more honorable and christian-like to steal the secret and then claim it as our own." But because neither of these options js open to him because of his lack of Chinese-language skills, he will solve the problem himself.

Magnetism, he writes, is "pure matter acting through a compound material substance," and he further defines the latter as "any kind of matter that is composed of two or more elements of matter of different kinds, such as rocks, water, iron, etc." Iron or steel is the medium through which the magnetic force acts. However, not just any chunk of iron or steel will do; it will first have to undergo an alteration of its molecules by having a charge of electricity run through it. Magnetism is pure matter, that is, matter "in its original, unadulterated, uncompounded ultra-gaseous state." Once electric current passes through iron or steel, it is said to be magnetized and will respond to the larger positive and negative forces that are constantly flowing in the atmosphere. Eubanks is alluding to recent discoveries of the magnetic fields present around the earth. The

positive and negative poles of the magnets thus respond to the positive and negative elements in the earth's magnetic field, according to
Eubanks.

In back-to-back articles in the *Advocate* of January 11 and 18, 1884,
titled "The Celestial Visitor," Eubanks examines a strange phenomenon he has sighted in the skies at dusk and dawn, red and yellow
hues that are of unnatural consistency and duration. In the first article, he describes the phenomenon, and in the second he looks at its
causes. Eubanks explains explosions on the sun and then goes on to
explain the earthly lights as being manifestations of these "sun-
spots." Although today's scientists would correct him on several
points, he makes a plausible argument for his theory on the basis of
available knowledge.

Continuing in this scientific vein, Eubanks next takes up the subject of meteorites, wrongly concluding that they arise in the earth's
atmosphere, and that their material is terrestrial. This theory relies
on Eubanks's study of magnetism and especially on the idea that the
earth acts as a giant magnet, accounting for the aurora borealis and
other phenomena. "Meteoric dust," he writes, "is the stuff of those
streaks of light across the nighttime sky." The earth possesses a
"magnetic atmosphere" that resembles the "aqueous" one necessary
for the hydrologic cycle. This magnetic atmosphere is full of metallic particles that respond to the magnetic fields of the earth. These
metallic particles, or meteoric dust, respond to the positive-negative
attractions of the North and South Poles and thus streak their way
across the sky, propelled by those attractions. This dust is subject to
extreme heat generated by electromagnetic sources that makes the
metallic particles glow. The result is visible on the surface of the
earth. From time to time, the metallic dust aggregates into larger
lumps, which then fall from the sky as meteorites.

In all these literary forays into the scientific realm, Eubanks is
blending his observations of the natural world with what is available for him to read about it. His printed sources of information took
the form mostly of works by amateur or hobbyist naturalists, a great
many of whom were publishing in the nineteenth century. Some of
these writers did in fact put forth compelling and valid arguments
about our physical environment; others were less reliable. It must
have been difficult for Eubanks, who was situated in a place where

access to reliable scientific information was limited, to separate the wheat from the chaff. But his scientific writing reveals a curious, discerning mind in a man with superior powers of observation, combined with a talent for writing. The result was interesting reading for his public.

When John Rollin Ridge headed to California in the middle of the nineteenth century to participate in the gold rush, he was not the only Cherokee to do so. Wagon trains were organized at Fort Smith, Arkansas, for the long journey, and many young Cherokees joined them, lured, like so many others, by the prospect of easy riches. Edward Wilkerson Bushyhead was such a man. He, like Ridge, abandoned the mining idea shortly after arrival in the new state and instead turned to a journalistic career.

Edward, or Ned, Bushyhead was born in Tennessee on March 2, 1832, just before his parents removed to the western Cherokee Nation. His father was Jesse Bushyhead, a leading man among his people who grew up bilingual and attended the American Board of Commissioners for Foreign Missions school at Candy Creek in Tennessee. Jesse was a close associate of Evan Jones in both Jones's religious and linguistic activities. Under Jones's tutelage, he was licensed to preach by the Baptists and was ordained to the ministry in 1833, when he was employed by the Baptist Board. Bushyhead was a good linguist, so he was called on to assist Jones in the translation efforts. In 1835, he was elected to the National Council and later became chief justice of the Cherokee Supreme Court.[12] When the Cherokees organized themselves into contingents for removal to the West, the elder Bushyhead led about a thousand people to the new lands.

The Bushyhead family settled just west of the Arkansas line at a place at first called Breadtown because there, rations were distributed to Cherokees arriving from the East. Jesse Bushyhead erected some buildings there that became the seat of Evan Jones's operations discussed in previous chapters, and the name was changed to Baptist Mission to reflect this. Jones's press, with both Cherokee and English fonts, was set up in one of Bushyhead's buildings, Ned Bushyhead began to learn the printer's trade at Baptist Mission, then leaving to work on the *Cherokee Advocate*, learning more about operating the press and setting type. Carolyn Foreman reports that he also worked in a printing office in Fort Smith, Arkansas.[13]

Ned Bushyhead got caught up in the California gold rush fever sweeping the country at midcentury and in 1850 joined a wagon train leaving for the West from Fort Smith and led by his brother, Dennis W. Bushyhead, who later returned to the Cherokee Nation and served as principal chief. Ned's train was made up of three different parties that banded together for the difficult journey. After an arduous trip, he landed at Placerville, a mining town in El Dorado County in northern California. Having no luck there, he moved to Tuolumne County and continued to search for the elusive metal. Still later he moved camp to Calaveras County, where he is listed as a miner in the 1860 census. Around this time, though, he abandoned mining and reentered the printing trade. In this endeavor, he took on a partner, William Jeff Gatewood, with whom he took over publishing the local newspaper, the *San Andreas Register*, by 1867.

By that time, the Civil War had ended and the gold rush had died, resulting in a loss of population for the mining districts and an economic downturn. However, southern California was just beginning to boom. Gatewood's brother-in-law was a businessman in San Diego and loved to regale the *Register*'s publishers with success stories of southern entrepreneurs. In 1859, the *San Diego Herald* had moved to San Bernardino, leaving the huge county without a newspaper. Seeing a perfect opportunity, Gatewood and Bushyhead, along with José Narciso Briseño, moved their newspaper to San Diego. Briseño, who had learned the newspaper trade in the *Register* office, now became a partner in the firm. Bushyhead accompanied the press and other equipment on a coastal steamer from San Francisco, while the others traveled by stagecoach. When they arrived in San Diego, they established the *San Diego Union* in 1859, which is still published today. At first, the paper struggled, with a subscription list of less than a thousand and meager advertising revenue. Gatewood sold his interest to Charles P. Taggart in 1869, but after this, things picked up. Taggart sold out to William S. Dodge, so Bushyhead had yet another partner. As revenue and profits grew, the paper increased in size and moved into larger quarters. In 1870, Dodge was replaced by Douglas Dunn, a *Union* employee, and it was in that year that

Bushyhead scored a newspaper coup when he published a speech by President Grant in its entirety after receiving the text by telegraph. The *Union* bragged that it was the only "country" newspaper to be able to accomplish this. In 1871, Bushyhead and his partners decided to make the *Union* a daily, a big step for the time. At the same time, they continued to print the weekly edition, which, Bushyhead claimed, was delivered to every household in San Diego. The daily turned out to be grueling work for everyone connected with the paper, including its editor. In June 1873, Bushyhead retired from newspaper work and received $5,000 for his stock in the company.[14]

Bushyhead did not return to the Cherokee Nation, even though by this time, his brother, Dennis W. Bushyhead, was a leading figure there, serving as principal chief from 1879 to 1887. But Ned Bushyhead had his own political career in San Diego, serving as deputy sheriff of the county from 1875 to 1882. In 1882, he ran for sheriff on the Republican ticket and won; he was reelected in 1884. Both times he was nominated by acclamation. From 1883 to 1886, he also held the post of tax collector. Later, in 1899, he became chief of police of the City of San Diego. Sometime after the death in 1901 of his wife, Helen Corey Nichols, a native of New York, Bushyhead moved north again, to Alpine, California. In that locality, he died in March 1907, at age seventy-five. His body was sent to Tahlequah, where he was buried. Bushyhead was a highly respected citizen of San Diego and California, a member of the Pioneer Society, reserved for early settlers from the United States, and a member of several lodges.

Bushyhead's writing was entirely journalistic. He reported on the events of the day in San Diego County, a huge area stretching from the Mexican border up close to Los Angeles and from the Pacific Ocean to Arizona, and covered other California news. He also wrote on politics, generally restricted to state and local elections, as well as the activities of the local political parties and their candidates. The intimate knowledge of public affairs processes thus gained doubtless helped him considerably when he later embarked on his political career.

John Rollin Ridge, DeWitt Clinton Duncan, William Eubanks, and Edward W. Bushyhead were all sophisticated Cherokee writers, the equal of mainstream writers in other parts of America. Ridge and

Bushyhead are looked on as pioneers in West Coast writing, standing with a few other notable figures, such as Samuel Clemens, and Joaquin Miller. Duncan's work appeared both in Indian Territory and in mainstream publications, but he and Eubanks chose to write largely for an Indian Territory audience. In one way or another, they share a debt to their common Cherokee heritage, with its reverence for the written word and the opportunities that that national respect afforded them.

An examination of these writers' works, especially those of Ridge, Duncan, and Eubanks, demonstrates an enormous range of intellectual interests and knowledge. The following two chapters will investigate the work of other Cherokee writers. They will show that the extent of interests and talent of authorship were not limited to these four, although they furnished inspiration to Cherokee writers and thinkers for generations to come.

CHAPTER 8

POLITICAL WRITERS AND FEUDERS

The nations of Indian Territory in the second half of the nineteenth century were faced with opponents who threatened their very existence, most notably those who would make Indian Territory a federal territory—that is, one destined for statehood once certain conditions were met. The Indian nations opposed this movement because with territorial status would come an end to tribal sovereignty, the demise of tribal governments, revocation of all treaties, and dissolution of tribal citizenship. The Indians would become U.S. citizens and would be forced to compete with an influx of white settlers for land and mineral rights that had formerly been owned in common with other tribal members. The territorial bills flooded Congress and were tied to other threats to Indian national security, such as grants of tribal land to railroad companies and of mineral rights on Indian lands to mining and energy companies and the opening to white settlement of "unused" tribal lands, such as the "leased district" west of the Muscogee (Creek), Chickasaw, and Choctaw Nations and the Cherokee Outlet. The territorial movement was tied to allotment, in which land held in common by tribal entities would be surveyed, split into individual farm plots, and "allotted" to individuals or families. The "surplus" lands would then be open to white settlement.

The idea of making Indian Territory like any federal territory, along with allotment of Indian lands, was proposed as a policy before the Civil War. In 1848, Representative Abraham R. McIlvaine of Pennsylvania introduced a territorial bill in the House Committee on Indian Affairs that stipulated that whites be allowed to settle on lands not being "used" by the Indians. McIlvaine's bill did not pass, but Senator Robert Johnson of Arkansas in 1854 introduced another bill calling for Indian Territory to be split into three federal territories, the land to be surveyed, and the Indian governments to be eventually dissolved. In the future, too, were allotment of land in severalty and white settlement of "surplus" lands. Johnson's bill did not pass, and the territorial issue was pushed to the back burner and the heat turned down as the Civil War neared.

However, as soon as the war was over, the issue was moved to the front, and the heat of demand for land by veterans, immigrants, and the landless poor was applied. Senator James Harlan of Iowa introduced a bill soon after the end of the Civil War in 1865 with the approval of the former superintendent of Indian affairs for the Five Nations at Fort Smith, Elias Rector of Arkansas, and Governor Robert J. Walker of Kansas. Harlan's bill did not pass, but government officials used it as a basis for the negotiations over the 1866 treaties with Indian Territory tribes.[1] Harlan's bill was so popular with territorial supporters that Harlan was appointed secretary of the interior in 1865 and thus was in a position to push his ideas forward. Harlan was not alone in promoting the territorial idea in the government. After 1866, from four to eight different territorial bills were introduced each year, mostly by representatives or senators from western states. Cherokee national policy was to oppose all such bills, and the nation's delegates were pledged to identify and combat these threats. The Cherokees realized that not only were they engaged in combat with territorial forces in Congress, but they needed to fight a propaganda war for control of public opinion as well. Three Cherokee writers who fought vigorously in this battle for tribal sovereignty, both for and against, were William Penn Adair, William Potter Ross, and Elias Cornelius Boudinot.

These men were well-educated intellectuals, and each in his own way applied his intellect to control situations and to direct events. More than men of deliberation and reflection, they were men of action who attempted to bring their ideas to fruition. At the height of their careers, they applied themselves to the major issue of the day for the nations of Indian Territory: the territorial question. A fourth writer, Johnson Harris, sought to assuage the damage to Cherokee culture from territorialism, loss of national sovereignty, and allotment. His major contributions to his people included planning and executing policy to hold the Cherokees together as they experienced extreme centrifugal pressures to atomize their culture and reminding them of a shared history reaching back into the distant past.

Boudinot, Ross, and Adair were often in contact and usually at odds. Adair and Ross often were on opposite sides in internal Cherokee Nation politics but shared antiterritorial aims in their dealings with the federal government. Boudinot, unlike his brother William, was ostracized from internal Cherokee affairs mainly because he was an assimilated Cherokee in every way, dedicated to bringing territorial government and white settlement to Indian Territory and imbued with the same capitalist business ambitions as his white counterparts. He was as much at home in Washington society as in the West, and even though he became amicable with the Cherokee leadership in his later years, most of his time was spent in western Arkansas rather than in the nation.

William Penn Adair is a figure who loomed large in Cherokee affairs after the Civil War. Born in the eastern Cherokee Nation in 1830, the year the Indian Removal Act became law, Adair was the eldest son of George Washington Adair and Martha Martin. Both sides of his family were prominent members of the nation and produced many leaders. The Adair family, along with Martha's father's family, removed to the West in 1837 in covered wagons; the contingent, made up of Cherokee adults and children and African-descended slaves and their families and transporting household goods, livestock, and provisions, took around three months to make the journey.[2] Upon reaching Indian Territory, the Adairs settled on Saline Creek near Salina, while the Martins located their home two miles south on the Grand River near Locust Grove.

When the Cherokee public school system became operational, William Penn was one of the more promising pupils. Later, he attended schools outside the nation and eventually studied law. Like many in his family, he entered politics at an early age and was elected senator from Flint District in 1855 and then reelected for two more terms. In 1861, he married Sarah Ann Adair, a second cousin, daughter of Walter Scott and Nannie Harris Adair. Sarah died while she was a refugee from the nation during the Civil War.

The Civil War split the Cherokee Nation along a rift that had opened before Removal. At first, John Ross tried to keep the nation out of the war, but people succumbed to the arguments and entice-ments of Confederate recruiters such as Albert Pike, on the one hand, and the vociferous abolitionist preaching of Evan Jones, on the other. But when the Cherokee Confederate and Union regiments were formed, the divide was not between slaveholding mixed-bloods on one side and antislavery full bloods on the other. Rather, the split was between the Ross Party and the Treaty–Old Settler Party, a ri-valry that antedated Removal.

Adair joined the Confederate regiment organized by Stand Watie, brother of the slain Elias Boudinot, and was appointed lieu-tenant colonel under Watie, a post much sought after and envied by the other officers. Watie later took command of other Indian troops as well, and his regiment fought in many battles and skirmishes, mostly in Indian Territory and northwest Arkansas. In 1863, Watie's men were fighting other Cherokees on the Union side, and when the Confederates occupied the Cherokee capital of Tahlequah, they burned the log capitol building. Watie during this same period burned Chief Ross's home, Rose Cottage, at Park Hill. Ross spent most of the war years in Pennsylvania with his family and thus escaped capture or injury. Once Ross left the nation, the Confeder-ate Cherokees organized a convention to form a government, and many in the Adair and Martin families served as delegates. Stand Watie was elected principal chief but, of course, was never recog-nized by the federal government in this capacity. A month or two before the war ended, Adair was captured by Union Cherokees at his home, which his family members had vacated when they had fled to Texas as refugees. It was in Texas that his wife, Sarah, passed away.

After the war, the federal government demanded that the Chero-kees sign a new treaty that would supersede the older treaties. This step was necessary, officials asserted, because some of the Chero-kees had taken up arms against the government, but other factors came into play as well, including the status of Indian Territory and tribal sovereignty. Because several other tribes of Indian Territory had had Confederate factions, they, too, were forced to negotiate new treaties. The federal negotiators played a canny game, pitting the old enemies against one another, and discussed terms with two sets of Cherokee delegates, one from the Confederate side (even though they had never recognized Watie's government) and one from the Union side, headed by John Ross. Initial meetings were held at Fort Smith, but later the two delegations traveled to Washington, D.C., to negotiate there. William Penn Adair was part of the Confederate, or Southern Cherokee, group, along with John Rollin Ridge, Elias Cornelius Boudinot, Richard Fields, and Saladin Watie. Saladin Watie was Stand's son, and Ridge and Boudinot were Watie's cousin and nephew, respectively. Boudinot had been the Cherokee delegate to the Confederate Congress during the war. Although the outcome may not have been a foregone conclusion in the minds of the federal officials, the treaty was eventually signed between the federal government and the Union, or Ross, Cherokees. Ross himself died during the negotiations.

Both delegations engaged in writing a series of statements that were published as pamphlets during this time. Often written in the form of "memorials," or official communications, to Congress, the pamphlets were designed to state the delegates' positions along with supporting arguments aimed at government officials charged with making decisions about the particular issue at hand. But they also served the purpose of galvanizing public opinion in support of their cause, and therefore, they were printed as pamphlets for wide distribution. Since the days of the *Phoenix,* the Cherokees had recognized the power of the printed word to shape public opinion and thus to influence government policy. Adair had a hand in writing these statements, although Ridge's and Boudinot's fingerprints may be discerned as well. Adair was to engage in this form of written expression for the rest of his political life, and his talents in this regard were forged in a very hot fire.

In 1868, Adair married Susannah McIntosh Drew, the daughter of William and Delilah Drew. They lived east of the settlement of Adairs on Spavinaw Creek, but the couple also spent a good deal of time in Washington, D.C., where Adair was a Cherokee delegate for much of the period between 1868 and 1879. During this time, he was also a negotiator for the Cherokees, along with Henry D. Reese, with those Shawnees who were adopted into the nation. As a delegate to Washington, he spent much of his time combating a number of forces, mainly territorial and railroad interests intent on introducing white settlement into Indian Territory and the exploitation of its natural resources for profit.

As the territorial fire raged, the Cherokees and other tribes knew that they could not stay at home and watch the blaze. The *Cherokee Advocate* reported that in 1871 alone, thirty-one bills were expected to be introduced.[3] Leaders of the Cherokees and other tribes decided that they needed to have delegations in Washington on a more or less permanent basis to monitor events and react to them quickly by issuing statements or rebutting testimony before Congress and its committees with testimony of their own. Adair's presence in the delegation was helpful to the Cherokee cause. His skills as a memorialist and pamphlet writer served him and the nation well in the years he spent in Washington fighting the "territorial ring," as the nexus of senators, congressmen, Department of the Interior officials, and lobbyists who supported breakup of the Indian nations was called. One of the important functions of the delegates was to report back to the nation about the state of their affairs in the capital city; this, in addition to official reports to the tribal officers, took the form of letters to the *Cherokee Advocate*, the official national newspaper. In one such missive, Adair enumerated issues that threatened his people. Reduction in government funding was one issue, but the others he identified were intertwined: plans to abolish treaties with Indian nations, as well as to ignore treaties already in force; territorial schemes; and railroad incursions into Indian lands. Compounding these issues was the confusion concerning the recent addition of the Fourteenth Amendment to the U.S. Constitution. Many in Congress claimed to believe that the amendment made all Indians U.S. citizens. Members of tribes were not covered by the measure, but this was not made clear until 1884 in a Supreme Court decision.[4]

Adair had become a peerless orator, and he led the 1870 delegation on a tour of eastern cities in a series of speaking engagements in which the delegates sought to sway public opinion and newspaper editors to the rightness of the Cherokee cause. On their journey, reminiscent of the tour Elias Boudinot and John Ridge had made in the 1830s in an attempt to stave off Removal, they found many people sympathetic to their cause, including some members of Congress.

Contemporaries recognized that the delegates' skill in using both oral and written language to persuade at least slowed down the powerful locomotive of the territorial ring.

William Potter Ross was one of Adair's colleagues as a Cherokee delegate fighting the territorial forces during the 1870s. Before this time, however, he had built a strong record of service to the Cherokee people. William was taught by his mother before entering a mission school under William Potter, for whom he was named. He later attended an academy in Tennessee before entering Hamil's Preparatory School in New Jersey, after which he entered Princeton University, at that time called the College of New Jersey, and graduated with honors in 1842. Many of the funds for his higher education were furnished by his uncle, John Ross.[5]

In the eastern Cherokee Nation, John Golden Ross operated a trading post and warehouse at Gunter's Landing on the Tennessee River. When the main body of Cherokees removed in 1838, the elder Ross was forced to abandon his holdings, as well as his home, and to join his brother-in-law's family in the contingent for the trek west led by John Drew, a nephew of John and Eliza's. The group traveled on flatboats down the Tennessee River to Tuscumbia, Alabama, where Chief John Ross purchased the *Victoria*, a steamboat. The party embarked and was taken down the Tennessee to the Mississippi, entered the mouth of the Arkansas River, and sailed up that stream to within a few miles of its destination.[6] John Golden Ross's family settled at Park Hill, near Tahlequah.

When he returned to the Cherokee Nation from Princeton, William Potter Ross taught school and then was elected clerk of the Senate of the National Council in 1843. When the National Council established the *Cherokee Advocate*, he was appointed its first editor. As clerk of the Senate, Ross had honed his writing skills in the drafting of state papers; as editor of the *Advocate*, his writing took another direction. Ross practiced law and served in the Senate after he left the *Advocate* in 1848; in all his work, his command of language, both written and oral, served him well. One biographer points out, "He rapidly developed into a most versatile writer and fluent public speaker and became so recognized among the Cherokees."[7] Later, when he was a delegate to Washington, educated whites also recognized his reputation in this regard.

The Civil War interrupted Ross's career, as it did so many others. He enlisted in the Confederate army as a lieutenant colonel in the First Cherokee Regiment of Cherokee Mounted Rifles in 1861 and fought at the battle of Pea Ridge, Arkansas, in March 1862. In the year after this battle, however, many of the members of his regiment went over to the Union side. In the summer of 1862, Union forces occupied Tahlequah and Park Hill, and their commander offered Chief John Ross a military escort to Ft. Scott, Kansas. William Ross, although a Confederate officer on "parole of honor," made the journey with his uncle and then returned to Fort Gibson. As John Ross made his way to Philadelphia, where he spent the duration of the war, William joined the Third Regiment of Indian Home Guards, a Union force, and became the sutler at Fort Gibson. After the war, he was a "Northern" Cherokee delegate to the Fort Smith treaty conference, at which his long-running feud with Elias Cornelius Boudinot began. After John Ross died in 1866, the Cherokee National Council elected William Potter Ross principal chief, a post in which he served until the 1867 election of Lewis Downing. Downing died in 1872, and Ross was appointed to serve out the remainder of his term.

Ross directed the rewriting of the Cherokee Constitution to conform to the terms of the 1866 treaty, and in 1867 he helped write the treaty with the Delawares under which they were adopted into the Cherokee Nation. His interest in education for his people was intense, and he was instrumental in enlarging the Male and Female Seminaries, as well as the establishment of the Cherokee Orphan Asylum. As a tribal official, he supported education unwaveringly. Ink seemed to flow in Ross's veins, for if he was not writing various state documents as a chief, senator, or treaty negotiator, he was writing for newspapers. As noted in Chapter 6, he became editor of the *Indian Journal* at Eufaula in 1875–76, the *Indian Chieftain* at Vinita in 1883–84, and the *Indian Arrow* at Fort Gibson and Tahlequah in 1888–89.

Ross's editorship of the *Indian Journal* began as a move in opposition to Boudinot's establishment of *Indian Progress,* a proterritorial newspaper that published its first issues in Muskogee in the Creek Nation. The Creek Nation's government was appalled by what it considered an incursion by an enemy and quickly had the *Progress* expelled. Boudinot moved his paper to Vinita, where it survived for a few months before being sold, but, ironically, the *Indian Journal* became a long-lived, thriving newspaper.

Ross's experience with drafting the rewritten Cherokee Constitution after the Civil War was helpful when he became a delegate to the Okmulgee Councils, international meetings of the Indian Territory tribes beginning in 1867 that were part of the stipulations of the postwar treaties. The first meetings were attended by wary delegates who feared loss of sovereignty, an entirely appropriate response, given the circumstances. However, the federal government became impatient and insisted that the Indians continue to meet and adopt a constitution for the territory. In September 1870, the council met at Okmulgee in the Creek Nation; attending, along with Central Superintendent Enoch Hoag of the Office of Indian Affairs, were delegates from the Creek, Cherokee, Seminole, Chickasaw, Ottawa, Eastern and Absentee Shawnee, Quapaw, Seneca, Wyandotte, Confederated Peoria, Sac and Fox, Wea, and Osage Nations. The group sent a memorial to President Grant asking him to prevent the establishment of a "federal" territorial government for Indian Territory and to respect the treaties. The process of considering a constitution began at that time, but the drafting was left mainly to Ross. Ross returned to a reconvened council in December with the Okmulgee Constitution, which provided for an elected governor, a bicameral legislature, and a court system. Ratification required a two-thirds majority of Indian Territory citizens. Federal officials made some changes, but neither the constitution nor a revision introduced in 1875 was ever ratified.[8] By that time, the territorial ring in Congress had built up a full head of steam and was aiming for a complete end to Indian sovereignty, and Ross's attention was focused on dealing with this threat.

Other aspects of his illustrious career notwithstanding, it was Ross's service as a delegate to Washington that distinguished him most of all. Here his talents as a writer and orator were put the test in front of the whole world. His essay on an attempt to introduce a territorial bill into Congress in 1874 is a model of well-reasoned, well-documented rhetoric that rivals or surpasses most other examples of persuasive writing that appeared at the time on either side.[9] Territorial bills were based on just a few ideas, and most embodied these ideas in one form or another. Major issues were organization of a "civil government" over Indian Territory for "the better protection of life and property," and land allotment. The two went hand in hand because treaties had made it clear that either the governments of the Indian Nations had to concur with opening their lands, or, if no tribal government existed, the issue would be decided by the federal government. If the territory was "reorganized" under a territorial rather than a tribal government, the road would be paved to allotment and the opening of "surplus" lands to white settlement. The excuse "better protection of life and property" was a canard, given that any "lawlessness" was due to restrictions the federal government had placed on the tribal judicial system. Ross's essay takes all the territorialist arguments and refutes them, logically, systematically, and without emotion.

First, Ross looks at the many treaties the Cherokees have made over the years and shows how, since before the Republic existed, the Cherokees had been recognized as a sovereign people with the power to make laws and enter into agreements with other nations. He argues that this status has been maintained until the present day; as recently as 1868, the Cherokees treated with the United States, which proves that the federal government regarded the Indian nations as self-governing entities. Ross presents this seventeen-page review of the treaties painstakingly, going over each carefully and highlighting the points he wishes to make. He includes litigation concerning the treaties, as well as the land patents granted according to their terms. One patent in particular is cited, that of 1838, which refers to the tribal land west of Arkansas later known as Indian Territory and the tract known as the Neutral Land. The patent states, Ross points out, that the land will belong to the Cherokees "forever, subject to certain conditions therein specified of which the last one is that the lands hereby granted shall revert to the United States if the said Cherokee Nation becomes extinct or abandons the premises."[10] By pointing to this stipulation, Ross demonstrates to his opponents that he is well aware of the fact that they are trying to subvert the spirit and the letter of the Cherokee land patent by imposing a replacement government on the people.

Later, Ross takes on the false assertion that a territorial government is needed to provide protection for life and property. In fact, the lives and property of the Cherokees were well protected by its criminal justice system through district courts and sheriffs. White intruders did not fall under Cherokee jurisdiction by federal law, but because their presence in Indian Territory was problematic to begin with, the Cherokees did not see their lives and property as the Indians' responsibility. But Ross goes further on this issue. In his identification of the persons and entities who have an interest in overturning tribal governments, he mentions the "border press and telegraph," which "chronicle and distort every unfavorable or unlawful action that occurs or is provoked" in Indian Territory.[11] He is referring to those editors of border-town newspapers up and down Indian country who spread panic and misinformation about Indians because doing so was popular with advertisers who catered to the crowds of people poised to overrun Indian lands. He then establishes the degree of assimilation reached by the Five Civilized Tribes before examining the criminal justice records of the states surrounding Indian Territory. "Kansas has its Benders, its mobs, and its shootings along the line of its railroads and border towns," he writes, while Arkansas is currently offering rewards for fourteen murderers, according to the newspapers, "to say nothing of the proceedings of white and colored mobs and individual acts of violence which occur in her swamps and mountains." Missouri, Ross says, is no safer, because "the knights of the road, in broad daylight, cause the gatekeepers of city fairs to stand and deliver; mobs stop railway trains, plunder or murder their passengers, or shoot down the officers of the law, in order to hang men who have been consigned to imprisonment." White America, Ross says, is less safe than "lawless" Indian Territory.[12]

The territorialists often interjected the freedmen issue into the territorial debate. The freedmen were the people of African descent who had been taken to Indian Territory as slaves and who had been freed by the 1866 treaties. Some of these complained that they were still not regarded as first-class citizens, a grievance shared by former slaves all across America. However, the territorialists asserted that the Indian governments carried out racist policies against the freedmen, and that a territorial government would redress these wrongs. Given the record of neighboring Arkansas, Texas, and other southern state governments, this claim was tenuous. Ross shows that the Five Civilized Tribes, the only nations that held slaves, had made laws freeing their slaves and entitling them to all the privileges of citizenship. The complainers, Ross adds, were those persons of African descent who had come later to Indian Territory, who were not citizens of any nation, and who had "no legal right to be there."

Another territorialist argument was that the Indian nations stood in the way of progress. This term could mean many things to different people, but in this context, it was used as a euphemism for Manifest Destiny, that quasi-spiritual force of history that destined white people to occupy the U.S. land mass from east to west and also implied an embrace of all things technological. "Progress" was also used to denote an economic system based on profits derived from investments and the sale of commodities and services.

If the Indians rejected progress because their very existence defied Manifest Destiny, then they were guilty on that count. However, Ross argues, the Indian nations are on record as accepting technology, and he points to their reception of railroads as an example. Moreover, he says, his people are "progressive, rapidly progressive, and self-sustaining," as statistics will show. The Cherokee expenditure for education, more than that of any of the surrounding states, shows that the Cherokees are readying their children for the future. The huge effort to teach them the English language so they will become literate citizens in a literate age, he argues, demonstrates a deep understanding of what it means to be progressive in a way that surpasses the efforts of their white neighbors.

At this point in his rejoinder, Ross looks at the plan for territorial government as expressed in the bill and raises specific objections. He objects to the bill's failure to provide protection of tribal "organizations, legislatures, rights, laws, privileges, and customs" and to the appointment of the superintendent of Indian affairs as the executive of the territory. But his major objection targets section 12, devoted to the right to vote. Suffrage, Ross states, is the "Trojan horse." It shall be granted on the basis of an individual's " 'adoption of the customs of civilized life;' that of citizen of the United States upon legal residence." He asks, "Upon what customs and upon what lawful residence? And who are to determine these questions? What are the customs of civilized life and how many of them must an Indian have to be allowed the right to vote in his own country, or to be deprived of that right?" He further comments on these nebulous customs: "The customs of civilized life, as we know it, are both numerous and somewhat mixed; and who are to determine the degree of advancement in these things, the exact standard of excellence or proficiency in these customs necessary for the exercise of this important right?" Ross goes further by pointing out that one of the bill's provisions is to make the Indians citizens of the United States. If they are U.S. citizens, he argues, then the suffrage provision is unconstitutional.

Ross ends his argument with a request and a prediction. The Indians of Indian Territory are "quiet, peaceable, progressive, and friendly. They ask simply for your protection." The larger society has already promised it, he says, so now extend it. In this way, he predicts, instead of their extermination in a few years, you will get what you say you want, that "they may be imperceptibly mingled in blood, sentiment, intelligence, and high aspirations with your own descendants." Ross expresses his belief that history, allowed to run its natural course, will lead inexorably to assimilation. Ross's work of reasoned argument is a rhetorical masterpiece the tone of which he maintains to the end, finishing not with bombast or an emotional appeal but with a simple statement that if his logical and thoughtful approach is followed, the result will be what his opponents have expressed their wish for.

It is fair to say that not all Cherokees were in accord in opposing the aims of the territorial ring, as hard as that may be to believe now. According to J. H. Beadle, writing in 1873, there were three reactions to the proposed Okmulgee Constitution: the territorialist position, in favor of a territory open to white settlement after each Indian had received some land; the constitutionalist position, in favor of the Okmulgee Constitution, with U.S. citizenship but no white settlement and no imposition of "federal" territorial status; and the position of those who favored the status quo.[13] One of the hard-core territorialists was Elias Cornelius Boudinot. Boudinot, a son of the assassinated Elias Boudinot and a nephew of Stand Watie, had been educated in the East, where his stepmother had taken the family after her husband's death. He returned to the Cherokee Nation as a young man and began his search for a meaningful life, which for him meant a rise in his fortunes and those of his family. The status of the Treaty Party as a minority voice in Cherokee affairs rankled him, and he made himself an implacable foe of John Ross and his supporters. Boudinot edited the *Arkansian,* a newspaper in Fayetteville, Arkansas, home of many of the Ridge-Boudinot-Watie faction, where he engaged in politics and caught the eye of some influential politicians in Little Rock. He was offered the editorship of a newspaper there, the *True Democrat,* and took the job, which increased his visibility as a writer and political handyman. When the state secession convention convened in 1861, he was elected secretary, and he voted with the majority to keep the state in the Union. When Fort Sumter was attacked in April, the secretary of war ordered the Arkansas governor to provide 780 men to join the Union war effort. When the governor refused, the secession convention was reconvened, and the members voted nearly unanimously to leave the Union. When the work of the convention was done, Boudinot headed for Indian Territory, where Stand Watie was organizing his Confederate regiment.

Boudinot campaigned for the post of lieutenant colonel in that regiment, but Watie chose William P. Adair instead, setting the stage for a long rivalry that was to blossom into hatred later on in Washington. Boudinot settled for the rank of major and fought with distinction in several battles and skirmishes involving the Indian troops. When the opportunity arose for the Southern Cherokee forces to send a delegate to the Confederate Congress in Richmond, Boudinot was chosen for this role. He did his best to procure scarce supplies for Watie's troops and for the Southern Cherokee refugees, mostly women and children, who had fled to Texas when Union forces controlled the Cherokee Nation.

After the war, Boudinot played a major role in the negotiations of the treaty at Fort Smith and later as a delegate to negotiations in Washington. At Fort Smith, he first became acquainted with the Harlan territorial bill, which he was to embrace later. He, his cousin John Rollin Ridge, and William P. Adair drafted responses to the statements of the Ross delegation and lobbied intensely for their version of the treaty. As noted, the government played the two sides against each other, not a difficult task, and forced concessions from both Cherokee delegations. In the end, the United States made its treaty with the Ross faction. Boudinot returned to Washington in 1868 as a Cherokee delegate for matters relating to the treaty but also for the sale of the Neutral Lands in Kansas. He had not yet burned his bridges to the Cherokee government or become the ardent territorialist that he was to be.

His attitudes were changed by one significant episode in his life, known now as the Cherokee Tobacco Case. After postwar treaty negotiations, Boudinot looked around for an opportunity to make money and to set himself up as a man of means. He hit on a plan to manufacture plug tobacco as his avenue to this end. Plug tobacco was more than a method of nicotine delivery at the time. In the years after the war in certain areas, money was almost nonexistent. Debts and other obligations were being fulfilled by a warrant system, little more than a bankless checking-account arrangement, or by direct barter. Plug tobacco in Indian Territory and surrounding states began to take on the aspects of currency and was used as such, so it was a commodity in high demand. Southwest Missouri and northwest Arkansas were prime regions for growing red burley, a tobacco variety used for plug, as well as an area in which abundant grapes grew, the juice of which was used to sweeten the product. Further, article 10 of the 1866 Cherokee treaty stipulated that no excise tax could be collected on any item manufactured by a Cherokee and offered for sale inside or outside Indian Territory. With these factors in his favor, Boudinot, along with his business partner, Stand Watie, built a tobacco-processing factory in the Cherokee Nation, albeit only about one hundred yards from the Arkansas border, and began to sell Watie and Boudinot plug at a price that was lower than those of competing brands because it was not taxed the thirty-two cents a pound that other brands were.

Naturally, other tobacco producers from as far away as St. Louis began to complain and convinced the federal tax collectors based in Arkansas that Boudinot was breaking the law. The argument reached a head when marshals from Arkansas crossed the border, destroyed the factory, and arrested Boudinot. He was released when his case came up in federal court, where he made the argument that treaty law superseded the excise statutes, especially because he had began the business before the tax became law. His case reached the U.S. Supreme Court, where the question was whether the revenue act of 1868 applied to Cherokee citizens, given the terms of Article 10 of the 1866 treaty. The prosecution argued that actions of Congress had precedence over treaties, and when discrepancies arose, it was up to Congress to set things right. In the Court's decision, 78 U.S. 616 (1970), three justices decided for the prosecution, three dissented and decided for Boudinot, and three did not participate. With this "majority," the issue was decided against Boudinot's position. He quickly saw the far-reaching effect for Indian sovereignty; in a letter to Watie, he announced the disappointing decision and declared it "the death-knell of the Nations." It showed that treaties could be discarded, disregarded, or altered at any time by Congress, and that their force in law was thus reduced ummeasurably. From this moment, Boudinot recognized that Indian governments could be wiped out with a stroke of the pen, and that fighting against the lawmakers was a futile exercise. He determined that henceforth he would devote his energies to working for a territorial plan that would benefit his people and, of course, his family and himself.

Boudinot embarked on his journey by using his contacts among politicians in Arkansas and Washington to open doors for him. One of these doors was to offices of railroad executives. He had drafted a bill in Congress in 1868 to incorporate "a Central Indian Railroad Company, to be owned and operated by the Indians of Oklahoma." Boudinot was farsighted enough to see that if the Indians were to be competitive in getting their goods to market, they would need rail transportation. However, many others in Indian Territory saw railroads as their enemy, a means of transporting white settlers to their lands. In addition, most of the territorial schemes included stipulations giving rail companies rights-of-way through the territory, along with land grants, supposedly for stations, work yards, and areas from which to harvest timber for ties and buildings. Some of the land grants were exorbitant, consisting of whole sections all along the right-of-way, that were clearly to be sold to settlers when the territory was "opened." However, the 1866 treaty provided for two railroads through the Cherokee Nation, one north-south, the other east-west. Two railroads were vying for the north-south route, one of which was the Missouri, Kansas, and Texas Railway Company, known as the Katy. Earlier, the Union Pacific Railroad, Southern Branch (UPSB), had been organized to take this route, and its stockholders tried to make a deal with the Cherokee Nation in which the Indians would contribute cash to complete the road and share in profits once it became operational. William Potter Ross and others on the Cherokee National Council were in favor, but the Southern Cherokees were against it because they believed that the Rosses would enrich themselves, while others opposed railroads altogether, so the deal fell through. The Katy was born when Levi Parsons, a Wall Street banker, bought controlling stock in the UPSB and re-named the line.

At this point, it was decided that the first railroad to reach the Cherokee border with Kansas would be awarded the right-of-way. The Katy began to build fast and furiously, and the Missouri River, Fort Scott and Gulf did the same via another route. At this point, Boudinot jumped into the fray on the Katy side, making friends with its superintendent, Robert Stevens, and agreeing to keep an eye on the competition and to report its progress to him. As part of the plan, Boudinot built improvements and put up fencing at Russell Creek, a few miles below the border, on prime grazing land. There he planned a cattle operation, including feed lots where cattle could be brought in from the range to be fattened up before boarding freight trains for points north and south. Stevens agreed to help bring Boudinot's plan to fruition. In the end, the Katy won the race to the border in June 1870, with Robert Stevens driving the last spike on the Kansas side while Boudinot drove the first spike on the Cherokee side. From that time on, Boudinot worked to advance the interests of railroads in Indian Territory, to the extent that he was identified as a railroad agent.

After serving as a Cherokee delegate in Washington in 1868, he traveled to New York City, where he had been invited by his old political cronies from Arkansas to be one of their delegation to the National Democratic Convention. His acceptance did not endear him to many other Cherokees because the Arkansas politicians were seen as part of the coalition from western states that was trying to extinguish Indian title to Indian Territory and open it to white set-tlement. In the next two or three years, Boudinot spent most of his time in Washington dealing with matters relevant to his tobacco case. Along the way, he made friends among the politicians who admired the writing and oratorical skills he used in his case, but he also won friends through his social skills; he was an entertaining presence at parties and other gatherings through his singing and

poetry recitations. In any case, he became known to the major territorialists, who saw the advantage in having an eloquent Cherokee
writing and speaking for their cause.

Boudinot was also active as a speaker, at first mostly at Indian
Territory venues, but later, as he became less and less welcome there
and as his fame grew among those favoring railroads, white settlements, and extinguishment of Indian government and land title,
throughout the country. He spoke to crowds in the western and
mid-western states and as would-be settlers flocked to Kansas and
areas close by, to large, enthusiastic audiences. At these gatherings
he distributed his pamphlets, supplying ammunition for the guns of
editors in small towns with merchants who catered to the influx of
whites. Thus while Adair was on the eastern speaking circuit trying
to garner support for the Cherokee position, Boudinot was speaking
in the Midwest and West to bolster the territorialist cause. Both addressed formal hearings in Congress, as well as speaking in rebuttal
to the assertions of the other side. From then on, a predictable cycle
began: a territorial bill would be introduced; William P. Adair or
William Potter Ross would argue against the bill, often by issuing a
memorial and a pamphlet containing the text of the memorial that
was sent to newspapers and made available to officials and the public; and E. C. Boudinot would respond, often reiterating the territorialist argument and adding points of his own. Of course, Boudinot
was also publishing his arguments in pamphlets financed by railroads and other territorial interests.

Boudinot's written arguments and speeches were crafted in rather
sophisticated ways and show him to be a master of classical rhetorical style. He used his education, specifically the teaching of Aristo-
tle and others on the forms of persuasive address, to press his views
on his audiences. These texts also show that he knew how to analyze an audience, and although the substance of what he had to say
seldom varied, his methods of delivery changed to suit his audience,
which usually was one of three types: government officials, especially congressional bodies; the people of Indian Territory; and
whites interested in the "Indian question" and, more specifically,
the question of opening territory previously reserved for Indians. For
each audience, he employed the three classical modes of rhetoric—
appeals to ethics, logic, and emotion—in varying degrees, depending

on his listeners. Adair and Ross used the same rhetorical techniques in both oral and written arguments. Ross and Adair were attempting to protect the status quo, but Boudinot believed that this course was folly, and that it was fruitless to try to stand up to the might of the U.S. government. He deemed it better to recognize the inevitability of the territorialist position and for the Indians to make the best arrangement possible for their people to live in the new world. After all, he argued, he had tried to stand on treaties to fight the Internal Revenue Service and had come away bloody.[14]

During the 1870s, the attacks on Indian nations' sovereignty intensified. The committees in both congressional houses that were charged with the oversight of territories were especially active. Ross, Boudinot, and Adair were present during many of the debates, Ross and Adair as Cherokee delegates, Boudinot representing "himself as a Cherokee," as he put it during testimony for an investigation instigated by his associate, Senator D. W. Voorhees of Indiana.[15] This hearing is worth examining because it not only clearly delineates the interests of the territorialists but also demonstrates the positions of the Cherokee delegates and of E. C. Boudinot, the thorn in their side.

The investigation began because of questions about bonds issued by the UPSB, mostly to Dutch investors. The railway had fallen on hard financial times after Boudinot helped it begin construction into the Cherokee Nation. Although the road was to extend into Texas, by the date of the hearing, it had advanced only to Vinita. The corporation, further, had been reorganized as the Missouri, Kansas, and Texas Railroad. The questions about the bonds had to do with whether the railroad had misrepresented to its creditors that it had received large land grants along the right-of-way from Kansas to Texas, which, if true, would have greatly increased the value of the bonds.

However, Voorhees widened the investigation to include two other issues, at least one of which had been inspired by Boudinot. Besides the bond question, the subcommittee charged with conducting the hearings took up the question whether money from the Indian nations' education funds had been diverted to support the delegations opposing "the organization of a civil government" over Indian Territory. Boudinot knew that the Cherokee government's accounting system did not make a distinction between the general fund and the education fund, so technically, the charge, as it related to the Cherokees, was correct. The third issue raised by Voorhees was "whether a civil form of government [i.e., a nontribal one] cannot be organized over the Indian Territory for the better protection of life and property," and whether the lands held in common by the tribes should not be "divided in severalty," that is, allotted.

What Voorhees had done was to adopt a tactic common to governments before and since: introducing issues unrelated to the one at hand in order to pass legislation that had less chance of passage through regular channels. The railroad investigation now became a sounding board for arguments made by the territorialists and others interested in dissolving tribal sovereignty and opening Indian Territory to exploitation by non-Indians.

The hearing began with the testimony of James Baker, attorney and railroad president, who denied the bond charges against his company. When cross-examination began, Adair demonstrated that his mastery of the English language was second to none in the building. He grilled Baker not only about railroad finances but also about the company's expectation for land grants along its right-of-way, as well as his views of Indian sovereignty. At one point, Adair asked him whether he had any knowledge of the Cherokee government, pointedly inquiring whether Baker had read the Cherokee Constitution, the nation's published laws, or other sources of information. When the attorney replied in the negative and admitted that he knew little about how the Indian nations were governed, Adair continued to press him. Probably unnerved by the Indian lawyer, Baker blurted out that although he did not know much about Cherokee government, he nonetheless considered it "an absolute mockery," a comment that betrayed a high level of ignorance, racism, and self-interest, fairly common among people in his position. When the committee chairman objected to Adair's line of questioning as "not proper," Adair and the other Cherokee delegate, Daniel H. Ross, protested that the Voorhees investigation was beyond the jurisdiction of Congress, an objection that was joined by the Muscogee (Creek) delegation. The hearing, however, went on.

The Choctaw and Chickasaw delegate argued that the tribes had a long history of self-government and that this history had been recognized by a series of legal precedents, chiefly *Cherokee Nation v. Georgia* (1831), in which the U.S. Supreme Court delivered a definition of sovereignty for Indian nations that stands today. Adair concurred in this argument and issued a formal protest to the committee disputing its jurisdiction on the matters of national sovereignty and internal allocation of tribal funds.

A series of protests were issued. At this point, it was Adair's turn to deliver the protest that he and Daniel H. Ross had prepared. Adair addressed in turn each of the resolutions on which the subcommittee was conducting its investigation. The first issue, that of railroad bond fraud, the Cherokee accepted. However, he objected to the second topic, that of the money expended on delegations and the possibility that some of it had come from education funds. "We object to such construction of said resolution as will enable your investigation to interfere with or molest our treaty and inherent rights of self-government, or with the disposition of our national funds after they are receipted for by our nation to the government under our treaties, except as to the school and orphan funds, to which we may submit, as an act of courtesy, for information for the Senate as well as the President."[16]

Adair's next point was directed to the third resolution, about which he said, "If this proposition relates to the establishment of a territorial government of the United States over our nation, we protest that, in view of our treaties and the necessities of the case, this cannot be done without the full and free consent of our nation and people." The Voorhees resolution notwithstanding, the territorial, allotment, and railroad bills that eventually were passed all stipulated the concurrence of a majority of the people affected. The fourth resolution concerned land allotment. Here, Adair pointed to a provision in the 1866 treaty that made allotting tribal land in severalty contingent on a request made to the federal government by the Cherokee government. Because no request was forthcoming, Adair argued, an investigation of this issue was uncalled for.

At this point, the Cherokee delegation issued a statement that "relates more directly to the freedom and liberty secured to our nation in the disposition of its own funds . . . [and] other views and facts in relation specially to the organization of a civil government or United States territorial government over our nation and people." In this part of the statement, Adair and Daniel Ross based their arguments on the treaties, especially the 1835 Removal treaty and the 1866 treaty. After citing the relevant portions of those documents, Adair said, "These treaty provisions, as interpreted by your Supreme court, and by the uniform practice of the Executive Department in dealing with our nation, recognize said nation to be beyond the pale of Congressional or departmental jurisdiction in its rights of self-government as expressed above. It has uniformly been so, and there is no instance that we know of where the reverse has been true."

Boudinot was a highly visible figure during this investigation; he gave testimony of his own and cross-examined witnesses, arguing with them when their views did not match his. At the same time as Adair announced his intention to file a protest, Boudinot declared that he disagreed entirely and wished to reply to the Indian nations' protests. Boudinot protested Adair's protest not only in the committee room but also in a pamphlet he issued for consumption in the East, Indian Territory, and its border states.[17] As a means of establishing his position, he took the opportunity to insert into the record two pieces of writing that he had done previously, one of which was the prospectus for the newspaper he had started, the *Indian Progress* (1875). The *Progress,* as its name implied, was an organ that advocated change in the status quo. It was unabashedly in favor of a reorganization of Indian Territory into a federal territory, U.S. citizenship for all Indians, and allotment of land in severalty. The prospectus synopsized these views. Boudinot had at first attempted to publish in the Creek Nation but had been forbidden by the national government there and had moved to Vinita in the Cherokee Nation. The paper caused quite a stir among the leading men of the Five Civilized Tribes, who considered Boudinot a viper in their midst. The *Progress* had been established on the precepts of the Caddo Resolutions, first given in Boudinot's speech in Caddo, Choctaw Nation, in 1875. As part of his rebuttal of Adair's protest of the hearings, Boudinot inserted the resolutions into the record. The resolutions consisted of the following points: reorganizing Indian Territory and dissolving tribal governments; recognizing a Grand Council, with members from all tribes, as the legislative body for the new territory; appointing a congressional delegate for the territory; forbidding any attempt at driving a wedge between full-bloods and other citizens; settling all Indian claims against the federal government; and barring any more resettlement of tribes in the territory.

But at the core of Boudinot's statement was the congressional act of March 3, 1871, which, together with the decision on his tobacco case, established that treaties were no longer to be made with the Indian tribes and, further, denied that the Indian nations were independent. This act and the tobacco case were the principles on which Boudinot based all his territorial machinations. If, he reasoned, Congress could supersede any treaties or agreements between the federal government and the nations, then the tribes had already lost their sovereignty and any semblance of self-determination. For Boudinot, the situation was very clear. In effect, Adair was arguing for the status quo as established by treaties. In his reply, Boudinot was insisting that the situation had changed drastically, even in the short time since the 1866 treaty had been signed.

The rivalry between William P. Adair and Elias C. Boudinot was a long one, going back to the Civil War, but it intensified over the years as they dueled with words, each constructing rhetorical edifices that the other sought to tear down with rhetoric. For the most part, they were evenly matched, with neither man gaining an edge. This led to frustration in each of them, and one day in 1880, their pent-up emotions came to a boil and resulted in physical assault. The two had joined some other men, Cherokee delegates and members of Congress, meeting in the office of the commissioner of Indian affairs. Upon leaving, the pair traded insults, and Boudinot attacked Adair with his walking stick. Further blows were exchanged, and the struggle ended with both on the floor. The frustration must have been powerful indeed, for at the time Boudinot was forty-five, and Adair, at fifty, was in the last year of his life. To fight like schoolboys in such a venue and in front of such witnesses must have proved embarrassing to both.[18]

A man whose writings attempted to hold the Cherokee Nation together at a time when pressure to fragment it was extreme was Colonel Johnson Harris, who served as principal chief after the death of Chief Joel B. Mayes. Harris was born in 1856 in Georgia to William and Susan Harris and received his Cherokee blood through his mother. William Harris died in 1865, and Susan brought her young son to the Cherokee Nation in the early 1870s, where they settled in the Canadian District. Other members of the family had come to Indian Territory in earlier years. Harris attended public schools in Georgia and later the Cherokee Male Seminary, after which he taught school for a while. He raised livestock in the Canadian District near Warner, where he married Nannie E. Fields, daughter of Cherokee notable Richard Fields and his wife, Rachel Elizabeth Goss. After Nannie's death in 1887, he married Mamie Adair, daughter of William P. Adair and his wife, Sarah Ann. The marriage lasted until Mamie's death in 1902, whereupon he married again, this time Caroline Alice Hall.

Harris was a competent man and was recognized as such by his fellow Cherokees. He was elected senator in 1881 and served until 1885, during which time he was elected president of the Senate. In 1889 and 1895, he was a delegate to Washington, and, in 1891 he was elected treasurer of the Cherokee Nation. Later that year, Principal Chief Joel B. Mayes died, and the National Council appointed Harris to serve out Mayes's term. During Mayes's first term, Harris had served as his secretary.

When Harris took the reins of office, the nation was in peril and knew it. Alarm bells were ringing in Washington because of the fires of rumor being set by unscrupulous land seekers and government officials eager to bring about dissolution of the tribes. A special Senate committee went to Indian Territory in April 1894 to investigate the rumors and returned with a report that claimed that Indian governments were "non-American" and "radically wrong," and that the situation was deteriorating rapidly. The Dawes Commission's first report of November 1894 informed Washington officials that the Indian governments had been taken over by persons with little or no Indian blood and that they had monopolized all the best land held by the tribes.[19] Harris could see that these damaging reports, as well as other rumors, might have the effect of splitting the citizens of the nation, not only creating a deeper rift between mixed-bloods and full-bloods but also fragmenting the freedmen and adopted citizens from other tribes, such as the Shawnees and Delawares. He also saw the immediate danger of these charges being used as evidence to advance the cause of those desiring territorial government, allotment of land and white settlement, and dissolution of tribal government.

As a defensive measure, he appointed a committee to confer with the Dawes Commission. He explicitly instructed the committee's members to insist on adherence to the treaty provisions that had guaranteed the right of the Cherokees to govern themselves in their own way. Further, he forbade them to discuss the allotment of lands in severalty, the whole point of the Dawes Commission's existence. As chief, he followed the same policy, refusing to negotiate with the commission on this issue. His bitter opposition to allotment continued after he was succeeded as principal chief by Samuel H. Mayes, who accomodated the Dawes men and opened the door to allotment of Cherokee lands. Mayes perhaps saw the futility of resistance, but Harris refused to budge an inch. His writing reflects his desire to maintain the status quo, but it also attempts to reach all segments of the Cherokee population to make them recognize the dangers confronting them all and see that their only salvation depended on their reinforcing their common bond.

Harris made a point of sharing his insights with his people. Whatever the issue, he was quick to prepare an address from the high office of principal chief to explain the problems that were before the Cherokee Nation. At a time when per capita payments were being made with the proceeds from the sale of the Cherokee Outlet, Harris saw a problem that needed addressing. Accordingly, he used newspapers to issue a warning. "To the Cherokee People" begins, "I deem it advisable, under existing circumstances to call your attention to the attendant dangers and the melancholy aspect of the present per capita distribution now going on in your midst, and to the necessary caution, on your part in your intercourse and dealings with the hundreds of adventurers, sharps, and tricksters now in the country for dishonorable purposes."[20] Harris was concerned not only for the welfare of individuals and families in this matter, but also for the damage these dishonorable men would do to the national reputation at a time when the Cherokee Nation was being painted as a lawless land of thieves and murderers. "The Good Lord knows," he wrote, "that we have to answer for enough bad characters in our country under ordinary circumstances, regardless of the flood that is pouring in from the adjacent states. Not only for their presence with us are we blamed, but for the crimes they commit, and by reason of them and their crimes we are threatened with political extinction and [they] subject us to the tender mercies of those who are encompassing our ruin." He finished with a plea to his compatriots not to support or encourage any of these intruders, and to remember that "much of our happiness and prosperity depends upon ourselves."

A few months later, in his "Third Annual Message," published in the *Cherokee Advocate* of November 7, 1894, he brought before his people the proposals of the Dawes Commission and added his responses to each. He begins with a statement concerning the general effect on the nation that the constant attacks from the territorialists have brought. "It is a wretched condition of a nation, with the solemn guarantee of the United States to protect it, to be always on the defensive simply with the arms of argument and the pitiful protestations of right and preference. Such a condition of affairs demoralizes industry, hinders progress and unsettles the aims of the people and keeps them in perpetual torment of apprehension." Further, he says, the state of affairs contributes to a belief that the Cherokee government is insecure, the title to our lands is shaky, and our culture is about to be demolished. This encourages intruders and criminals, further adding to the nation's difficulties. Harris then delineates the "findings" of the Dawes Commission, published as a series of recommendations:

Alloment of lands in severalty.
Removal of all "unauthorized" persons from homesteads.
Allotments to be "inalienable" for 25 years.
Claims against the United States to be settled.
Per capita payments of all tribal funds except education funds and money derived from the sale of town sites and mineral rights.
Boards to determine citizenship and the freedmen roll.
Territorial government, if the Cherokees concur.
Present government to continue until after allotment.
Intruders to be removed.

After presenting this list, Harris advises that a delegation to Washington be appointed and held in readiness because Congress's present term is due to run out shortly and "all business will be done with necessary dispatch." He then addresses the issues. "The fact cannot be denied that the lands of our Nation are the very foundation of our political existence and the source of our livelihood," he begins. Holding the land in fee simple is the only way for the Chero-kees to be "absolutely secure" in keeping their land. Once the na-tion succumbs to the belief and practice of the business world that land is "property," to be bought and sold like livestock or goods, the land will be lost. The Cherokees can hope to keep their land only if they adhere to Cherokee law, the basic tenet of which is that "every citizen owns, in his own right, a certain quantity of the Nation's un-divided land, of which he cannot be deprived as long as he remains in the country. By no manner of argument, consistent with our con-stitution can any citizen, as further evidence, claim, on account of possession, the land he occupies with any reasonable belief that he never will be molested while there is a single citizen, having equal rights with himself in the common property, is without his share. Room in the common home of the nation is provided for all." This basic rule, Harris believes, is at the core of Cherokee heritage, and once it is violated, the demise of the people will follow.

Harris's eloquence was appreciated by his people, and many were doubtless inspired by his words, but in the end, the opposition over-whelmed him and his people with sheer numbers and the great power of the federal government. After he left the chief's office, Har-ris continued to serve the nation in various roles that did not require public writing, but he continued to publish on topics not directly related to politics. He had a knowledge of Cherokee history and be-gan a series of articles on that topic, hoping to keep before the Cherokees a sense of their past, even though many of their institu-tions had been demolished.

One of his pieces, published in the *Tahlequah Arrow* of March 9, 1907, "Old Cherokee Laws and Treaties," traces written law as far back as anyone can remember. Harris describes that first regulation as one that instituted "regulating parties" in each district; their du-ties included pursuing horse thieves and other robbers, as well as making sure that heirs received their parents' property, and gener-ally looking after things in their areas. This written law was passed by the head chiefs and warriors in a national council at Broom Town in the eastern nation on September 11, 1808. At the time, Harris says, the Cherokees had three head chiefs: Black Fox, principal chief, Path Killer, second chief, and Toochaler, third chief. This act was the be-ginning of a formal Cherokee government. Harris writes, "From this time written laws gradually superceded usage and custom; the enactment and enforcement of laws being done by members of a body termed 'council' and the head chiefs, until May 6, 1817, when it was agreed that there should be thirteen members elected as a standing committee, whose legislative action should be concurrent with that of the council and the head chiefs." Harris then traces the political evolution of the nation through the early years to the first constitution in 1827 and the institution of a republican form of government. He then writes about the new constitution of 1839, formulated after the Cherokees were forcibly removed from their homeland, and the new laws imposed under the post–Civil War treaties. With the following epitaph for the nation as he knew it, Harris ends his piece: "The Cherokee Indians enacted their own laws, lived in their own vineyard, educated their children to a higher life and it may be said of them 'thou hath done well.'"

Harris, like other Cherokees before him, used his writing and rhetorical skills in defense of his people and to confound their enemies. His logic, appeals to common sense, and command of both bald facts and nuances of meaning made him a formidable opponent in the halls of Congress and in the public forum. Harris is near the end of a long line of Cherokee statesmen who rival the great American masters of rhetoric and writing that enlivened the intellectual climate of the nineteenth century.

CHAPTER 9

A STEADY STREAM OF
CHEROKEE WRITERS

The literary history of the Cherokee Nation includes several figures who wrote in various genres. Examples discussed in previous chapters are John Rollin Ridge, DeWitt Clinton Duncan, and Colonel Johnson Harris. But others were a part of this tradition as well; many started out as newspapermen during a century when journalists were called on to provide political or literary essays and so naturally branched out from their duties as news chroniclers. Among these writers was William Penn Boudinot, son of a man who was anathema to many in the Cherokee Nation.

Much of nineteenth-century Cherokee history was marked by the antipathy between the Ross faction and the Boudinot-Ridge-Watie supporters, but the animosity began to abate somewhat in the 1870s, largely because of a practical political alliance between former rivals who had opposed each other from at least 1835. With the 1875 tribal election fast approaching, it appeared that William Potter Ross, leader of the National Party, sometimes called the Ross Party, was a sure winner for principal chief. However, many Cherokees vehemently opposed Ross. When the National Council appointed Ross principal chief upon the death of Lewis Downing in 1872, the Southern Cherokees were greatly disturbed because they expected a renewal of the reprisals taken against them after the Civil War. Ross had opposed Downing in the 1867 election and lost, perhaps because most Cherokees were sick of bloodshed and the feuding of the two factions. The people who opposed Ross's election in 1875 were each influential among certain groups, but none could lead a majority of Cherokees. Lewis Downing, an early convert of Evan Jones, was a founder of the party that opposed Ross in 1875. Although Downing was not a full-blood, he commanded respect among that segment of the population. With the support of Jones and his son John, who had been close associates of John Ross and the Northern Cherokees before and during the Civil War, Lewis Downing set out to reach a rapprochement with Stand Watie and the Southern Cherokees. Watie, William Penn Boudinot, and William Penn Adair were at the time important leaders among the "treaty men." The factions came together to form the Downing Party. Their candidate, Charles Thompson, was elected principal chief in 1875, the last full-blood to take that post.[1] With Thompson's election, members of the Boudinot-Ridge-Watie faction regained some of the national prominence they had held before 1835. Chief among these was William Penn Boudinot, in whose footsteps followed his sons Elias Cornelius, Jr., and Frank Boudinot.

As noted in Chapter 6, William Penn Boudinot was the son of Elias Boudinot, who had been assassinated by members of the Ross faction of Cherokees in 1839 for being a leader of the Treaty Party, the Cherokees who had signed the 1835 Treaty of New Echota that provided for the removal of the tribe. He was the nephew of Stand Watie, who succeeded to the leadership of the "treaty men," as they were known, after the deaths of the elder Boudinot, John Ridge, and Major Ridge. William Penn's brother, Elias Cornelius Boudinot, also discussed in earlier chapters, became a spokesman for the "territorial ring" and was for a long time regarded as an enemy of the Cherokee Nation by many Cherokee citizens. Nonetheless, William Penn Boudinot became an important public man in the nation; his value to his people lay primarily in his writing and editing skills.

Boudinot was born in 1829 to Elias and Harriet Ruggles Gold Boudinot in the eastern nation. He was named for the pen name William Penn used by Jeremiah Evarts in writing a series of essays for the *National Intelligencer* titled collectively *The Present Crisis in the Condition of the American Indians*. This work of 1829 was a well-reasoned but impassioned argument against Removal of the eastern tribes. As a fellow writer and a campaigner for the same cause, Elias Boudinot had great admiration for Evarts. When William was a young boy, his mother died, and, shortly before the Cherokees removed to the West, Boudinot married another white woman, De-light Sargent. Once the main body of Cherokees arrived in Indian Territory, some of those bitterly opposed to Removal assassinated Boudinot, John Ridge, and his father, Major Ridge, all on the same day. Delight Sargent fled the Cherokee Nation with the Boudinot children and traveled to the East, where she had relatives who provided her and the children refuge.

William Boudinot was raised by and educated with relatives in Connecticut, Vermont, and Philadelphia, where he learned ornamental jewelry engraving. In a letter to Stand Watie in 1848, he describes his skill at engraving but also voices a desire to return to the Cherokee Nation.[2] By the spring of 1850, he was living in Fort Smith, Arkansas, on the Cherokee border. His skills as a writer and editor must have been apparent when he returned to his people because in 1852 he was appointed editor of the *Cherokee Advocate* and served until the following year. As editor, Boudinot increased the amount of Cherokee news and reduced the reprinted material from other publications. His editorials defended Indian rights with forceful and logical arguments, and he injected humor into his writing. The paper closed shortly afterward because of a lack of funds.

During the Civil War, Boudinot served in the Confederate regiment headed by Stand Watie. During the war, the "Southern" Cherokees, as the Confederate adherents were called, met in a convention, first at Tahlequah and later in the Canadian District, to form an alternative government in the vacuum created when Chief John Ross left Indian Territory for the East. William Boudinot was elected secretary of the convention, at which Stand Watie was elected principal chief. After the war, when the Ross "loyalists" regained control, Boudinot and his Southern or Confederate compatriots lost their property and citizenship rights until they were restored by the postwar treaties with the Union.

Boudinot subsequently rejoined the mainstream Cherokees; in 1870, he was appointed editor of the newly revived *Cherokee Advocate* by the National Council and remained in that position until 1873. He edited the newspaper again in 1876–77 and 1888–89. Boudinot served in various capacities in the government, representing the Cherokees as a delegate to Washington and working as executive secretary to Principal Chief Dennis W. Bushyhead.

Boudinot was nearly seventy when he died under rather mysterious circumstances. On March 13, 1898, Boudinot traveled from Fort Gibson with his son Frank to Kansas City to get treatment for his morphine addiction at an institution there. Frank returned home but later received a letter posted from East St. Louis, Illinois, on March 15 from his father saying that he had been dissatisfied with the treatment he was receiving, so he had left the clinic, would seek treatment elsewhere, planned to return home when he was cured, and promised to write again. Frank received one more letter, dated April 8 and sent from Chicago, saying that he was not doing well and that he expected to be away for some time. Frank, sensing from the letter that his father needed help, traveled to Chicago and visited the hotel where William said he had been staying, but found that no one there had seen him.[3] That summer, a story circulated in the Cherokee Nation that Boudinot had either jumped or fallen from a steamer on Lake Michigan between Chicago and Milwaukee.[4]

William Boudinot's writing, unlike that of his brother, Elias Cornelius, had little bombast and few rhetorical flourishes. Instead, it was polite, reasoned, and full of common sense that his readers valued. A good example is an article on the Old Settler claims published in the April 11, 1884, issue of the *Cherokee Advocate*. The Old Settlers maintained that payment for their land and improvements vacated in Arkansas upon their removal to Indian Territory had not been made in full. Under the treaty of 1846, the Cherokee Nation in Indian Territory had been united as one political body, including the Ross Party, the Treaty Party, and the Old Settlers. As a result, the Old Settlers had difficulty making legal claims because they had lost their status as an independent body. It was not until 1874 that the nation instructed its Washington delegates to pursue the matter with the federal government. By 1884, an investigating agent for the secretary of the interior had found that the claim was indeed justified. It took until 1896, however, before a way was found to pay the money owed to the Settlers and their offspring. Boudinot's article attempts to find a fair method to do this.

The issue provoked heated debate among certain Cherokees about the best tactics to use in the cause, and Boudinot's first move in his article is to quench the fire. In his opening paragraphs, he addresses one William W. Wilson, who has dismissed opinions other than his own as "silly" and "impertinent." Boudinot gently chastises Wilson, saying that Wilson is "certainly entitled to his opinion, but so are others, who are as much concerned as he is." He continues that Wilson is "so incensed to find that others do not think precisely as he does, but does not see how it can be helped." He points out that when "writers lay their opinions before the public, they are not allowed to dictate what the public shall think of these opinions." These remarks establish the tenor of his article in the *Cherokee Advocate* for April 11, 1888, which then makes some suggestions about how the Old Settlers should be paid and gives some recent history of the matter. He concludes in the same fashion as he began: "If other Old Settlers do not concur in the action proposed, that is all there is of it. No one needs be angry, for any person interested has a right to propose, and a simple proposal cannot possibly do any harm."

Boudinot's article on the possibility of establishing a federal court in Indian Territory is also moderate in tone but no less compelling. The issue was somewhat complicated by the fact that the "territorializers," to use Boudinot's term, had made the court a condition for the establishment of a territorial government that would extinguish or eviscerate tribal governments. His argument opposes both this proposition and the petition made by the Chickasaw delegate to establish the federal court in Denison, Texas, near the Chickasaw Nation. Boudinot begins by reminding the Chickasaws that many whites would love to have the court in a white town because of economic factors. Trials draw defendants, lawyers, friends, and spectators, all of whom spend money for food, lodging, and entertainment; a court and its jail need employees, and these mostly come from the community. In short, the federal court will be a cash cow that will give its milk to a white community instead of an Indian one if the Chickasaws have their way.

On the other hand, Boudinot argues, the court and territorial government are separate issues, and that fact should be made clear before discussions of locality begin. This is the stance, he says, of the Cherokee, Muscogee (Creek), Choctaw, and Seminole delegates. They promote a U.S. court in the territory, he explains, for the economic impact and so that people will not have to travel far from home to procure justice. "There is no implication, intimation, or admission of the necessity of a territorial government before such a

Court can be established in the Territory," he continues, adding, "It is an unwise, unwarranted and dangerous position for them or any of them now to take, that the agreement to have a Court *might* be an agreement to have a territorial government." Reporting as a Cherokee delegate from Washington, he seeks to make the Cherokee position clear on the matter and, just as important, to assure people at home of their delegation's intentions. His words, characteristically, do not attack or ridicule but rather explain and reassure.

This is not to say that his writing could not take on a hard edge when he felt it was needed, especially in dealing with the "territorializers." Writing as a delegate from Washington in the *Cherokee Advocate* for April 4, 1888, Boudinot comments on a bill in Congress introduced by Representative Springer of Illinois, chair of the House Committee on Territories, that would open Oklahoma, that is, the lands lying to the west of the Indian nations, to white settlement and create a "Territory of Oklahoma." The Indians, of course, saw this action as a springboard to opening their own country to settlement. Boudinot's piece reacts to Springer's speech in introducing the bill. Despite a Democratic administration's promise "never again to make our nations a prey to the violent embraces of a U.S. Territory or State," he begins, "a prominent Democrat now proposes . . . to do that very dishonorable thing." He writes further, in a tone of outrage just barely under control, "The savage nature of the proceeding is so plainly apparent that some of its supporters even are inclined rather to try the arts of seduction first, and to postpone the act of violence until the gratification of overpowering lust for Indian possessions become a *'necessity'*—a necessity of *'civilization'*—just think of it." However, he feels certain that the government and the people will consent to see the Indians "consigned to the brutalities of conscienceless 'boomers.'" He then derides some of the bill's stipulations, for example, the provision that the Cherokees would be paid a dollar and a quarter an acre for their land only if they gave their consent. "Thus the imprisoned victim is condemned to take the poor nourishment offered by his jailer or to starve to death." He thus casts the Indian nations as captives of the United States instead of sovereign entities.

This article also reports on an interesting event, the meeting of all the Indian delegations in Washington at that time, including those from the Five Civilized Tribes, as well as Iroquois, Stockbridge, and

Ojibwe delegates, representatives from tribes Boudinot does not name, and North Carolina Cherokees. He reports in the *Cherokee Advocate* for April 10, 1889 that the combined advice of the Indian Territory delegates was for the other tribes to embrace the ways of "progressive humanity" as the surest way of holding on to what they had left, education being the best means toward this end. This is interesting advice in that it came during a time of growing awareness of the imminent "disappearance" of the Indians. It is a call for all Indian nations to muster and nurture their intellectual resources to protect their cultures and sovereignty.

As the sovereignty of the nation was eroded by attacks from several directions late in the century, the Cherokees began to accept the allotment of land in severalty as a certainty, and many thinkers began to wrestle with the various implications of that momentous change in national life. One of the fears voiced by John Adair and others was the threat of "monopoly," that is, the accumulation of property and improvements by some individuals that would leave others landless and destitute. Largely, they viewed the threat as coming from unscrupulous mixed-bloods and whites who would exploit the ignorance of full-bloods, to whom the concept of private property was vague, if not foreign. Boudinot begins a discussion of this issue in an article in which he uses the standard rhetorical tactic of anticipating the opposing view.[5] Freedom, he says, is to blame if monopoly occurs, because it is the result of individuals freely entering into agreements to transfer property and money. His next step is to examine the concept of freedom in a democratic society. There is, he writes, "one thing in a free country that is fully as important and essential to the success and happiness of a people as freedom itself, namely: The wisdom that will enable the people to use their freedom so that it will be a blessing and not a curse." Here, Boudinot seems to be echoing earlier writers on the matter, such as Matthew Arnold and John Stuart Mill. Unless "a people be wise as well as free—unless, with the power of locomotion and the power to go in any direction they may choose to go, they have their eyes opened and understandings enlightened so as to see which way to go and how to keep on going that that way . . . unless a people are educated and enlightened as well as free, it will be another case of the 'blind leading the blind' and all parties 'fall into a ditch.'" Boudinot continues his idea: "It is not to be inferred from this that a nation should not be allowed to govern itself until it is able to do so wisely, but that the right to govern itself carries with it and imposes the duty of becoming able." In other words, a democratic government may not be wise in all its decisions, but it should strive for wisdom to do the right thing.

At this point, he takes issue with the Cherokee Nation's educational policy, complaining that since the school system was put into effect, the nation has made no attempt to use the Sequoyan syllabary to educate full-bloods who speak little or no English. Thus, he writes, the nation is ignoring the educational needs of over one-half of its population. He sees this neglect as exacerbating the monopoly problem by keeping full-bloods ignorant of their rights and of legal processes. This neglect flies in the face of the advice he has offered to the other tribes, that is, to develop all their intellectual stocks.

William Boudinot was also a poet, not surprisingly, given his obvious respect for and love of language. Unfortunately, only one of his poems is extant, although it was published in a number of venues. In a foreword to the poem in *Twin Territories*, the editor says that the poem was written around 1850, around the time when the poet returned to the Cherokee Nation. Titled "The Spectre," it is written in the cadences of Edgar Allen Poe's "The Raven," and seems to mirror its diction, if not its theme. It begins:

> *There is a spectre always haunting*
> *All the living things of earth;*
> *Like a constant shade attending*
> *Every mortal from his birth;*
> *And his likeness is a demon's*
> *Horrible with mocking mirth.*

The haunter, of course, is Death, which, to the impressionable young man, seemed to hover closely as one grows old.

> *For we feel its icy fingers*
> *Tracing wrinkles on our brow,*
> *While its breath so cold and deadly*
> *Turns the raven hair to snow;*
> *As we hobble on our journey*
> *With a stumbling step and slow.*

The poem was published in *Twin Territories* in December, 1889, shortly after Boudinot's disappearance and rumors of his death. It is an interesting work when read in the context of his addiction to morphine.

Writers in the Cherokee Nation were, of course, not limited to writing official documents or literature intended to persuade readers to adopt the writer's political views. A good example is Henry D. Reese, or White Horse; although he did participate in writing political pieces as a delegate for the Cherokee Nation in Washington and as a newspaper editor, some of his most significant writing was his historical account of the Cherokees in times past. Reese was born in the eastern nation in 1820, son of Charles Reese and Nellie McKoy. His early education took place in Jasper County, Georgia, at Constitution Hall. He must have been an exceptional student because at age fourteen he was appointed clerk of the circuit court of Georgia. When the Cherokees were removed to the West, Reese moved with them in 1837 and settled in Tahlequah. There he was clerk of circuit and district courts until 1850, when he was appointed clerk of the Cherokee Supreme Court, serving until 1861. In 1852, he took on the duties of superintendent of schools while still attending to his Supreme Court responsibilities and served in that capacity until 1867. He served as a delegate to the U.S. Congress from 1867 to 1869, during which time the Cherokees and other Indian Territory tribes were negotiating with the federal government concerning their future status. He and William P. Adair negotiated with the Shawnees; out of these talks came the Cherokee-Shawnee Agreement of 1869. The agreement transferred an annual $5,000 payment from the Shawnees to the Cherokees plus a one-time payment of $50,000, which was the amount received from the sale of the Absentee Shawnee lands in Kansas. In return, the Cherokees agreed to cede unoccupied land to the Shawnees, as well as to incorporate them into the Cherokee Nation on equal terms in every respect. When Reese returned from Washington, he took on the duties of treasurer of the nation in 1871. In the late 1870s, he was a prosecuting attorney and district judge. He also edited the *Cherokee Advocate* in 1878.

It was in the pages of the *Advocate* that White Horse began to publish his historical pieces under the titles "Old Times" or "Long Ago." Initially, most of these were firsthand accounts from Reese's memory involving some momentous occasions in Cherokee history. Others were of general historical interest, such as descriptions of dwellings and other buildings, as well as of various occupations of the inhabitants. One early account tells of white "ancestors" who had come to the nation in earlier years, had intermarried, and had become Cherokee citizens, much as his own forebears had done. Reese is at pains to describe these men as educated gentlemen, rather than border ruffians, and tells of the origins of the Ross, Rogers, Adair, Hicks, Brown, and Lowrey families.[6]

In another interesting account, Reese tells of an examination at Brainerd School in 1828. These examinations were conducted by school inspectors hired by the school's administration and were open to the public. The schools regarded them as public relations events and endeavored to showcase their successes. Brainerd had been established in 1817 and was one of the early missionary schools built to serve the Cherokees. By the time at which Reese witnessed the examination, the school's fame had spread throughout the nation, and the event attracted many people. Assistant Principal Chief George Lowery was there, and later in the day, Elias Boudinot and John Ridge arrived with their brides from Connecticut, riding in a "fine coach." The young boys gathered around to see a wagon with glass windows, truly a novelty. Students and their teacher from Creek Path School were in attendance as well. As a preliminary to the examination, the teacher introduced Ridge, Boudinot, William Coody, William Hicks, and others as young Cherokees who had benefited from an education and urged the children to use them as examples for their own lives. Reese then describes other educational efforts in the Cherokee Nation at the time.[7]

Because he fears that the young Cherokees of the 1870s do not understand the "troubles with the state of Georgia," he endeavors to re-create those times for his readers. He begins with the Georgia Compact of 1802, in which the state surrendered its land claims to present-day Alabama and Mississippi to the federal government in exchange for $1,250,000 and a promise that the United States would extinguish the Indian title to lands within the limits of the state as "early as it could be done on fair and reasonable terms." Between 1802 and the 1820s, Reese continues, the Cherokees had made "rapid advances in the arts of civilized life, had adopted a constitution and enacted wholesome laws." The Cherokees clearly were determined to hold on to their land. As tensions rose, the Georgians passed a series of onerous acts, including a survey of Cherokee lands and a land lottery based on that survey. Settlers who "won" land in the lottery moved to take possession at once, forcing Cherokees from their homes and confiscating their crops and livestock. "Pony clubs" of thieving marauders often raided Cherokee farms and were sanctioned by state authorities. Pleas for help from President Jackson brought only the response that he could do nothing and the advice that the Cherokees should remove to the West. Reese then writes of the oppressive laws leading to the imprisonment of missionaries Samuel A. Worcester and Elizur Butler.[8]

Reese gives an account of the battle of Lookout Mountain from a conversation with Major George Lowery, who had been a participant in that conflict as a young man. Lowery's description of the battle involves a regiment of Tennessee troops heading for Lookout Mountain, where they were met by Cherokees who had taken up positions on the high ground. Earlier raids by Tennesseans had prompted a quick response by the Indians, and they were ready when the white troops advanced. The battle itself was short, and a number of white soldiers were killed by a fierce fusillade sent down by the Cherokees, who registered only one casualty.[9]

In the "Old Times" piece of January 27, 1877, Reese takes an interesting tack. Acknowledging that he is trying to reach young readers with no memories of the old nation, he invites them to take a "ramble" with him to "see the people, the farms, and all matters of interest." The imaginary journey takes place in 1829 in New Echota, the Cherokee capital, and proceeds eastward to Spring Place, the home of Joseph Vann. Here Reese describes the house and the farm of the man the Cherokees called "Rich Joe," the large brick family dwelling, rivaling that of any white Georgia planters, the row of brick houses for the more than one hundred slaves, and the five hundred acres of farmland that the slaves cultivated. He mentions a second farm and a ferry some miles away that Vann has been forced to evacuate because of the pony-club raids, and the steamboat that the Cherokee operated on the Tennessee River. A second steamboat built by Vann, the *Lucy Walker,* named for one of his favorite horses, plied the Mississippi. It was while Joseph Vann was on board this boat that his life came to an end when the engine exploded, killing several other people as well. Upon leaving Spring Place, Reese's journey brings him to another farm, that of Davie McNair, married to Vann's sister. This farm, too, was the equal of the finest in Georgia.

As Reese continues his travels in subsequent articles, he follows this fictive frame. In so doing, he is able not only to describe the landscape and the lifeways of the inhabitants but also to reflect on the lives of some of the leading Cherokee figures. He goes to Wills Valley to visit the home of Charles Hicks, a prominent figure who built the first mill in the Cherokee Nation and was active in political, literary, and religious affairs. He visits Brainerd and takes the opportunity to tell the story of the early missionaries to his people. After Brainerd, he travels to the home of John Ross, who would shortly replace Charles Hicks as principal chief, then toward Lookout Mountain to where Daniel Ross, John's father, lived. He describes the scenery in the Lookout vicinity in almost reverent tones as he goes up the mountain and to the valley with the same name. There he describes the home of John Benge, a two-story house and large farm on which graze "six or seven hundred head" of cattle. Beyond Benge's farm is John F. Baldridge's, where even more cattle graze, along with a hundred peacocks and peahens. Then the road takes him to Wills Valley, home to Wee-ley, for whom it is named, as well as to George Lowery's place and the former home of George Guess, or Sequoyah, who had gone to Arkansas by 1829. At Wills Town, the national festivals of the green corn dance and the "physic-dance" were held, attended by all the Cherokees. He then describes the mission established there. With the March 7, 1877, issue of the *Advocate*, Reese discontinued his historical ramble, but not before passing on valuable information on the persons and places of the former Cherokee Nation. His intentions are clear: first, to be sure that this firsthand history of the Cherokee people is preserved, and second, to reinforce a sense of nationhood in a society that outside forces seem determined to destroy.

Some of the writers publishing in Indian Territory newspapers during the nineteenth century used Indian names to identify themselves or as pen names. Many of these are readily identifiable to present-day readers, like DeWitt Clinton Duncan's use of the name Too Quah-stee. Others, however, are more difficult to identify;

although the writer may have been well known to contemporary readers, he or she remains elusive today. One of these elusive figures is U-Na-Kuh, a writer whose work is interesting not only for what it says about current affairs in the nation at the time but also for the attempt to portray a Cherokee speaking English in a distinctive dialect, thus capturing, perhaps, the sounds of the language as spoken by Indians of that time and locale. Some of U-Na-Kuh's pieces resemble the dialect humor familiar to readers of mainstream newspapers, antedating the work of fellow Cherokee Roger Royal Eubanks and Wyandotte writer Hen-Toh (Bertrand N. O. Walker).

However, U-Na-Kuh's first articles are commonplace enough, consisting of reports of people and events from Flint District. Aiming to keep citizens aware of what was happening in other areas, the *Advocate* carried these reports from all districts in the nation from correspondents who lived there. These first attempts by U-Na-Kuh, like their counterparts in other districts, consisted of squibs on marriages, deaths, births, resident arrivals and departures, the weather, and crop conditions. In one, he writes "—'Grub' somewhat 'skase,'" followed by "—Now is the season of our discontent—larder empty." In a piece that appeared in the November 2, 1878, *Advocate,* though, he furnishes a commentary that refutes those territorialists who assert that the Cherokees stand in the way of "progress," writing that the nation's schools have a larger attendance as a percentage of population than either of the "progressive" states of Arkansas and Texas. He then describes the high quality of agricultural products and livestock raised in the nation and sent to markets in St. Louis and elsewhere. U-Na-Kuh writes that these facts are beginning to influence people in the East who see the antiprogress arguments of the railroads and the "land-sharks" as spurious.

By February 19, 1879, his language has begun to evolve into the dialectal patterns that mark his later writings. In his column for this date, he starts out with a report on the weather: "It raineth muchly." In the *Advocate* of December 17, 1879, he introduces his main foil, his wife, Miranda Emmeline, and begins to develop the persona of a lazy layabout, possibly an intermarried white man.[10] Here, too, he begins occasionally to omit the hyphens from his name; this leads to a variety of spellings, Unakuh, Una-kuh, U-Na-Kuh, although these changes may have been due to typesetters' preferences or mistakes. The persona uses an affected educated vocabulary, eroded by misspellings and dialectical pronunciation. He begins his article by quoting Miranda Emmeline: " 'Is it possible' exclaimeth my good wife as she hastily scanneth the last issue of the *Advocate*, 'that we are not entirely forgotten, here good husband U-Na-Kuh; rouse up thy drooping energies, the Editor calleth for thee, seize thy pen, write, and unburden thyself of the woes which seemeth to oppress thy spirits.' " Here, the writer is referring to the fact that on at least two occasions, the *Advocate*'s editor[11] had printed invitations to U-Na-Kuh to send him material. His "latent ambition" aroused, the writer looks around him for inspiration. He describes the desolate December landscape with its dead vegetation, his hungry livestock, the incessant rain that "falleth in streams through the roof," and his dwindling fuel supply. He then turns his attention to his wife, whom he describes as displaying the ravages of want on every feature as she works while he writes. She mends his old trousers, tends the fire, and prepares "con nah ha nuh"[12] for his breakfast. All around him are the signs of poverty and misery. He introduces his child, who in his innocence shows not an indication of trouble, "but everything seemeth to be bright to him; he knoweth not, or seemeth not to know that he is surrounded by squalid poverty; that the smoke house has long since been empty, that the corn bin is void of all, save its own emptiness."

U-Na-Kuh then anticipates his editor's response to this tale of woe by answering the obvious question, "Why this thusness? Why dost thou not labor? The harvest is plentiful and the laborers are few." U-Na-Kuh's reply is that he is a third-grade teacher employed by the Cherokee schools, "ekeing out a miserable existence on one hundred and fifty dollars per session, until his credit is bankrupt," his supplies are cut off, and he is "floating like a ship without a rudder." He ends his article in the *Cherokee Advocate* of November 2, 1878, with a verse

Alas I am a third grade teacher
My salary already "eksho"[13]
And unless my grade is raised,
To the poor house I'll go.

U-Na-Kuh's complaints were not lost on his readers, and in a subsequent issue, a writer using the pen name "Indian" replied to his piece. In an article titled "The Contented Indian," he identifies himself as a fellow third-grade teacher, but he describes his life as different from U-Na-Kuh's, one of economical happiness with his hardworking wife, Kate. He makes bold to draw up a budget for U-Na-Kuh's yearly salary, including money to patch the roof, which leaves a surplus of $100, which he advises his fellow teacher to invest in an interest-bearing account. To end his piece, he composes a quatrain:

> *Only a third grade teacher am I.*
> *Poor pay, and hard living I know,*
> *But to the top of the hill so high,*
> *Kate and I if employed will go.*

In U-na-kuh's next article, in the October 5, 1878 issue, he writes of his New Year's holiday, and how his outlook has brightened considerably, first because of the words of his wife. In reply to his query regarding her perspective on her life, Miranda Emmeline replies, "I am contented with my lot. The 'bright side' of life consisteth in being content with what the good Lord giveth thee, when we so beeth, all appeareth fair to us." As U-Na-Kuh shakes his head in disagreement, a number of schoolchildren appear at his gate bearing a large basket filled with food. As he feasts on these delicacies, he reflects on the simple pleasures of life, and Miranda Emmeline's optimism is vindicated.

His status as an elementary-school teacher established, the writer in his next piece in the January 11, 1879 *Advocate* sets up his persona as an intermarried white. "Unakuh Dialogueth with Miranda Emeline [*sic*]. They Argueth the 'Indian Question'" begins with the persona asking his wife why prejudice exists between the red and white races, and before she can answer, he asks, "What are the great wrongs which the whites commiteth against the red man, that they mistrusteth us all?" Miranda Emmeline asks him in return whether he has read any history. Knowing full well that he has, she says, "Thou knowest all these things but too well—thou only mocketh me with these questionings."

Un-Na-Kuh replies that history shows that the Europeans brought civilization to the savage Cherokees and brought them religion, for which the Cherokees should be thankful. His wife agrees that the Indians have learned much from the whites. However,

> while the white man was teaching us right by *precept*, they taught us wrong by *example*. While they were teaching us "to love one another" they were secretly plotting our ruin, they taught us falsehood, they taught us deceit, they taught us to steal, they stirred up strife among the tribes of red men, they blinded our eyesight with the demon alcohol, and while the poor untutored savage standeth and listeneth to those great things which the white man telleth him, of how Christ died to save the world of men from destruction, of how he must do to receive eternal life, and gain a portion of the great "tree of life"—I say, while the white man was teaching us these things they stole from us our inheritance, they drove us from our homes, herded us together as so many dumb beasts, marched us a thousand miles into an unknown wilderness, without habitation, without shelter from the winds of winter, without the necessities of life.

These facts, she concludes, make up the Indians' history and cause them to dislike the white man.

U-Na-Kuh's reply to this heated discourse is to admit that a few white men have acted in bad faith toward the Indians, but this is not reason enough to hate all white men. Besides, he asks, did not the Cherokees sign a treaty with the whites and agree to remove to "a better country"? Did not the federal government do all that it was obliged to do under the terms of the treaty? His wife's rejoinder is that the Cherokees were forced to go, that the government had left them no choice. She then recounts the Indians' sorrow at leaving their ancestral homes and the graves of their relatives, as well as the hardships suffered on the Removal routes. She ends with the words "But Unakuh, I see I astonish you with these recitals, and so we will now defer the conversation 'til some other time."

By 1884, U-Na-Kuh had perfected his dialect form, and his works took on a more comic form. His concerns now seem to be less serious, and in "Unakuh's Troubles," in the February 11 *Advocate* he tells about one of them. The narrator is found one spring morning, sitting in his chair on the south side of his door, enjoying the warm sun and listening to the "steddy thump, thump, ov the corner ha-ne pessel, az Miranda Emmeline poundeth the corn fur hour evenin meel," when a question enters his mind and "almost knockt me crank sided with its force. What cud I ever du without Miranda?" The elementary-school teacher segment of his persona seems to be shed, as well as most of the rules of English orthography, and the writer is thus allowed to experiment with the sounds of Indian Territory dialect speech. In his reverie on Miranda's qualities as a wife and homemaker, he suddenly hears a scream, and a slapstick scene ensues in which "the old swine came roun the corner of the cabin, like az if she had bin shot from a 'batterin ram' closely pursude bi Miranda Emeline, whose only words which explaineth the cause, was—'catch her' 'catch her?' 'She's got it, she's got it.'" Bewildered, U-Na-Kuh writes that the hog "sought to take reffuge under the cheer on which Unakuh setteth, but the carpenter which made the cheer kontemplatch no such a contingence, and provideth not for the same; and hence, Unakuh, cheers, swine, etc., becom intercommixed muchly, and worse, the mud hole neer bi, wher the geese and ducks sporteth, fell athwart the spot wher providence ordaineth—or at least Meester Editor, the place whur I lit, was right in the middle of same." Sitting there in the mud, he felt like a "stewed akscident, and looked like the hip straps of bad luck." Miranda, coming on him, then berated him because he had allowed the pig to have "et that year of corn" that had been designated little Unakuh's supper. Having been upbraided, U-Na-Kuh thinks to himself, "The tru worth ov such a woman az Miranda Emeline forced itself upon me agin—and I sayeth nothing."

Another noted Cherokee writer in the second half of the nineteenth century was John Lynch Adair, who was born in the eastern Cherokee Nation in 1828. His father, Thomas Benjamin Adair, and mother, Rachel Lynch, died when John was young, so he was raised by relatives. After Removal, he was sent to a Moravian mission school before being sent to Bentonville, Arkansas, where he entered a school operated by Cephus Washburn, the missionary and teacher formerly attached to the Cherokees in Arkansas before Removal and who taught many Cherokees afterward. Later, Adair studied at the Ozark Institute near Fayetteville. He did well in school, where the study of language was his favorite subject. He learned Latin and some Greek and was well versed in literature and history. He had no money to continue his schooling beyond the institute, so he took the course that other Cherokees did and joined one of the wagon trains heading for the gold fields of California in 1849. Disillusioned with the rush for quick riches, he returned to the Cherokee Nation in 1853, when he married and began to farm.

The Civil War interrupted his life, and he enlisted on the Confederate side. After the war, he settled at Tahlequah, where he took part in Cherokee affairs and government. He served as national auditor, clerk of the Cherokee Senate, and executive councilor under Chief Lewis Downing; in addition, he traveled to Washington on the nation's behalf, where he served as a delegate three times, taking part in the forays against the territorial ring and other interests trying to wrest control of Indian Territory from its inhabitants. He helped write memorials to Congress and various reports on the delegates' work in the capital and engaged in the effort to gain supporters among the white population of the East.

Adair wrote for and edited several Indian Territory newspapers, including the *Cherokee Advocate* (1873–75) and the *Tahlequah Courier* (1893) at Tahlequah and the weekly *Indian Chieftain* (1885–89), the *Daily Indian Chieftain* (1891), and *World* (1891) at Vinita in the Cherokee Nation. In these publications' pages, he voiced the same opposition to anti-Indian interests that he had as a delegate to Washington and weighed in on internal matters as well, such as funding the nation's schools.

John Lynch Adair was also well known as a poet among Indian Territory readers. Although he supposedly wrote a number of poems, only two seem to have survived. The poems are written on universal and not "Indian" subjects and demonstrate Adair's knowledge of the English and American literary conventions that he learned in school. His poem "Hec Dies, "for example, is somber in tone but imparts a message of hope for a life beyond this one. That eternal life, Adair seems to believe, is real, while our mortal lives are but dreams. This of course, is the stuff of many religions and of contemporary Neoplatonism as expressed by romantic writers such as Percy Shelley.

HEC DIES

To him, whose hopes are far away,
        To where life's sunset scene discloses
        First of spring flowers and roses,
        Of summer next, and winter snows
        Further on, knows or thinks he knows
That far this scene beyond is day.
That to behold it, as we may,
        It's but little more than a dream,
        And of events, this turbid stream—
        Beginning, ah where? And ending,
        Ah, where? And forever wending—
Is not a real scene to-day.
That we'll fall to sleep, as we say,
        And weary, would have it night
        While the sun is yet warm and bright;
        Will wake from sleep to find
        That all we saw and left behind
Was nothing but a dream that day.
Wonder how long we slept that way.
        Think we've been dreaming—nothing more—
        And to those who had woke before
        From sleep, will wish to tell our dreams,
        Of the unaccountable scenes,
We beheld as we slept that day.
That our loved we'll find, as we pray,
        Who had grown weary and had slept,
        And in their dreams had laughed and wept
        O'er scenes that were so real
        That nothing could be ideal
Of what they saw and felt that day.
Believe we were dreaming, some way,
        When we thought it was more than sleep—
        It was so cold and calm and deep—
        In which they lay, and sorrow's tears
        We'll think were strange, as were the fears,
That made sad our dreaming that day.
That the gleams from the faraway
        We sometimes have of better things—
        Like strange birds upon helpless wings,
        Blown from some isle in tropic climes—
        Are memories of other times,
And we'll find when we wake that day. [Cherokee Advocate, May 27, 1876]

Adair pursues the theme of immortality here and finds comfort in the thought, in the midst of grief for a lost friend, by juxtaposing sleep and wakefulness. He takes the conventional metaphor of death as sleep after long toil and turns it on its head by referring to mortal life as sleeping and dreaming and immortal life as waking into eternal day. What makes this poem different from other poems with religious overtones is the skillful interplay of sleeping, dreaming, and wakefulness in which he declares that what we think are dreams are but emanations from the spiritual world, intimations of what lies beyond this life. The poem's sophistication lies not so much in the subject as in the execution of the controlling idea.

Adair's other extant poem is more overtly religious and is the prayer of a Christian begging for the protection of his God against the vicissitudes of life and the dangers of unbelief.

JOY RETURNETH IN THE MORNING
A great storm had blown out the stars
*   And the winds, rushing from their caves,*
*   Lashed the sea into mountain waves;*
And the ship, under bending spars,
In utter darkness plowed the deep.
*   Unto Him whom the winds obeyed*
*   On Galilee, I humbly prayed*
That in his keeping I might sleep.

In a haven, calm and bright
*   With tropic sunshine, where the scent*
*   Of orange blooms made redolent*
The breeze that was so soft and light
That scarcely there a wavelet broke
*   Upon the bosom of the bay,*
*   When next morn' our good ship lay—*
To glad consciousness I 'woke.

So may it be, good Lord of all,
*   When into darkness sinks my sun*
*   And my stars go out, one by one,*
To such calm slumber may I fall.
And that which only faith had been,
*   Awake to find a truth to be,*
*   Where no white sails go out to sea,*
But are forever coming in. [Cherokee Advocate, June 17, 1876]

As a delegate to Washington and a journalist, Adair wrote on the affairs of his nation during this turbulent time in its history. One of the issues that Adair addressed was that of monopoly. With allotment pending, Adair and others saw a disturbing trend in the Cherokee Nation: the population was growing, but the people being added to citizenship rolls were those who were less than half Cherokee by blood. Although it is true that the Cherokees did not recognize degrees of citizenship based on blood quantum and that as a nation they were perhaps more accepting of mixed-bloods than other Indian groups, it was not hard to see what was happening. People saw the chance for free land in Indian Territory; the price was admission to the citizenship rolls. The result was that people with rather nebulous ties to the nation were for the first time declaring their Cherokee-ness. The Cherokee government had set up a citizenship committee to screen these applications, but the numbers of "less-than-halves," as Adair dubbed them, continued to rise.

Compounding the monopoly issue was the fact that many of the Cherokee mixed-bloods, who as a group were more savvy about landownership and the value of holding property than the full-bloods, were claiming lots in the newly established towns that were being platted in the nation. Legal notices asserting such claims appeared in every issue of the *Cherokee Advocate* during the early 1890s. Adair feared that the monopolies would crowd the full-bloods out of the best land allotments and relegate them to rocky, hillside farms far from the towns. When Alice Robertson, testifying before the House Committee on Territories when Adair was a delegate in 1890, came out against these trends, Adair readily agreed. He writes that she chided the Cherokee Nation (which she was representing) for its "mismanagement of public affairs. The steady increase of a population of less than half Indian, and the exercise of political power by them to the exclusion of others on the other side of the line, was a matter of much concern to her. The occupancy of lands by the less-than-halves amounting to a monopoly and detriment of the others, was another cause of complaint."[14] Adair then presents a vibrant metaphor but does not indicate whether it is Robertson's or his: "She thought that to cut the dog's tail off at one fell stroke would be much more merciful than taking it off by inches until it became so short that it was a mere stump and a joke on its former dimensions."

Adair continued to attack the monopolies as time went on. He saw this as an issue that needed to be settled before a final allotment bill became law. The way to that end lay in the Cherokee government enacting a law, and so Adair, enlisting the help of several other prominent Cherokees, set out to see it passed.[15] As that day loomed closer, the urgency of his position was reflected in his writing, in which he sought to point out potential difficulties and to propose ways of averting them. One of the biggest arguments involving the issues was what to do about noncitizen laborers hired to work in the nation. At first glance, this may not seem to pose a problem; however, unrestricted importation of labor led Cherokee entrepreneurs to extend "improvements"—fences, barns, and other buildings—to large tracts of land, thus, under Cherokee custom, taking control of that land from the public domain. Of course, a family can work only so much land, which seems to have been the idea when the nation was young and heavily full-blood. However, the use of outside labor allowed Cherokees to lay claim to and work much bigger tracts and to engage in large-scale farming and stock raising. Adair urged the nation to adopt rules restricting the use of this labor and thus preventing individuals from monopolizing tribal lands. Land monopoly, in Adair's eyes, did away with the ancient premise that all Cherokees shared equally in the land base.[16] Land monopoly in the Cherokee Nation, Adair asserted, was analogous to "an English Lord holding an estate in Ireland."

To head off these difficulties, Adair put forward a proposal based on the assumption that allotments would go to each man, woman, or child who was a citizen, and that the size of these allotments would be 160 acres each. His proposal states that Cherokee citizens have the right to combine these allotments when they are contiguous. Further, Adair proposed that Cherokees might apply for permits to employ noncitizen laborers, but that these employees would be limited to the number of those who were needed to work a 160-acre allotment. For example, a two-year-old Cherokee child might be granted an allotment but be hard pressed to work it. The child's parents could employ noncitizen labors to farm that allotment or tend livestock on it. Anyone attempting to cheat the system would be fined. Adair was one of many who voiced their opposition to monopolies, fearing that the worst aspects of the white man's capitalism would become part of their own culture, just as it had corrupted the world of "progress." While mainstream newspapers screamed against monopolies in railroads, industry, and other aspects of the business world, the Cherokees saw a similar threat in Indian Territory.

Ora V. Eddleman, raised in a newspaper-publishing family, became widely known in Indian Territory in the waning years of the nineteenth century and into the twentieth. Her writing was popular and consisted mainly of short fiction, usually based on Indian Territory people and subjects, written under the pseudonym Mignon Schreiber. Eddleman also wrote some poetry, history, and sketches of other Indian writers. She went on to become publisher of *Twin Territories*, a literary magazine, and later, editor of the "Indian Department" of *Sturm's Oklahoma Magazine*. She wrote for publications in the East, was the first woman member of the Indian Territory Press Association, and in the 1920s managed a radio station.[17] She married Charles A. Reed, an official with the Dawes Commission, and took his name.

Born in 1880 near Denton, Texas, Eddleman owed her Cherokee heritage to the Bunch family on her mother's side. In 1894, her family moved to Muskogee, where she attended Henry Kendall College, which later moved to Tulsa and still later became the University of Tulsa. When her father bought the *Muskogee Morning Times*, the first daily in Muskogee, she worked in the newspaper office and learned many aspects of the publishing business. Among other things, she was "telegraph editor," taking news off the wire and rewriting it for Indian Territory readers. The *Times* was the first newspaper in the territory to subscribe to the Associated Press, so this became a major job and excellent experience for a young reporter. When her sister and brother-in-law began *Twin Territories: The Indian Magazine* in 1898, she was hired as editor and feature writer. As editor, Eddleman made Indian Territory material the magazine's main subject matter, promoting the work of Indian writers, discussing current issues, and providing history of the various tribes and cultures represented in that region. She included local club and school news, a children's page, and a page containing interesting matter for farmers and livestock raisers. One prominent feature was profiles of local young women and photographic portraits of persons, schools, and homes to show that "civilized" and "progressive" people lived in the area and to dismiss the notion that Indian Territory was filled with criminals and cutthroats. In 1900, Lura A. Rowland bought a half interest in the magazine and moved it to Fort Gibson in the Cherokee Nation. Within two years, though, the publication was beset with financial difficulties, and Ora Eddleman had the controlling interest again. She moved the magazine back to Muskogee and, in 1902, sold it to E. C. Dighton. The last issue appeared in May 1904.[18]

Eddleman later worked as editor of the "Indian Department" of *Sturm's Oklahoma Magazine,* which was published and edited by Oliver Perry Sturm, a journalist from Missouri. The publication was designed for wide appeal to both urban and rural audiences, and at one time, its circulation was around 10,000. It provided a voice for many writers of the area, but its main mission was to promote the towns of the new state. *Sturm's* continued until May 1911.[19] Eddleman's husband, Charles Reed, went into the oil-exploration business, and this work took the family from place to place. Mrs. Reed wrote for a newspaper in Casper, Wyoming, and had a radio program there. Later, she published articles in various Oklahoma newspapers and magazines until her death in 1968 in Tulsa.

Eddleman's work came at a time of great transition in Indian Territory, and her fiction work reflects this, often finding its themes, characters, and tensions in the coming together of cultures. She writes of white farmers and ranchers who flooded into the area from the late 1880s onward, as well as the Indian peoples who had been dispossessed and who were struggling to make sense of this new world. Eddleman was well aware of the special time and place in which she was writing and took it on herself to chronicle what she knew was a changing world. Perhaps her salutatory piece in *Sturm's* in June, 1904, as she began her work there, "The Object of the Indian Department," says best how she viewed her subject and her mission: "The Indian Department has been set apart by the editor of this magazine for the study of Indian history and literature—to perpetuate the story of the Red Man and to record the progress he has made and is making in the world of civilization." This statement sets Eddleman's mission apart from those writers seeking to preserve—at least in print, recordings, and photographs—the old ways of American tribal people, writers who were convinced that anthropological aspects of the "disappearing race" must be captured for the education of posterity. She points out that she intends to record accounts of Indian culture as passed down by older people, but she also intends to publish the work of the more educated and acculturated tribal people. "An expression of their beliefs, ideas and opinions of the day" is what she wants to publish and, therefore, preserve. After pointing out that *Sturm's* is the only magazine in the country with such a mission, she continues, "The Indians themselves should feel that this department is theirs." In this way, Eddleman hoped that she could continue promoting the work of Indian writers, as she had in the pages of *Twin Territories.*

In most of her fiction dealing with Indians, Eddleman portrays them as possessing a wisdom that provides the white people with whom they are in contact a deeper understanding of their common situation and relationships. This fiction appeared in *Twin Territories.* On both sides, often, a native naïveté is displayed that is disarming and even charming. A good example may be found in her short story, "Billy Bearclaws, Aide to Cupid." The story revolves around three central characters, Betty Merwin, a teacher at a government Indian school and daughter of the straitlaced superintendent; Martin Strong, a white rancher, in love with Betty, a straight shooter, and spouter of every cliché about Indians known to humankind; and Little Eagle Tom, a pupil at the school who has a schoolboy crush on Betty and a deep respect for Strong. Superintendent Merwin has forbidden Strong's courting of his daughter, so the two remain apart, both yearning for their loved one. As the story opens, Little Eagle Tom has run away from the school, which, with the exception of his lovely young teacher, he hates. He vows never to return, echoing the sentiments of thousands of tribal people since that time. Little Eagle knows about the situation between Miss Merwin and Strong, and the plot revolves around his efforts to assuage the situation. He goes so far as to offer to return to the despised place of incarceration, as he views it, if that will bring the two together. Strong, typically, does not know or bother to learn Little Eagle's real name and finds it easier to bestow the nickname Billy Bearclaws on him. In the end, the wisdom, as well as the scheming, of Little Eagle wins the day, and the young rancher and his new prize possession, as he sees her, ride off together to his ranch.

Eddleman touches on several elements of Indian Territory life at the end of the nineteenth century. The characters could very well have been drawn from real-life models: the macho rancher and hard-nosed government school official, the strong but feminine young woman, and the resentful Indian pupil who was removed from his family (who are never mentioned) and forced to attend school and live in a barracks-like atmosphere. But she keeps her story light and romantic, hoping to appeal not only to her local audience but also to readers from other parts of the country who regarded the American West as an exotic land. This may be seen in the substantial reader-ship of the *Indian Magazine* in the Midwest and East, as well as in the popular Wild West show tours and Indian "villages" set up at the expositions held around this time in large American cities.

Another of Eddleman's pieces deals with the sagacity of the Na-tive people, especially that of the full-bloods. In "Indian Tales be-tween Pipes," she writes of stories told by the Dawes Commission crews who traveled throughout the Cherokee Nation and other In-dian lands to enroll the people for allotment. It is clear that many of these white men, recruited from states in the East, had not known any tribal people before and most likely arrived with preconceived ideas about their savagery and lack of intelligence. Her husband, Charles, was one of the Dawes men, and Eddleman probably learned some of these stories through him. In some ways, the anecdotes as told by the white men are self-deprecating as they recount instances in which the "benighted" people are able to best the white man, mainly through the application of common sense. The piece shows, too, the appalling lack of a sense of history of the Dawes men. For example, as they approach a full-blood settlement, the men are away, so when the women and children sight the white men, they flee to the woods. The whites chalk up this action to shyness, nor realizing that in the not-so-distant past, the approach of a party of white men meant extreme danger for the unprotected women, children, and elderly persons.

In "Father of 90,000 Indians," appearing in the April 1904 issue of *Twin Territories*, Eddleman writes of the time when tribal dissolution was taking place, Oklahoma had not yet become a state, and Indian Territory was administered by an appointee of the secretary of the interior. The piece is written from the point of view of the admin-strator and is sympathetic to the difficult task he is called on to per-form. J. George Wright's duties range from the seemingly trivial problems of individuals to decisions that affect large numbers of people. Many of these issues involve various payments made by the government to individual Indians, whose money-management skills vary to a high degree. Eddleman's take on the situation is that it is a "strenuous" time for whites and Indians alike, and the end of it will be welcomed by all.

Ora Eddleman wrote historical pieces as well. In these pieces, she relies heavily on the work of white historians but offers readable accounts of the major events in the tribal past. Her essay "The Choctaws and the Chickasaws" in the November, 1905 issue of *Sturms* relies on D. C. Gideon's *History of Indian Territory* (New York: Lewis Publishing Co., 1901) and James Adair's *History of the Indians* (London: Edward and Charles Dilly, 1775) for her basic facts. But Eddleman takes these stories, mostly attributed to "tradition," and puts them in a contemporary context, bringing the history to the present day. The result is a readable piece that furnishes her readers with an idea of some of the beliefs surrounding the founding of the nations, as well as the more recent and more easily documented history. She introduces Indians to a white audience who may have had barely an inkling of who they were.

The fact that a literary magazine such as *Twin Territories* could have been contemplated in Indian Territory attests to the presence of a literate public, a sizable portion of which was Cherokee. The existence of such a large group of readers was due to a steady accumulation made possible by a vibrant school system that, although limited in its scope of clients, did an amazing job, given its location and its time. The other factor that made such a readership possible, of course, was an active newspaper presence. Eddleman's efforts to dispel the image of Indian Territory as an uncultured, dangerous place was a daunting task, given the propaganda put out for so long and so relentlessly by the territorial forces. It is ironic that many of the white people who had come into the region thanks to allotment, dissolution of tribal government, and white settlement now also sought to eradicate this image by portraying Indian Territory as a progressive place where it would be safe to settle one's family and to enjoy the fruits of a civilized existence.

By the end of the nineteenth century, Cherokee literature was blooming. The writers of that nation wrote in various genres, ranging from fierce political debate to philosophical treatises and to humorous commentary. Their writing appeared in many Indian-edited publications, but by the time the century ended, some were breaking into regional and even national publications. This Cherokee literary flowering established the standards for Native writers from other nations and ultimately set the stage for Indian literature of today.

EPILOGUE

Literacy for the Cherokees came about through a series of events, all tied to a national will to survive. The acceptance of education as presented by the missionaries was a response to the threat of white encroachment on their homeland. The overwhelming initial embrace of the Sequoyan syllabary may be attributed as much to national pride as to its being perceived as a practical instrument of communication; but as the people found more uses for it, from sending greetings to far-off relatives to recording sacred texts, it became vital to the transmission of ideas among the Cherokees. As a people who had always valued the power of rhetoric expressed orally, the Cherokees hoped that the printed word and modern rhetoric could be turned against opposing forces and used to protect the political and social institutions that had evolved earlier in the century. At the same time, traditionalists among the Cherokees used literacy in their language to help preserve the Cherokee Nation's ancient religious and cultural heritage by creating texts to be handed down to succeeding generations. Thus the written expression of the language, the Sequoyan syllabary, became ingrained in Cherokee culture.

At the same time, the ability to communicate with the larger society in its own language took on a similar value. If the people's representatives were to negotiate treaties and influence the whites' policies, thorough fluency in English was required. Once the threat of land loss and Removal became a reality, literacy grew even more important as the threat of new intrusions on Cherokee territory emerged from whites seeking free or cheap land. When this threat later crystallized into a coordinated attack by the combined forces of railroad and land interests, populist politicians pandering to white voters, and an increasingly anti-Indian government policy, the need for educated persons to fight the enemy with words rather than guns became apparent.

Although the acquisition of the ability to read and write in either Cherokee or English did not ultimately alter the outcome of the struggle—the land was allotted, the Native governments were disbanded, and the land was opened to white settlement—the facility with written language prepared the Cherokees, as well as other Native peoples, in a perhaps unexpected way: the people were able to adapt to the new order in ways that tribes placed on reservations and thoroughly dependent on the largess of the federal government were unable to do. The ability to adapt became a source of pride to the Cherokees and was even woven into the fabric of their culture. Was not the invention of the syllabary itself a way to adapt to changing circumstances? Were not the early adoption of a constitution and the organization of a rather complex tribal government ways of adjusting to change? Shortly after Oklahoma statehood and the demise of tribal sovereignty, individual Cherokees, as well as Choctaws, Chickasaws, and others, ran for office. They not only sought local posts but also campaigned at the state and national levels. This adaptive spirit may be illustrated by a publication that appeared in 1926 called the *Super-Civilized Indian,* which included much political news and advice, as well as advertisements for candidates, Indian and non-Indian.[1] The audience for this monthly was obviously a literate, politically aware group whose members saw themselves as distinct from the larger society but in no way inferior to it. These were people who had not only ability and confidence in their language skills but also the self-assurance to face up to changing societal and political rules. In the present-day Cherokee Nation, this willingness to adapt is amply illustrated by efforts to link the use of the syllabary to the latest electronic means of communication. Thus this talent for coping with a larger society that is continually modifying itself continues.

Obviously, the Cherokee language did not disappear with tribal dissolution or the creation of the state of Oklahoma early in the twentieth century. It has continued in both its written and spoken forms until today. During World War I, for example, Cherokee troops were the first of the Indian "code talkers" to use their language to transmit and conceal critical information. Cherokees in the 30th Infantry Division in the Second Battle of the Somme sent telephone messages to other Cherokee signal men, often creating colorful terms for such equipment as tanks, airplanes, and machine guns for which no native equivalent words existed.[2] Cherokee troops in the 36th Division were trained as code talkers and assigned to the telephone service. Later, the more famous Navajo and Choctaw signal men used their languages in the same effort. In World War II, seventeen tribes were represented among the code talkers, including Cherokees.[3]

Use of the Cherokee language did dwindle after World War II because of a variety of factors, including Relocation, in which people moved away from the nation, and the prohibition of native languages in government schools. However, a significant effort to teach the language to young people began in both the Oklahoma and the Eastern Cherokee Nations in the last decades of the twentieth century and has increased in recent years. Some spectacular strides have been made. In Oklahoma, the Cherokee Nation passed the Act Relating to the Tribal Policy for the Promotion and Preservation of Cherokee Language, History and Culture in 1991. This law ensured, among other things, that Cherokee, along with English, was the official language of the government. Henceforth, business would be conducted in both languages, much as it had been in the nineteenth century. Additionally, the act called for the establishment of an extensive educational campaign that would focus not only on the schools but also on adult learning. Classes in the people's heritage were organized, and their teachers traveled to various population centers where significant numbers of Cherokees lived. The Cherokee Heritage Center expanded its offerings along these lines at Park Hill, drawing Cherokee and non-Native visitors from distant places. The centerpiece of this revival of interest in all things Cherokee, however, was the language-instruction programs, with their emphasis on the Sequoyan syllabary.

The Cherokee Immersion School was created in 2001 by the nation's educational services department. The major impetus for the

EPILOGUE 249

school was the realization that the language was in imminent danger of dying out; most of the speakers were over age fifty, and young people had not learned to speak Cherokee. The school operates according to a step-by-step method. It started with three-year-olds and then added a new class every year, kindergartners, first-graders, and so on, until high school. At Sequoyah High School, the students take a regular curriculum plus a class in the Cherokee language each year until graduation. The program anticipates that by graduation, students will have attained a mastery of the language to the extent that they can become translators.

Although modern communications technology has no doubt contributed over the years to children not learning the language of their forebears, it has been embraced by enterprising young people engaged in Cherokee-language education. Joseph Erb and Roy Boney, Jr., have been able to introduce learners of Cherokee to using the syllabary to access texting devices, search engines, such as Google, and other electronic tools. They use methods they and software engineers at electronics/software firms developed, employing two types of keyboards. One is a virtual keyboard with "keys" for each of the Sequoyan symbols; the other is a specially adapted QWERTY keyboard on which the user types a transliteration of the Cherokee sound in Roman alphabetic characters, and the program transforms these into the Sequoyan symbols. Young Cherokee speakers set up their Facebook pages using Sequoyan and text and e-mail one another in Cherokee, thus reinforcing the skills learned in the immersion classroom. This is yet another example of the Cherokees adapting to changing technology in order to preserve their culture. Erb, Boney, and others are following in the footsteps of Sequoyah and Elias Boudinot in this regard. It is hoped that the twenty-first-century adapters will be as successful as their forebears.

Similarly, the literary legacy of the Cherokees continues to the present day. Several writers in English rose to national and regional prominence in the first half of the twentieth century, benefiting from their nation's educational and literary heritage. Conspicuous among these are Rachel Eaton, Will Rogers, Mabel Washbourne Anderson, John Oskison, Royal Roger Eubanks, and Lynn Riggs. Eaton became a historian of note; Rogers, the well-known humorist and columnist for the *New York Times,* had an international reputation;

Anderson was a journalist and historian; Oskison became an essayist and correspondent; Eubanks was a teacher, artist, and writer; and
Lynn Riggs gained attention as a poet and dramatist.

Rachel Caroline Eaton was born soon after the Civil War in 1869,
when the nation was still in turmoil and beset by the terms of the
postwar treaty. She was the daughter of George W. Eaton, a white
man, and Nancy Williams Eaton, a Cherokee. Eaton attended the
national schools and graduated from the Female Seminary in 1887,
after which she earned her B.A. at Drury College, followed by an
M.A. and a Ph.D. from the University of Chicago, where her doctoral
dissertation was "John Ross and the Cherokee Indians." She then
entered her lifetime career as a teacher and researcher, teaching at
Erie College in Ohio and Trinity University in Texas, as well as at the
Female Seminary. Later she became superintendent of schools for
Rogers County, Oklahoma. Her historical research is valuable because it draws not only from written accounts but also from the oral
tradition. Rachel Eaton died in 1938.

Although Will Rogers, the well-known humorist, made his initial
foray into show business as a cowboy, he was a Cherokee and billed
himself as "the Cherokee Kid." Born in 1879 at Oolagah, Cherokee
Nation, he was the son of Clement Vann Rogers and Mary Schrimp-
sher Rogers. Clem Rogers was the proprietor of a large ranch and a
Cherokee politician, and Mary Rogers had attended the Female
Seminary. Both parents had high aspirations for Will, who attended
Cherokee schools before the Rogerses sent him to Kemper Military
Academy. After a year of military discipline, however, he left to become a cowboy in Texas and worked there for four years before leaving in 1902 to see the world. In South Africa, he joined Texas Jack's
Wild West Circus as a trick rider and roper; when the entourage returned to the United States in 1904, he joined another Wild West
show, which eventually led him to vaudeville. As a showman, he
appeared in musical productions, joining the Ziegfeld Follies in
1916. During the 1920s, he went on lecture tours and became involved in radio shows that broadcast his wit and humor across
America. He also acted in a number of films between 1925 and 1935,
making the transition from silent pictures to "talkies."

Rogers turned his attention to current events and in 1922 began a
weekly newspaper column that commented on happenings in the

nation and the world. He also wrote books, including *The Illiterate Digest* (1924), *Letters of a Self-Made Diplomat to His President* (1926), *There's Not a Bathing Suit in Russia* (1927), and *Ether and Me* (1929). Rogers was embraced by the common people because he talked their language. He exposed false intellectuals, the pretentious rich, pompous politicians, and other pretenders, using a conversational tone, slang, ungrammatical structures, and deliberate misspellings. Very much in demand, he traveled the world, representing what most people agreed was the best America had to offer. He was on such a journey when his plane, piloted by aviation pioneer and fellow Oklahoman Wiley Post, crashed near Point Barrow, Alaska, in 1935. Much of what he said and wrote may be applied to today's world.

Mabel Washbourne Anderson was born in the Cherokee Nation in 1863, attended the nation's public schools, and graduated from the Female Seminary in 1883. She was related to two families important in Cherokee history: her maternal grandfather was John Ridge, and her paternal grandfather was Cephas Washburn (the name came to its current spelling later), both mentioned numerous times in preceding chapters. After graduating from the seminary, she became a teacher and married John Anderson in 1891. The couple lived at Pryor Creek in the nation and later moved to Tulsa.

While continuing to teach, Anderson began writing for newspapers and making appearances before local literary societies in 1890. She wrote poetry, fiction, and essays in which she explored Cherokee history, folklore, biography, and literature. Her work was widely known in Oklahoma and was published outside the Cherokee Nation and the state as she became more widely recognized. One of her most famous works is a biography of her grandfather John Ridge's cousin, Stand Watie, whom she immortalized as the last Confederate general to surrender. Most of her historical work is considered nostalgic today, but it reveals the almost romantic reverence with which later Cherokees regarded their existence before tribal dissolution. It also demonstrates a certain amount of the pride that Cherokees exhibit in their status as a civilized nation. Anderson continued to write and publish until her death in 1949.

John Milton Oskison had a long career as a fiction and prose writer of some note. Born at Vinita, Cherokee Nation in 1874, Oskison attended Willie Halsell College there, where he was a friend and classmate of Will Rogers. He finished college at Stanford University in 1898 and entered the graduate literature program at Harvard. He had begun writing short stories at Stanford, and in 1899 he published "Only the Master Shall Praise" in *Century Magazine,* winning that publication's award competition for college graduates. He continued to write short fiction, using the Cooweescoowee District, where he had spent his boyhood, as a setting. He took his characters, both Indian and white, from the same area. Subsequently, Oskison published in *Century, Overland, Frank Leslie's Monthly, North American Review, Everybody's,* and *McClure's,* benefiting from the popularity of regional writing at the time.

He next turned to journalism and edited a newspaper in Ossining, New York, from 1903 to 1912. Oskison also wrote editorials and financial pieces for *Collier's* and was a syndicated writer for other periodicals. Later, he turned to writing novels, publishing *Wild Harvest* (1925), *Black Jack Davy* (1926), and *Brothers Three* (1935); in these novels, he returned to the settings, characters, and themes of his earlier fiction, depicting the Indians, missionaries, outlaws, and white immigrants of Indian Territory in the late nineteenth and early twentieth centuries. He also published two book-length biographies, *Texas Titan: The Story of Sam Houston* (1929) and *Tecumseh and His Times* (1939), recounting the lives of a white man adopted by the Cherokees and a Shawnee and pan-Indian leader.

Royal Roger Eubanks was born at Tahlequah in the Cherokee Nation in 1879, the son of writer and polymath William Eubanks and Eliza Thompson Eubanks. Educated in the Cherokee public schools, he graduated from the Male Seminary in 1897. He then taught school, first in a small community and then at the Cherokee Orphan Asylum, and in 1901 became a teacher at the Male Seminary. He became its superintendent in 1905. Eubanks was a gifted artist and pursued this talent as he taught young men and women. He published political cartoons in Cherokee newspapers before moving to Chicago, where he joined a cartoon syndicate. He left Chicago to return to his teaching career but continued to work in commercial art.

Upon his return, he began to write dialect tales and short stories, all of which involved Cherokee history and culture, perhaps as part of the movement at that time of preserving aspects of the past Indian civilization that were in danger of disappearing. He took part in a similar project by a Wyandotte writer, B. N. O. Walker, or Hen-Toh, who wrote *Tales of the Bark Lodges* and employed Eubanks to illustrate the volume. The Cherokee wrote a number of animal tales reminiscent of Joel Chandler Harris's *Nights with Uncle Remus,* using the Cherokee dialect, but he wrote other stories as well that reflected the clash of cultures as the whites poured into Indian Territory. Eubanks spent his later years in Berryville, Arkansas, where he taught school and engaged in commercial art.

When Lynn Riggs died in 1954, he left behind a reputation as one of the premier American playwrights of the 1920s and 1930s. Born at Claremore, Cherokee Nation, in 1899, he attended Oklahoma public schools. He became a journalist after high school, working for newspapers in Chicago, New York City, and Los Angeles, before enrolling at the University of Oklahoma in 1920. At Oklahoma, he wrote poetry for school publications and, upon leaving the university, published his work in *Poetry,* the *Nation,* and the *Bookman.* When he moved to Santa Fe, New Mexico, upon medical advice, he turned to writing plays and gained such attention in this area that he was offered a Guggenheim fellowship in 1928–29. During this time, he traveled to France, where he wrote what he called his "folk play," *Green Grow the Lilacs.* The play was later produced as the musical *Oklahoma!,* which was subsequently made into a popular film. His other plays brought him critical and popular acclaim as well. During the 1930s, he worked as a scriptwriter for major movie studios but continued to write for the stage and to compose poetry. Riggs was another Cherokee writer who drew on the later years of Indian Territory and the Cherokee Nation in particular, taking his settings and characters from that time and place.

Although the superb intellectual activities of the Cherokees in the nineteenth century did not succeed in stopping the forces of Removal and allotment, they nevertheless provided the foundation for learning and literary efforts that continue today. Men and women of Cherokee descent have reached pinnacles in the literary world. Cherokee writers have also inspired other Native Americans to take up the pen and write not only about their nations' pasts but also about their present and future. Their literary efforts were given a strong impetus by an unlettered Cherokee working alone in a cabin, thinking his project through and completing it with perfection.

NOTES

Chapter 1

1. Orly Goldwasser, "How the Alphabet Was Born from Hieroglyphics," *Biblical Archaeology Review* 36:2 (March–April 2010): 38–50.

2. "Mesoamerican Writing Systems," Ancientscripts.Com, http://www.an cientscripts.com/ma_ws.html (accessed November 20, 2012).

3. David Tavárez, "Zapotec Time, Alphabetic Writing, and the Public Sphere," *Ethnohistory* 57:1 (Winter 2010): 73–85.

4. John F. Chuckiak IV, "Writing as Resistance: Maya Graphic Pluralism and Indigenous Elite Strategies for Survival in Colonial Yucatan, 1550–1750," *Ethnohistory* 57:1 (Winter 2010): 87–116.

5. James Constantine Pilling, *Bibliography of the Iroquoian Languages*, Bureau of American Ethnology (Washington, D.C.: Government Printing Office, 1888), 191ff.

6. Barbara Williams and Maria del Carmen Jorge y Jorge, "Aztec Arithmetic Revisited: Land-Area Algorithms and Acolhua Congruence Arithmetic," *Science* 320:5872 (April 2008): 72–77.

7. Phillip H. Round, *Removable Type: Histories of the Book in Indian Country, 1663–1880* (Chapel Hill: University of North Carolina Press, 2010), 21. Round's work, surprisingly, pays little attention to Cherokee literary and printing efforts.

8. Ives Goddard and Kathleen J. Bragdon, *Native Writing in Massachusetts*, Memoirs of the American Philosophical Society (Philadelphia: American Philosophical Society, 1988), 14.

9. Ives Goddard, "Native Writing Systems," in Willard B. Walker, *Handbook of North American Indians*, vol. 17. Edited by William C. Sturtevant (Washington, D.C.: Smithsonian Institution, 1996), 159–60.

10. Round, *Removable Type*, passim.

11. David M. Oestreicher, "Unmasking the *Walum Olum*: A Nineteenth-Century Hoax," *Bulletin of the Archaeological Society of New Jersey* 49:1 (1994): 1–44.

Chapter 2

1. Althea Bass, *Cherokee Messenger* (Norman: University of Oklahoma Press, 1936), 43–44.

2. William G. McLoughlin, *Cherokees and Missionaries, 1789–1839* (New Haven: Yale University Press, 1984), 33.

3. Ibid., 2.

4. Francis Paul Prucha, *American Indian Policy in the Formative Years: The Indian Trade and Intercourse Acts, 1780–1832* (Cambridge, Mass.: Harvard University Press, 1962), 213–16.

5. Ard Hoyt, "Brainerd Journal," June 24, 1818, American Board of Commissioners for Foreign Missions Papers, (hereafter cited as ABCFM Papers), 18.3.1, Reel 73 Houghton Library, Harvard University.

6. William G. McLoughlin, *Cherokee Renascence in the New Republic* (Princeton: Princeton University Press, 1986), 355. President James Monroe introduced an Indian removal plan in the year after his advocacy of the civilization act. This is a good example of the government's mixed attitudes toward the Indian "problem."

7. McLoughlin, *Cherokees and Missionaries*, 103.

8. Joseph Tracy, *History of the American Board of Commissioners for Foreign Missions* (Worcester, Mass.: Spooner and Howland, 1840), 46.

9. McLoughlin traces the fortunes of these early missionaries in *Cherokees and Missionaries*, 35–81. Other factors were involved in the missions' difficulties besides language issues. For example, some of the missionaries had engaged in Cherokee politics by taking sides in internal disputes, and one was accused of selling whiskey.

10. Ibid., 106–107.

11. ABCFM, Annual Report, 1816, quoted in Bass, *Cherokee Messenger*, 291.

12. McLoughlin, *Cherokees and Missionaries*, 4–5.

13. Stephen Brandon, "Sacred Fire and Sovereign Rhetorics: Cherokee Literacy and Literature in the Cherokee and American Nations, 1760–1841" (Ph.D. diss., University of North Carolina at Greensboro, 2003), 220.

14. William G. McLoughlin, *Champions of the Cherokees: Evan and John B. Jones* (Princeton: Princeton University Press, 1990), 345.

15. William G. McLoughlin and Walter H. Conser, Jr., "The Cherokees in Transition: A Statistical Analysis of the Federal Cherokee Census of 1835," *Journal of American History* 64:3 (December 1977): 692.

16. McLoughlin, *Champions of the Cherokees*, 34.

17. Thomas McKenney to Cyrus Kingsbury, April 10, 1826, quoted in John A. Andrew, *From Revivals to Removal: Jeremiah Evarts, the Cherokee Nation, and the Search for the Soul of America* (Athens: University of Georgia Press, 1992), 147.

18. *Latter Day Luminary* 1:154. Published in Philadelphia from 1818 to 1826, the *Latter Day Luminary* was the official organ of the Baptist Foreign Mission Board; it contains many of the early letters of the Baptist missionaries to the Cherokees.

19. McLoughlin, *Champions of the Cherokees*, 35.

20. Tracy, *History of the American Board*, 147.

21. Bass, *Cherokee Messenger*, 88.

22. Evan Jones Journal, November 22, 1829, quoted in McLoughlin, *Champions of the Cherokees*, 83.

23. *Latter Day Luminary* 3:311.

24. McLoughlin, *Champions of the Cherokees*, 26.

25. *Latter Day Luminary* 3:311–13.

26. Grant Foreman, *Sequoyah* (Norman: University of Oklahoma Press, 1938), 9–10.

27. Daniel S. Butrick's Journal, February 24, 1823, ABCFM Papers, 18:3:1, Reel 738.

28. McLoughlin, *Champions of the Cherokees*, 36.

29. Foreman, *Sequoyah*, 10.

30. McLoughlin, *Cherokees and Missionaries*, 136–37.

31. John Pickering, *Essay on a Uniform Orthography for the Indian Languages of North America* (London: Cambridge University Press, Hilliard and Metcalf, 1820).

32. Daniel S. Butrick to Jeremiah Evarts, August 31, 1821, ABCFM Papers, 18:3:1, Reel 738.

33. John Pickering. *Grammar of the Cherokee Language* (Boston: Mission Press, 1830).

34. Foreman, *Sequoyah*, 11.

35. Bass, *Cherokee Messenger*, 37.

36. Daniel S. Butrick to Jeremiah Evarts, February 22, 1825, ABCFM Papers, 18:3:1, Reel 738.

37. Daniel S. Butrick to Jeremiah Evarts, May 28, 1825, ABCFM Papers, 18:3:1, Reel 738.

38. Daniel S. Butrick to Jeremiah Evarts, April 6, 1825, ABCFM Papers, 18:3:1, Reel 738.

39. Ard Hoyt to Jeremiah Evarts, June 30, 1825, ABCFM Papers, 18:3:1, Reel 739.

40. Daniel S. Butrick to Henry Hill, May 4, 1825, ABCFM Papers, 18:3:1, Reel 738.

41. McLoughlin, *Champions of the Cherokees*, 91–92.

42. Carmeleta L. Montieth, "Literacy among the Cherokee in the Early Nineteenth Century," *Journal of Cherokee Studies* 9:2 (Fall 1984): 63.

43. Henry T. Malone, *Cherokees of the Old South: A People in Transition* (Athens: University of Georgia Press, 1956), 156–57.

44. Elias Boudinot, "Address to the Whites," Philadelphia: n.p., 1826.

45. McLoughlin, *Cherokees and Missionaries, 1789–1839* (New Haven: Yale University Press, 1984).

46. Between 1888 and 1890, James Mooney was able to procure some manuscripts written in the syllabary that became the basis for his *Myths of the Cherokee* (Washington, D.C.: Government Printing Office, 1900).

47. See McLoughlin, *Cherokees and Missionaries*, 185–86; McLoughlin, *Cherokee Renascence*, 350; and McLoughlin, *Champions of the Cherokees*, 39–40.

48. William Chamberlin's Journal, October 25, 1824, ABCFM Papers, 18:3:1, Reel 739.

49. Isaac Proctor to Jeremiah Evarts, January 25, 1825, ABCFM Papers, 18:3:1, Reel 739.

50. McLoughlin, *Cherokee Renascence*, 353.

51. Daniel S. Butrick to Jeremiah Evarts, November 26, 1824, ABCFM Papers, 18:3:1, Reel 739.

52. Daniel S. Butrick to Rufus Anderson, September 27, 1825, ABCFM Papers, 18:3:1, Reel 739.

53. *Missionary Herald*, February 1826, 47–48.

54. William Chamberlin's Journal, January 25, 1825, ABCFM Papers, 18:3:1, Reel 739.

55. Foreman, *Sequoyah*, 29.

56. Ibid., 28–29.

57. Jace Weaver, *That the People Might Live: Native American Literatures and Native American Community* (Oxford: Oxford University Press, 1997), 216.

58. McLoughlin and Conser, "Cherokees in Transition," 690.

59. *Cherokee Census of 1835*, Monograph 2 (Tulsa, OK: Trail of Tears Association, Oklahoma Chapter, 1986), especially 66.

60. Bass, *Cherokee Messenger*, 35.

61. Ellen Cushman, "The Cherokee Syllabary from Script to Print," *Ethnohistory* 57:4 (Fall 2010): 642.

62. McLoughlin, *Cherokees and Missionaries*, 185.

63. John Gambold to Thomas L. McKenney, August 30, 1924, quoted in McLoughlin, *Cherokee Renascence*, 353–54.

64. *Missionary Herald*, February 1826, 49.

65. Isaac Proctor to Rufus Anderson, March 27, 1826, ABCFM Papers, 18:3:1, Reel 739.

66. Brandon, "Sacred Fire and Sovereign Rhetorics," 132.

67. Isaac Proctor to Jeremiah Evarts, July 20, 1825, ABCFM Papers, 18:3:1, Reel 739.

68. William Chamberlin's Journal, October–November 1824.

69. Daniel S. Butrick to Jeremiah Evarts, February 22, 1825, ABCFM Papers, 18:3:1, Reel 739.

70. Isaac Proctor to Jeremiah Evarts, July 30, 1825, ABCFM Papers, 18:3:1, Reel 739.

71. Daniel S. Butrick to Jeremiah Evarts, December 8, 1826, ABCFM Papers, 18:3:1, Reel 739.

72. Daniel S. Butrick to Jeremiah Evarts, April 9, 1827, ABCFM Papers, 18:3:1, Reel 739.

73. McLoughlin, *Champions of the Cherokees*, 39.

74. Ibid., 80–83.

75. Nevada Couch, *Pages from Cherokee Indian History, as Identified with Samuel Austin Worcester, D.D., for 34 Years a Missionary of the A.B.C.F.M. among the Cherokees* (St. Louis: R. P. Studley and Co., 1884), 5–6.

76. Foreman, *Sequoyah*, 12–13.

77. Ibid., 7.

78. Samuel Worcester to Rufus Anderson, March 27, 1826, ABCFM Papers, 18:3:1, Reel 738.

79. *Missionary Herald*, February 1826, 48.

80. *Missionary Herald*, July 1827, 213.

81. *Missionary Herald* 25:1 (January 1829): 10; 24:5 (May 1828): 162–63.

82. Return J. Meigs to Col. Alexander Smyth, February 27, 1811; National Council at Oostenali to Meigs, May 5, 1811, Bureau of Indian Affairs, National Archives M-208.

83. Blair was a white man who had helped the Cherokees expel intruders and criminals.

84. For further details on the Rocky Mountain vision, see McLoughlin, *Cherokees and Missionaries*, 84–98.

85. McLoughlin and Conser, "Cherokees in Transition," 690–91.

86. Brandon, "Sacred Fire and Sovereign Rhetorics," 219.

87. McLoughlin, *Cherokee Renascence,* 355.

Chapter 3

1. *Laws of the Cherokee Nation* (Tahlequah, (Cherokee Nation: Cherokee Nation Press, 1852), 84–85.

2. See, for example, Barbara Luebke's profile of the *Phoenix* in Daniel F. Littlefield, Jr., and James W. Parins, *American Indian and Alaska Native Newspapers and Periodicals, 1826–1924* (Westport, Conn.: Greenwood Press, 1984); and Theda Perdue, ed., *Cherokee Editor: The Writings of Elias Boudinot* (Knoxville: University of Tennessee Press, 1983).

3. For Wheeler's account, see *Indian Record,* October, November, and December 1886 and January, February, and March 1887. The March 1887 number of the *Indian Record,* published at Muskogee in the Creek Nation, may have been the last. Wheeler's history was unfinished with that issue. An abbreviated version of his account may be found in Pilling, *Bibliography of the Iroquoian Languages,* 41–42.

4. *Indian Record,* October 1886, p. 1 col. 4.

5. Ibid.

6. See Luebke, *"Cherokee Phoenix* and Indians' Advocate," for a discussion,

7. Cullen Joe Holland. "Cherokee Indian Newspapers, 1828–1906: The Tribal Voice of a People in Transition" (Ph.D. diss., University of Minnesota, 1956), 53.

8. *Cherokee Phoenix,* April 24, 1828, 3:3.

9. *Indian Record,* December 1886, 1:4–5.

10. *Indian Record,* February 1887, 1:2. The account here of the legal proceedings between Worcester and the Cherokees and the Georgia authorities follows Wheeler's account in the February and March 1887 issues of the *Indian Record* and that of Bass, *Cherokee Messenger,* 137–77.

11. Bass, *Cherokee Messenger,* 126–28.

12. Ralph H. Gabriel, *Elias Boudinot, Cherokee, and His America* (Norman: University of Oklahoma Press, 1941), 114.

13. Holland, "Cherokee Indian Newspapers," 70.

14. Tracy, *History of the American Board,* 39.

15. Brandon, "Sacred Fire and Sovereign Rhetorics," 222.

16. Henry Clay, December 25, 1825, quoted in McLoughlin, *Champions of the Cherokees,* frontispiece.

17. Samuel Carter, *Cherokee Sunset: A Nation Betrayed* (Garden City, N.Y.: Doubleday, 1976), 160.

18. Elias Boudinot to Stand Watie, February 28, 1833, quoted in Kenny A. Franks, *Stand Watie and the Agony of the Cherokee Nation* (Memphis: Memphis State University Press, 1979), 17.

19. Franks, *Stand Watie,* 21. See also Luebke, *"Cherokee Phoenix* and Indians' Advocate," 89–90.

Chapter 4

1. "Message of the Principal Chiefs of the Cherokee Nation, October 13, 1828," reported in the *Missionary Herald* 24:12 (December 1828): 391.

2. McLoughlin, *Cherokees and Missionaries,* 108.

3. Daniel S. Butrick to Jeremiah Evarts, August 31, 1821, ABCFM Papers, 18.3.1, Reel 738.

4. William G. McLoughlin, *After the Trail of Tears,* (Chapel Hill: University of North Carolina Press, 1993), 87.

5. Ard Hoyt to Jeremiah Everts, August 7, 1823, ABCFM Papers, 18.3.1, Reel 738.

6. Humphrey Posey to Corresponding Secretary, Baptist Board of Foreign Missions, November 18, 1819, reported in the *Latter Day Luminary* 2:11 (February 1820): 28.

7. Abraham Steiner to Gen. Calvin James, July 17, 1820, in *Latter Day Luminary* 2:217 (May 1821): 330–31.

8. "Cherokee," *Encyclopedia of Arkansas History and Culture,* http://encyclopedia ofarkansas.net (accessed August 25, 2012).

9. Robert Howard Skelton, "A History of the Educational System of the Cherokee Nation, 1801–1910" (Ed.D. thesis, University of Arkansas, 1970), 72.

10. Ibid., 75–76.

11. John Ross, Annual Message, 1840, Papers of John Ross, in Gary Moulton, *Papers of John Ross* (Rome: University of Georgia Press, 2004), 2:404.

12. McLoughlin, *Champions of the Cherokees,* 204–207.

13. Annual Report of the Prudential Committee to the ABCFM on the Cherokee Mission, 1860.

14. "An Act Relative to Public Schools," December 18, 1841, in *Laws of the Cherokee Nation: Adopted by the Council at Various Periods* (Tahlequah, Cherokee Nation: Cherokee Advocate Office, 1852), 59–61.

15. *Cherokee Advocate,* April 3, 1845.

16. "Amendment to the Cherokee Treaty," *Cherokee Documents,* I, 2 (Misc. Docs. 148, 41st Cong., 2d Sess.)

17. Cherokee Delegation to the Committee on Indian Affairs, House of Representatives, (Washington, D. C.: Government Printing Office, 1878), 6.

18. McLoughlin, *After the Trail of Tears,* 88–89.

19. *Annual Report of the Commissioner of Indian Affairs* (Washington, D. C.: Government Printing Office, 1849), 560.

20. An exception to this statement was the *Cherokee Advocate,* first published in 1844, which emulated the *Phoenix* in its use of the syllabary to supplement its English content.

21. Report, April 18, 1854, in ABCFM; quoted in McLoughlin, *After the Trail of Tears,* 93. It is difficult to assess the accuracy of these numbers.

22. Samuel A. Worcester to S. B. Treat, June 5, 1854, ABCFM; cited in McLoughlin, *After the Trail of Tears,* 94.

23. "Memorial of John Beeson, etc.," 43d Cong., 1st Sess., Sen. Misc. Docs.; also *Cherokee Documents* 12, 1.

24. Emmet Starr, *History of the Cherokee Indians and Their Legends and Folk Lore* (1921; repr., Baltimore: Genealogical Publishing Co., 2006), 228.

25. Skelton, "History of the Educational System," 134.

26. Ibid., 156.

27. Cherokee Nation, *Laws of the Cherokee Nation, 1839–1867* (St. Louis: Missouri Democrat Printing, 1868), 64.

28. *Report of the Commissioner of Indian Affairs.* (Washington, D.C.: Government Printing Office, 1873), 203; also Skelton, "History of the Educational System," 136.

29. John B. Jones's report, September 1871, in *Annual Report of the Commissioner of Indian Affairs* (Washington, D.C., Government Printing Office, 1871), 563–69.

30. John B. Jones's report, September 1872, in *Annual Report of the Commissioner of Indian Affairs* (Washington, D.C., 1873), 236.

31. *Cherokee Advocate,* March 7, 1874.

32. *Cherokee Advocate,* May 9 and June 6, 1874.

33. Jones's 1873 report was included in the *Report of the Commissioner of Indian Affairs, 1874* (Washington, D. C., Government Printing Office, 1874), 204.

34. Starr, *History of the Cherokee Indians,* 229.

35. Skelton, "History of the Educational System," 150.

36. *Constitution and Laws of the Cherokee Nation* (Foley Printing, 1893), 282.

37. "An Act Making Further Provisions for Carrying into Effect the Act of the Last Annual Session of the National Council, for the Establishment of One Male and One Female Seminary or High School," November 11, 1847, in *Laws of the Cherokee Nation: Adopted by the Council at Various Periods,* 59–61.

38. Starr, *History of the Cherokee Indians,* 142.

39. Althea Leah Bass, *A Cherokee Daughter of Mount Holyoke* (Muscatine, Iowa: Prairie Press, 1937), 13.

40. See Brad Agnew, "A Legacy of Education: The History of the Cherokee Seminaries," *Chronicles of Oklahoma* 63 (Summer 1985): 128–47, for a history based on official records and interviews with former students.

41. Ibid., 134.

42. Ibid., 140.

43. Although the newspapers do not carry many details of the societies' activities, notices of meetings are found throughout their pages in the years after the Civil War.

44. McLoughlin, *Champions of the Cherokees,* 213. McLoughlin also attributes the rise of church membership in the nation to the breakdown of the clan system. He posits that church activities, such as revivals and camp meetings, replaced busks (traditional gatherings for dances and feasts held on busk grounds) and other socioreligious ceremonies in Cherokee life, especially among full-bloods, as Christianity gradually replaced the traditional belief system.

45. *Laws of the Cherokee Nation: Adopted by the Council at Various Periods,* 182.

46. Starr, *History of the Cherokee Indians,* 243–46.

47. "Report: An Act Authorizing the Locating Permanently of the Orphan Asylum and the Home for the Insane, Deaf, Dumb, and Blind of the Cherokee Nation , and for Other Purposes," November 29, 1873, Cherokee National Records, Sequoyah National Research Center, University of Arkansas at Little Rock, Cherokee (Tahlequah)—Orphan Asylum, October 23, 1866–September 18, 1909, Roll CHN 67.

48. McLoughlin, *After the Trail of Tears,* 321–23.

49. "Orphan Asylum Roll," Cherokee National Records, Cherokee (Tahlequah)—Orphan Asylum, October 23, 1866–September 18, 1909, Roll CHN 67.

50. "Third Annual Report, Cherokee Orphans' Asylum, 1874," Cherokee National Records, Cherokee (Tahlequah)—Orphan Asylum, October 23, 1866–September 18, 1909, Roll CHN 67.

51. "Senate Bill No. 14," Cherokee National Records, Cherokee (Tahlequah)—Orphan Asylum, October 23, 1866–September 18, 1909, Roll CHN 67.

52. John D. Benedict to W. C. Rogers, July 31, 1906, Cherokee National Records, Cherokee (Tahlequah)—Orphan Asylum, October 23, 1866–September 18, 1909, Roll CHN 67.

53. See T. L. Ballenger, "The Colored High School of the Cherokee Nation," *Chronicles of Oklahoma* 30 (Winter 1952–53): 454–468.

Chapter 5

1. Janine Scancarelli, "Cherokee," in *Native Languages of the Southeastern United States*, ed. Heather K. Hardy and Janine Scancarelli (Lincoln: University of Nebraska Press, 2005), 351.

2. Ibid., 364–65.

3. James Mooney, *The Sacred Formulas of the Cherokees* (Washington, D.C.: U.S. Bureau of American Ethnology, 1885–86). A digital version is available at http://www.sacred-texts.com/nam/cher/sfoc/sfoc26.htm. (accessed August 25, 2012).

4. Mooney, *Myths*, "Introduction," 1.

5. Jack Frederick Kilpatrick and Anna Gritts Kilpatrick, transl. and eds., *The Shadow of Sequoyah: Social Documents of the Cherokees, 1862–1964* (Norman: University of Oklahoma Press, 1965). The account here of some of these papers is deeply indebted to this important work.

6. See Alan Kilpatrick, "The Inoli Letters," *American Indian Quarterly* 19:3 (Summer 1995).

7. Kilpatrick and Kilpatrick, *Shadow of Sequoyah*, 24.

8. That is, the supreme being. The reference is probably to Christian religious texts.

9. Kilpatrick and Kilpatrick, *Shadow of Sequoyah*, 54.

10. Ibid., 62–63.

11. *Tahlequah Arrow*, March 14, 1903.

12. *Cherokee Advocate*, October 26, 1892.

13. See Chapter Four.

14. Jones did manage to get his textbook project under way, however, and published his *Elementary Arithmetic, in Cherokee and English, Designed for Beginners* in 1870 under the authority of the Cherokee National Council (Tahlequah: Cherokee National Press).

15 Raymond Yamachika, "Cherokee Literature: Printing in the Sequoyan Syllabary since 1828, with a Bibliography" (M.A. thesis, University of Oklahoma, 1961). Yamachika's bibliography, gleaned from earlier sources, is very helpful for tracing patterns in publications in the syllabary. Much of the information for this discussion of Cherokee publishing has been obtained from Yamachika's work.

16. Ibid., 159.

17. Ibid., 165.

18. *Missionary Herald* 32 (March 1836): 4, 110.

19. Lon H. Eakes, "Rev. Amory Nelson Chamberlin (1821–1894)," *Chronicles of Oklahoma* 12:1 (March 1934): 97–102.

20. D. W. C. Duncan, "Sample Pages of Cherokee Grammar," Microfilm 397, Cherokee. Archives of the Bureau of American Ethnology, Smithsonian Institution, Washington, D.C.

21. D. W. C. Duncan to James Constantine Pilling, January 3, 1888, Duncan Files, Sequoyah National Research Center, University of Arkansas at Little Rock.

22. To W. P. Campbell, Oklahoma Historical Society, Oklahoma City, Okla., from D. W. C. Duncan, Vinita, Okla., February 2, 1909, Duncan Files, Sequoyah National Research Center, University of Arkansas at Little Rock.

23. C. L. Webster, "Prof. D. W. C. Duncan's Analysis of the Cherokee Language," *American Naturalist* 23 (September 1889): 775–81.

24. William P. Thompson, "Courts of the Cherokee Nation," *Chronicles of Oklahoma* 2:1 (March 1924): 63–74. This article includes a history of the Cherokee judicial system and a lawyer's recollections of court procedures during the last three decades of the nineteenth century.

25. Nathan E. Bender, "Cherokee Shorthand: As Derived from Pitman Shorthand and in Relation to the Dot-Notation Variant of the Sac and Fox Syllabary," *American Indian Culture and Research Journal* 15:3 (1991): 63–76. Bender compares the English and Cherokee shorthands, but also compares Eubanks's work with the development of the Sac and Fox syllabary and shows possible influence.

26. Ibid., 64.

Chapter 6

1. A history of the *Advocate,* as well as the other newspapers discussed in this chapter, may be found in Littlefield and Parins, *American Indian and Alaska Native Newspapers and Periodicals,* 63–76 and passim.

2. Morris L. Wardell, *A Political History of the Cherokee Nation, 1838–1907,* 2nd ed. (Norman: University of Oklahoma Press, 1977), 312–20.

3. Cherokee, "Sentiment," *Cherokee Advocate,* March 25, 1851.

4. "Letter," Cherokee, *Cherokee Advocate,* February 4, 1851.

5. Copies of the *Cherokee Advocate* published before the Civil War are extremely rare. The only nearly complete set known to the author is bound into volumes in the Periodicals section of the Library of Congress. Attempts by the author to digitize it have been denied by librarians there. Comments on and descriptions of the content in the present work are from notes by Daniel F. Littlefield, Jr. and James W. Parins from the Library of Congress set in the *Cherokee Advocate* file in the Press History Collection of the American Native Press Archives, Sequoyah National Research Center, University of Arkansas at Little Rock.

6. See "The Weekly Chieftain," in Littlefield and Parins, *American Indian and Alaska Native Newspapers,* 390–95, for a full description of this publication.

Chapter 7

1. See James W. Parins, *John Rollin Ridge: His Life and Works* (Lincoln; University of Nebraska Press, 1990). An edition of his poems is available at http://anpa.ualr.edu/digital_library/digital_library.html (accessed January 2, 2013).

2. "Fatal Recontre in the Cherokee Nation," *Fort Smith (Ark.) Herald,* June 6, 1849, p. 2, col. 5.

3. Edward Everett Dale and Gaston Litton, *Cherokee Cavaliers: Forty Years of Cherokee History as Told in the Correspondence of the Ridge-Watie-Boudinot Family* (Norman: University of Oklahoma Press, 1990), 63–64.

4. *Fort Smith Herald,* January 24 and 31, 1851; reprinted in *Northwest Arkansas Times* (Fayetteville), March 10, 11, 12, 13, and 14, 1973, p. 1, col. 1.

5. Dale and Litton, *Cherokee Cavaliers,* 83.

6. Parins, *John Rollin Ridge,* 103–107.

7. For a full description of Ridge's career in journalism, see ibid., 113–93.

8. *Cherokee Advocate,* July 22, 1876. See American Native Press Archives, "The Too Quah-stee Collection," http://anpa.ualr.edu/digital_library/TooquasteeCollection.htm, December 2, 2012, for edited writing by Duncan.

9. *Cherokee Advocate,* October 21, 1876, quoting from the *Independent,* September 4, 1876.

10. "The Doctrine of Karma or the Law of Retribution," *Indian Sentinel,* May 20, 1898.

11. Augustus Le Plongeon, *Sacred Mysteries among the Mayas and the Quiches* (New York: R. Macoy, 1886).

12. McLoughlin, *Champions of the Cherokees,* 91–92.

13. Carolyn Thomas Foreman, "Edward W. Bushyhead and John Rollin Ridge: Cherokee Editors in California," *Chronicles of Oklahoma* 14 (September 1936): 296.

14. For an account of the founding of the *Union,* see Richard B. Yale, "The Birthplace of the *San Diego Union,*" Journal of San Diego History 14 (October 1968). See also William E. Smythe, *History of San Diego County, 1542–1907,* vol. 2 (San Diego: History Company, 1907), 479–84. Smythe's remarks on Bushyhead are based on interviews with the editor. See also Teri Thorpe, "Early Journalism in San Diego: *The San Diego Herald* and the *San Diego Union,*" Journal of San Diego History 28 (Summer 1882): 194–204.

Chapter 8

1. Wardell, *Political History of the Cherokee Nation,* 187.

2. Cherrie Adair Moore, "William Penn Adair," *Chronicles of Oklahoma* 29 (1951): 32–41.

3. *Cherokee Advocate,* December 9, 1871, 2.

4. Wardell, *Political History of the Cherokee Nation,* 261–62.

5. John Barlett Meserve, "Chief William Potter Ross," *Chronicles of Oklahoma* 15:1 (March 1937): 21–28.

6. Daniel F. Littlefield, Jr., and James W. Parins, *Encyclopedia of Indian Removal,* vol. 1 (Santa Barbara, CA: Greenwood Press, 2011), 193.

7. Meserve, "Chief William Potter Ross." 21–29.

8. "Okmulgee Constitution," http://digital.library.okstate.edu/encyclopedia /entries/O/OK093.html (accessed December 2012).

9. William P. Ross, *Remarks in Opposition to the Bill to Organize the Territory of Oklahoma by William P. Ross, Principal Chief of the Cherokee Nation, before the Committee on Territories of the House of Representatives, Monday, February 9th, 1874* (Washington, D.C.: Gibson Brothers, Printers, 1874).

10. Ibid., 14.

11. Ibid., 18.

12. Ibid., 23.

13. J. H. Beadle, *The Undeveloped West; or, Five Years in the Territories* (Philadelphia and Chicago: National Publishing Company, 1873).

14. For more information on the rivalry among these opposing Cherokees, see James W. Parins, *Elias Cornelius Boudinot: A Life on the Cherokee Border* (Lincoln: University of Nebraska University Press, 2006), 175–202.

15. 45th Congress, 3d sess., Senate Report 744, February 11, 1879. His testimony as reported here was given in the previous year.

16. See ibid., 72–76, for the protest.

17. Elias C. Boudinot, *Argument of Elias C. Boudinot, Submitted to the Senate Committee on Territories, January 17, 1879. The Committee Having under Consideration the Resolutions of Hon. D. W. Voorhees, Relating to the Indian Territory* (Washington, D.C.: T. McGill and Co., 1879).

18. Parins, *Elias Cornelius Boudinot*, 191–92.

19. John Bartlett Meserve, "Chief Colonel Johnson Harris," *Chronicles of Oklahoma* 17:1 (March 1939): 17–20.

20. Johnson Harris, "To the Cherokee People," *Cherokee Advocate*, May 30, 1894.

Chapter 9

1. Wardell, *Political History of the Cherokee Nation*, 210, 334, 341.

2. William P. Boudinot to Stand Watie, April 26, 1848, in Dale and Litton, *Cherokee Cavaliers*, 62–63.

3. *Fort Gibson Post*, April 12, 1898.

4. *Tahlequah Arrow*, April 30 and June 25, 1898.

5. *Cherokee Advocate*, October 26, 1892.

6. *Cherokee Advocate*, December 9, 1876.

7. *Cherokee Advocate*, December 16, 1876.

8. *Cherokee Advocate*, January 6, 1877.

9. *Cherokee Advocate*, January 13, 1877.

10. U-Na-Kuh is similar to the Cherokee word for white man, *yonega.* Although many white men married Cherokee women and became respectable, responsible citizens, some married only to gain access to land and to a woman who would feed and clothe them and attend to other needs.

11. Probably Elias Cornelius Boudinot, Jr., son of William P. Boudinot.

12. A traditional Cherokee dish made of corn, spelled in English in a variety of ways, including *cor-nau-ha nauh* and *con-nau-ha-nali.*

13. That is, spent, depleted.

14. *Indian Chieftain*, January 23, 1890, 2.

15. Adair mentions these men in an article, "Last Hit at Monopoly," *Cherokee Advocate*, October 26, 1892. They are "Col. Boudinot, the Old Roman; Rev. Walter A. Duncan, the preacher warrior; W. H. Davis, who knows more than he puts on; S.[penser] S. S.[tephens], although there in the fray, adds much to the proposed plan."

16. *Cherokee Advocate*, August 31, 1908, 2.

17. O. P. Sturm, "The Oklahoma Literati," *Sturm's Oklahoma Magazine* 2 (February 1911).

18. http://digital.library.okstate.edu/encyclopedia/entries/T/TW002.html (accessed March 13, 2012).

19. http://digital.library.okstate.edu/encyclopedia/entries/S/ST058.html.

Epilogue

1. Newspaper files, 1926, Sequoyah National Research Center, University of Arkansas at Little Rock.

2. *20th Century Warriors: Native American Participation in the United States Military*, Government Documents Paper Materials, D 1.2: W 2. (Washington, D.C.: 1996).

3. Phillip R. Quochytewa II, "Native American Code Talkers Came from 17 Tribes, Not Just Navajo," http://www.aaanativearts.com/article1433.html (accessed January 21, 2011).

Selected Bibliography

Agnew, Brad. "A Legacy of Education: The History of the Cherokee Seminaries." *Chronicles of Oklahoma* 63 (Summer 1985): 128–47.

Andrew, John A. *From Revivals to Removal: Jeremiah Evarts, the Cherokee Nation, and the Search for the Soul of America.* Athens: University of Georgia Press, 1992.

Baptist Foreign Mission Board. *Latter Day Luminary.* Philadelphia: Baptist Board of Foreign Missions, 1818–26.

Bass, Althea. *A Cherokee Daughter of Mount Holyoke.* Muscatine, Iowa: Prairie Press, 1937.

———. *Cherokee Messenger.* Norman: University of Oklahoma Press, 1936.

Bender, Nathan E. "Cherokee Shorthand: As Derived from Pitman Shorthand and in Relation to the Dot-Notation Variant of the Sac and Fox Syllabary." *American Indian Culture and Research Journal* 15:3 (1991): 63–76.

Brandon, Stephen. "Sacred Fire and Sovereign Rhetorics: Cherokee Literacy and Literature in the Cherokee and American Nations, 1760–1841." Ph.D. diss., University of North Carolina at Greensboro, 2003.

Caywood, Elzie Ronald. "The History of Northeastern State College." M.A. thesis, University of Oklahoma, 1950.

Confer, Clarissa. *The Cherokee Nation in the Civil War.* Norman: University of Oklahoma Press, 2007.

Couch, Nevada. *Pages from Cherokee Indian History, as Identified with Samuel Austin Worcester, D.D., for 34 Years a Missionary of the A.B.C.F.M. among the Cherokees.* St. Louis: R. P. Studley and Co., 1884.

Cushman, Ellen. *The Cherokee Syllabary: Writing the People's Perseverance.* Norman: University of Oklahoma Press, 2011.

Debo, Angie. "Southern Refugess of the Cherokee Nation." *Southwestern Historical Quarterly* (1932): 255–57.

Evarts, Jeremiah. *Cherokee Removal: The "William Penn" Essays and Other Writings.* Edited by Francis Paul Prucha. Knoxville: University of Tennessee Press, 1891.

Foreman, Grant. *Sequoyah.* Norman: University of Oklahoma Press, 1938.

Foster, George E. *Se-quo-yah, the American Cadmus and Modern Moses*. Philadelphia: Office of the Indian Rights Association, 1885.

———. *Story of the Cherokee Bible*. New York: Democrat Press, 1899.

Gabriel, Ralph H. *Elias Boudinot, Cherokee, and His America*. Norman: University of Oklahoma Press, 1941.

Goddard, Ives. "Native Writing Systems." Vol. 17, in *Handbook of the North American Indians*, by Willard B. Walker, edited by William C. Sturtevant, 158–84. Washington, D.C.: Smithsonian Institution, 1996.

Holland, Cullen Joe. "Cherokee Indian Newspapers, 1828–1906: The Tribal Voice of a People in Transition." Ph.D. diss., University of Minnesota, 1956.

An Illustrated Souvenir Catalog of the Cherokee National Female Seminary, Tahlequah, I.T., 1850–1906. Chilocco, Okla.: Indian Print Shop, 1906.

Johnston, Carolyn Ross. *Cherokee Women in Crisis: The Trail of Tears, Civil War, and Allotment, 1835–1907*. Tuscaloosa: University of Alabama Press, 2003.

Kilpatrick, Jack F. *Sequoyah of Earth and Intellect*. Austen, Tex.: Encino Press, 1965.

Kilpatrick, Jack F., and Anna Gritts Kilpatrick, eds. *New Echota Letters*. Dallas: SMU Press, 1968.

——— trans. and eds. *The Shadow of Sequoyah: Social Documents of the Cherokees, 1862–1964*. Norman: University of Oklahoma Press, 1965.

Leeds, Georgia Rea. *The United Keetoowah Band of Cherokee Indians in Oklahoma*. New York: Peter Lang, 1996.

Lowrie, Walter, Walter S. Franklin, and Matthew Clark. *American State Papers, Class II, Indian Affairs*. Washington, D.C.: Gales and Seaton, 1832, 1834.

Malone, Henry Thompson. "*The Cherokee Phoenix*: Supreme Expression of Cherokee Nationalism." *Georgia Historical Quarterly* (September 1950): 163–88.

———. *Cherokees of the Old South: A People in Transition*. Athens: University of Georgia Press, 1956.

McLoughlin, William G. *Champions of the Cherokees: Evan and John B. Jones*. Princeton: Princeton University Press, 1990.

———. *Cherokee Renascence in the New Republic*. Princeton: Princeton University Press, 1986.

———. *Cherokees and Missionaries, 1789–1939*. New Haven: Yale University Press, 1984.

McLoughlin, William G., and Walter H. Conser, Jr., eds. *The Cherokees and Christianity, 1794–1870: Essays on Acculturation and Cultural Persistence*. Athens: University of Georgia Press, 1994.

———. "The Cherokees in Transition: A Statistical Analysis of the Federal Cherokee Census of 1835." *Journal of American History* 64 (December 1977): 678–703.

Mihesuah, Devon A. *Cultivating the Rosebuds: The Education of Women at the Cherokee Female Seminary, 1851–1909*. Urbana: University of Illinois Press, 1993.

Monteith, Carmeleta L. "Literacy among the Cherokee in the Early Nineteenth Century." *Journal of Cherokee Studies* 9:2 (Fall 1984): 56–75.

Mooney, James. *Myths of the Cherokees. U.S. Bureau of American Ethnology, 19th Annual Report, 1897–1898*. Washington, D.C.: Government Printing Office, 1900.

Morris L. Wardell. *A Political History of the Cherokee Nation, 1838–1907*. 2nd ed. Norman: University of Oklahoma Press, 1977.

Perdue, Theda, ed. *Cherokee Editor: The Writings of Elias Boudinot*. Knoxville: University of Tennessee Press, 1983.

———. *Cherokee Women, Gender and Culture Change, 1700–1835.* Lincoln: University of Nebraska Press, 1998.

———. "Rising from the Ashes: *The Cherokee Phoenix* as an Ethno-historical Source." *Ethnohistory* (Summer 1977): 207–18.

Pilling, James Constantine. *Bibliography of the Iroquoian Languages.* Bureau of American Ethnology Bulletin 6. Washington, D.C.: Government Printing Office, 1888.

Prucha, Francis Paul. *American Indian Policy in the Formative Years: The Indian Trade and Intercourse Acts, 1780–1832.* Cambridge, Mass.: Harvard University Press, 1962.

Ray, Grace E. *Early Oklahoma Newspapers: History and Description from Earliest Beginnings to 1889.* University of Oklahoma Bulletin, New Series 407, Studies 28, (Norman, OK: University of Oklahoma Press, June 15, 1928.)

Riley, Sam G. "A Note of Caution—The Indian's Own Prejudice, as Mirrored in the First Native American Newspaper." *Journalism Quarterly* (Summer 1979): 44–47.

Round, Phillip H. *Removable Type: Histories of the Book in Indian Country, 1663–1880.* Chapel Hill: University of North Carolina Press, 2010.

Routh, Eugene C. "Early Missionaries to the Cherokees." *Chronicles of Oklahoma* (December 1937): 449–65.

Royce, Charles C. *The Cherokee Nation of Indians: A Narrative of Their Official Relations with the Colonial and Federal Governments.* Washington, D.C.: Bureau of American Ethnology, Smithsonian Institution, 1887.

Salvino, Dana Nelson. "'The Word in Black and White': Ideologies of Race and Literacy in Antebellum America." In *Reading in America,* ed. Cathy N. Davidson, 140–56. Baltimore: Johns Hopkins University Press, 1989.

Schwarze, Edmund. *History of the Moravian Missions among the Southern Tribes of the United States.* Bethlehem, Penn.: Times Publishing Company, 1923.

Skelton, Robert Howard. "A History of the Educational System of the Cherokee Nation, 1801–1910." Ed.D. thesis, University of Arkansas, 1970.

Starr, Emmet. *History of the Cherokee Indians and Their Legends and Folk Lore.* Oklahoma City: Warden Company, 1921.

Strickland, William. "Cherokee Rhetoric: A Forceful Weapon." *Journal of Cherokee Studies* (Fall 1977): 275–84.

Tracy, Joseph. *History of the ABCFM Compiled Chiefly from the Published and Unpublished Documents of the Board.* New York: M. W. Dodd, 1840.

Tyner, Howard Q. "The Keetoowah Society in Cherokee History." M.A. thesis, University of Tulsa, 1949.

Walker, Willard. "Notes on Native Writing Systems and the Design of Native Literacy Programs." *Anthropological Linguistics* (1969): 148–66.

Weaver, Jace. *That the People Might Live: Native American Literatures and Native American Community.* Oxford: Oxford University Press, 1997.

Williams, Barbara, and Maria del Carmen Jorge y Jorge. "Aztec Arithmetic Revisited: Land-Area Algorithms and Acolhua Congruence Arithmetic." *Science* 320:5872 (April 2008): 72–77.

Yamachika, Raymond. "Cherokee Literature: Printing in the Sequoyan Syllabary since 1828, with a Bibliography." M.A. thesis, University of Oklahoma, 1961.

Index

Academy for teachers, 76
Adair, Hugh Montgomery, 138
Adair, John Lynch, 114, 146, 158, 234–35; allotments, 238–39; editor, 235; poetry, 235–37
Adair, William Penn, 191, 192, 68, 191, 219–21
Adair School, 73
Adams, John Quincy and Cherokees, 59
Adopted citizens, 134
African Americans, 48, 108
Allotment, 190
Allotment bill, 1848, 190
Almanacs, 117
American Bible Society, 7, 115
American Board of Commissioners for Foreign Missions (ABCFM), 16
American Tract Society, 7
Analysis of the Cherokee language, 119
An Analysis of the Cherokee Language, pamphlet, 120
Anderson, Mabel Washbourne, 251
Arch, John (Asti), 29
Arkansas, Cherokees in, migration to, 46, 71
Arrest of whites in Cherokee Nation, 61
Arrests of missionaries, 63
Aupaunut, Hendrick, 6

Baird, Spencer F., 119
Bancroft, Hubert H., 162
Baptist Memorial, 141
Beadle, J. H., 202
Beeson, John, 82
Benedict, John D., 98
Bible texts, in syllabary, 40, 115
Bilingual teachers, 79
Billings, Josh, 147
Blunt, James G., 117
Boarding schools, 20
Boney, Roy Jr., 249
Boston Courier, 62
Boudinot, E. C., Jr., 136, 148
Boudinot, Elias, marriage of, 30; An Address to the Whites of, 51; fund-raising tour of, 51; "Prospectus to the Chrokee Phoenix," 52; resigns as editor, 65; views on Removal changing, 64
Boudinot, Elias Cornelius, 136, 167, 191, 192, 202, 203; colony of, 136; huge impact of, 138–39; and *Indian Progress*, 211; "Letter" of, 137; military career of, 203; and railroads, 205; rivalry with William Penn Adair, 207, 212; as "territorialist," prose of, 207–8
Boudinot, William P., 132, and Cherokee textbooks, 110–11; poetry, 225–26; prose, 221–23

Brainerd ABCFM school, 18
Breadtown, 76
Brown, David, 12, 28, 56, 73
Bryant, William Cullen, 141
Buffington, Mary J., 138
Bunch, Rabbit, 98, 148
Bureau of American Ethnology, 119
Bushyhead, Edward, 186–87
Bushyhead, Jesse, 31
Butler, George Oliver, 139
Buttrick, Daniel S., 27
Butrick, Samuel S., 27ff

Caddo Resolutions, 211
California historians, 162
California Police Gazette, 161
Campbell, W. P., 121
Candy, John, 62
Canup, William T., 148, 150
Carmel and Creek Path schools, 18
Carter, David, 130
Cartier, Jacques, 5
Central Railroad, 205
Chamberlin, Amory Nelson, 118
Chamberlin, William, 39
Chenango, 143
Cherokee (pen name), 143
Cherokee Advocate, 128; resumption of, 114
Cherokee Constitution, 59–60, rewriting of, 197
Cherokee Female Seminary, 89
Cherokee Immersion School, 248
Cherokee Insane Asylum, 98
Cherokee language, description of, 101–2; use of increased, 145
Cherokee language analysis, 26
Cherokee language preservation, 248
Cherokee Male Seminary, 89
Cherokee Messenger, 128
Cherokee middle class, 48, 81
Cherokee Nation, 1827 Constitution of, 116
Cherokee Ophan Asylum Press, 151
Cherokee Orphans Asylum, 94
Cherokee Outlet, 96
Cherokee Phoenix, content of, 56–57, 58; last issue of, 65; opposition to by Georgia, 59

Cherokee Pictorial Book, With Catechism and Hymns, 118
Cherokee schools, 197; federal control of, 98
Cherokee school system, 68; annuities in support of, 70
Cherokee shorthand, 123; use of in courts, 124
Cherokee Telephone, 149
Cherokee Tobacco Case, 204
Christian Philosophy, 58
Citizen Soldier, 141
Civilization Policy, 14, 18; economic effects of, 15
Civil War, Cherokees in, 193
Clay, Henry, 64
Clemens, Samuel, 189
Code Talkers, 248
Coffee, John, 47
"Colored" high school, 98–99
Confederate, Cherokee regiments of, 193
Cornwall, Barry, 141
Cornwall School, 29–39
"Crazy Snake" affair, 140
Cunningham, Jeter Thompson, 150
Curtis Act, 139, 164, 171

Dawes Commission, 139, 148, 151, 213–14; "findings" of, 215
Death notices, in syllabary, 108
Delawares, adoption of, 197
Denili Tsisghwa, 110
Depredations against Cherokee citizens, 62
Dick, John Henry, 149
Dodge, William S., 187
Dorsey, J. O., 119
Downing, Lewis, 218
Downing, S. H., 136
Downing Party, 98, 219
Drew, John, 147–48
Duncan, DeWitt Clinton, 118–19, 163–69; Cherokee grammar of, 122, 140
Duncan, Helen R., 119
Dunn, Douglas, 187
Dwight Mission, 72

Early missions, failure of, 17
Eastern Cherokee claims, 96

Eaton, Rachel, 250
Eddleman, Ora V., 240–41; editor and publisher, 241; fiction of, 242; prose, 242–43
Education, Cherokee control of, 74–75; financial support of, 78
Edwards, Jonathan, 6
Eliot, John, Bible of, 5
Emancipations Proclamation, 117
Erb, Joseph, 249
Ethnic stereotypes, 135
Eubanks, Royal Roger, 175, 252
Eubanks, William, 123, 140, 174–76, 189; and anthropology, 181–82; and Cherokee mythology, 182–83; and science, 184–86
Evarts, Jeremiah, 16, 28

Fairfield School, 73
Federal courts, 96
Final Settlement, 140
Foreman, Stephan, 78, 131
"formulae," Cherokee, 103–6
Fort Smith Picayune, 147
Freedman Compromise, 140
Friend of Youth, 141
Full blood, definition of, 20; high drop-out rate of, 20

Gahuni manuscript, 104
Garcia, Manuel, 160
Georgia, expends jurisdiction, 60; Georgia Guard established, 61
Gitigwanasti manuscript, 105
Goodman, D. Ellen, 141
Grant's "Peace Policy," 114
Green Peach War, 136
Gregory, James Roane, 140
Guess, George, 32
Gu-tla-Ona-Wv, 143

Harlan, James, 191
Harris, Col. Johnson Harris, 191, 212–13; and Dawes Commission, 213; prose of, 216
Harris, Isaac, 54, 61
Haskell, Charles N., 92
Hemans, Felicia, 141
Hesperian, 162
Hicks, Charles R., 26, 30, 65, 70

Hicks, Leonard, 29
Hindman, Thomas, 117
Hitchcock, Asa, 116
Hittell, Theodore, 162
Hollingsworth, William, 146
Home Journal and Citizen, 141
Horseshoe Bend, Battle of, 46
Hoyt, Ard, 15, 30, 70
Hoyt, Sylvia, 29
Hudson, Waddie, 139, 148
Hurons, writing by, 5
Hymnals, in syllabary, 116

Inalia manuscript, 104
Indian Chieftain, 145–46
Indian Journal, 146, 147–48
Indian Progress, 197
Indian Removal Act, 67
Indian-White relations, 165
Inoli manuscript, 107
Instructional duration, 27
Intercourse laws, 117
Intruders, 60, 167
Ivey, Gus, 146

Jackson, Andrew, election of, 47, 59
Jefferson, Thomas, 14, 47
Johnson, George Washington, 135
Johnson, Robert, 191
Jolly, John, 72
Jones, Evan, 70; 75 219; Cherokee literacy promoted by, 24; "preacher academy" proposed by, 70
Jones, John Buttrick, 83, 113; Cherokee textbooks of, 113

Kanaheta Ani-Tsalagi Eti, 104
"Katy" Railroad, 206
Keetoowah Society, 109–10, 148
Kilpatrick, Anna Gritts, 106–10
Kilpatrick, Jack Frederick, 106–10
Kingsbury, Cyrus, 15
Know-Nothing Party, 162
Knox, Henry, 14

Land grants, to railroads, 190
Landrum, Hiram Terrell, 134
Language of instruction, 21, 23, 80, 83, 112; after 1875, 113–14; debated, 85
Lawson, J. B., 110

Leased district, 190
Lenni Lanape, 8
LePlongeon, Augustus, 183–84
Life and Adventures of Joaquin Murieta, The Celebrated Calfornia Bandit, 160
Literacy, value of, 11; factors in, 11; treaties as a factor in development of, 12
Literary and dramatic societies, 93
Loeser, William T., 140
Long, W. N., 104
Longfellow, Henry Wadworth, 141
Louisiana Purchase, 7
Love, Harry, 160
Lowery, George, 40, 56

Mahican language, 6
Malan, Cesar, 116
Marshall, John, 63–64
Maryville Herald, 156
Massachusetts language, 5
Mayans, writing by, 5
Mayes, Joel B., 97, 98
McIlvaine, Abraham R., 190
Meigs, Return J., 45
Melton, Wiley James, 140
Mesoamerica, 3–5
Mesoamerican syllabaries, 4
Middle Class, Cherokee, 48
Mide Societies, 9
Milford, M. E., 146
Missionaries, literary efforts among, 16
Missionary Herald, 44, 58, 115
Mixed bloods, acculturation of, 48
Modoc War, 167
Monitor method, 19
Monroe, James, 15
Mooney, James, 102–5

Nahl, Charles C., 161
National Council, move to Red Clay, TN, 63; control of schools, 74
National Party, 137, 147
Natural resources, 136
New Orleans *True Delta,* 156
Newspapers, in Cherokee Nation, 127
New York *Journal of Commerce,* 62
New York Observer, 62

Oestericher, David M., 9
Ojibwes, symbols and pictographs of, 9
O-Ka-Cho-Tsee, 143–44
Okmulgee Conference, 198; constitution of, 198
Old Settler Claims, 221
Olmecs, writing by, 4
Orthographies, use of by missionaries, 9
Osage Dreamer, 143
Oskison, John Milton, 251–52
Owen, Robert L., 146

Parks, Jefferson Thompson, 150
Parley, Peter, 128
Payne, David L., 136, 167
Payne, James M., 79
Pen names, 229–30
Pickering, John, 6, 28
Pilling, James Constantine, 120
Pitman shorthand method, 123, 124
Poetry, 58; by Cherokees, 141–43
Posey, Humphrey, 70
Presses, Catholic, in Great Lakes area, 6
Printing, advances in; press, Cherokee, 113–14; resumption of after Civil War, 84
Proclamation of Pardon and Amnesty, 117
Proctor, Isaac, 35
Public Education Act, 77
Public lands, 137

Quinney, John, 6

Racial conflict, 160
Railroads, 190; through Cherokee Nation, 205
Rector, Elias, 191
Red Stick War, 46
Reese, Henry D. (White Horse), 136, 226; historical writing, 226–29
Refinesque, Constatin Samuel, 8
Religious tracts, in syllabary, 40
Removal, threat of, 13, 44–45, 47, 59
Richmond, Leigh, 116
Ridge, John, xv, marriage of, 30
Ridge, John Rollin, 189, 152–62; poetry of, 156–59
Ridge assassinations, 153

R. M. S., Cherokee poet, 142
Rocky Mountain Vision, 45–46
Rogers, W. C., 98
Rogers, Will, 250
Roman alphabet, use of, 26
Ross, Daniel Hicks, 130, 136
Ross, John, 69, 129
Ross, Lewis, 96
Ross, William Potter, 129, 196, 197; prose of, 198–202
Ross-Treaty Party rift, 193
Rustic Bard, 143

Sallisaw Gazette, 151
San Diego Union, 187
Saturday Evening Post, 141
Sawyer, Sophia, 87
Schermerhorn, John F., 74
Schoolcraft, Henry Rowe, 9
Scientific American, 141
Seminaries, Cherokee, 86; closure of, 92; curricula of, 90–91; reopening, 92; use during Civil War, 92
Sentinel, 150
Sequichie, Joseph R., 140
Sequoyah, xiv, syllabary of, 32; acceptance by Cherokees of, 32; acceptance of by missionaries, 32; life of, 33; reaction to by missionaries, 34; readership of, 32–34
Sequoyah High School, 249
Sequoyan documents, 106
Sergeant, John, 63
Sigourney, Lydia, 141
Sioux "uprising," 1862, 165
Smith, G. C., 116
Southern and Western Literary Messenger and Review, 141
Southey, Robert, 141
Spaulding, Henry, 6
Springston, John Leaf, 134
State of Sequoyah Constitution, 1905, 140
Stone, B. H., 148; shooting of, 137
Stone, Emma, 148
Student publications, 93
Subscriptions, from outside Cherokee Nation, 56
Sutherland, Kate, 141

Swimmer manuscript, 105–6
Swisshelm, Jane, 165S
Syllabaries, advantages of, 10
Syllabary, xiii; invention of, 102; type set in, 50, 51–52; used in advertising, 144
Syllabary, transliteration of, 249; in digital format, 249

Taggert, Charles P., 187
Tahlequah Courier, 151
Teacher recruitment, 77
Teachers' examinations, 82
Tehee, Charles, 138
Tennyson, Alfred, 141
Territorial bills, 190
Territorial ring, 195
Territorial status, 190
Textbooks, 112; in Cherokee, 110–11
Theosophy, 176–80
Thomas, William Holland, 107
Thompson, Charles, 83, 97, 219; election of as Principal Chief, 1875, 114
Thompson, Eliza, 175
Thompson, S. J., 146
Thompson, William Abbot, 150
Three-Fingered Jack, 160
Tinsawatee and Oothcala schoos, 18
Too Quah-stee, 163, verse of, 171–74
Tracts in the Cherokee Language, 116
Translations into Cherokee, 25; pre-Sequoyah, 31
Transliteration, English into Cherokee, 27
Treaties Between the United Sates of America and the Cherokee Nation, from 1785, 117
Treaty of 1817, 46, 72
Treaty of 1866, 117, 194
Tribal sovereignty, 190
Tsu-hu-o-tii, 143

U-nah-kah, 230–34
Universal History, 128

Valley Towns, Baptist schools at, 18
Vann, James Shepherd, 130
Vest, George G., 167
Vinita Leader, 151
Vinita Vidette, 151

Wafford, James, 27
Walum Olum hoax, 8
Ward, Artemus, 147
Watie, Stand, 117
Webster, C. L., 123
Weekly Capital, 150
Western Literrry Magazine, 141
Wheeler, John C., 147
Wheeler, John F., 54, 66, 147
Wheeler, Nancy Ridge, 66
Wheelers' Western Independent, 147

Whirlwind, 31
White Path Rebellion, 49
Whitmore, Ellen, 86
Whittier, John Greenleaf, 141
Wirt, William, 63
Worcester, Samuel A., 41, 52, 74
A Wreath of Cherokee Rose Buds, 93
Wright, Asher, 6
Wylie, John Fletcher, 138

Zapotecs, writing by, 4

Printed in the USA
CPSIA information can be obtained
at www.ICGtesting.com
CBHW050504270224
4716CB00002B/59

9 780806 193151